CISTERCIAN STUDIES SERIES: NUMBER

BEDE THE VENERABLE

EXCERPTS FROM THE WORKS OF SAINT AUGUSTINE ON THE LETTERS OF THE BLESSED APOSTLE PAUL

CISTERCIAN STUDIES SERIES: NUMBER ONE HUNDRED EIGHTY THREE

BEDE THE VENERABLE

EXCERPTS FROM THE WORKS OF SAINT AUGUSTINE ON THE LETTERS OF THE BLESSED APOSTLE PAUL

TRANSLATED BY DAVID HURST
Monk of Portsmouth Abbey

CISTERCIAN PUBLICATIONS
Kalamazoo, Michigan
1999

This translation has been made from
Bede. *Bedae Venerablilis Opera.* Edited by C. W. Jones and D. Hurst. Corpus Christianorum. Series Latina. 118A, etc. Turnholti: Brepols, 1955.

Cistercian Publications
Editorial Offices
Institute of Cistercian Studies
Western Michigan University
Kalamazoo, MI 49008

Available from
Cistercian Publications (Distribution)
Saint Joseph's Abbey
167 North Spencer Road
Spencer, MA 01562–1233

and

Cistercian Publications (UK)
Mount Saint Bernard Abbey
Coalville, Leicester LE67 5UL

The work of Cistercian Publications
is made possible in part by support from Western Michigan University
to The Institute of Cistercian Studies
Library of Congress Cataloguing available upon request.
ISBN 0-87907-583-X

Printed in the United States of America

TABLE OF CONTENTS

TRANSLATOR'S INTRODUCTION

OUTSTANDING SCHOLARS OF THE PAST one hundred years, pre-eminent among them John Henry Newman, Adolf von Harnack, Jean Daniélou and Jaroslav Pelikan, have provided us today with a history of the development of theological thought originating in the exegesis of the Scriptures. Few students of theology are unaware that our contemporary synthesis of religious ideas had its beginnings in the exegetical writings of those who have come to be regarded as Fathers of the Church, whose works go back to sub-apostolic times. The Scriptures themselves, both the Old and New Testaments, are a more or less heterogeneous collection of tales and sayings about religion compiled at various times, but they present an amazing continuity from the centuries preceding the advent of Christ to the formation of what we have come to regard as the Church founded by him. Nevertheless, they contain many seeming contradictions and inconsistencies that from the outset have caused their readers difficulties. The earliest christian thinkers wrote about the words and thoughts believed to have been divinely inspired to resolve these incongruities, as well as to expand or enlarge upon the events and teachings of the Scriptures.

One of the foremost theologians to deal extensively with these fuller explanations of the Scriptures and to attempt to reconcile some of their seemingly incompatible passages, was Saint Augustine, bishop of Hippo in North Africa during the fourth and fifth centuries of the christian era. So comprehensive were his writings, and so clear were his interpretations and resolutions of problematical passages, that he came to be regarded as the most authoritative exegete of the christian mediterranean world.

A century later, one Eugippius, abbot of a monastery at Castellum Lucullanum near Naples, desired to compile a collection of excerpts from Augustine's writings for his monks. Fortunately for him, the virgin or nun Proba—a relative of his contemporary, Cassiodorus, and like him a collector of manuscripts of the writings of earlier expounders of divine and humane subjects—possessed a library containing a large number of Augustine's exegetical works. From these Eugippius extracted some three hundred forty-eight passages that he considered crucial or helpful for the understanding of the letters of Paul. A copy of these extracts evidently made its way northward to England about the same time as the text of the New Testament known as the Lindisfarne Gospels. They were taken there by a greek monk, Theodore of Tarsus, whom Pope Vitalian appointed archbishop of Canterbury during the seventh century in place of the Anglo-Saxon Wighard, whom the kings of Northumbria and Kent sent to Rome to be consecrated, but who died before he was ordained.

Bede the Venerable must have found a copy of Eugippius's extracts among the two hundred or so books in the library at the Northumbrian monastery of Jarrow. Bede is best known today as the author of an *Ecclesiastical History of the English Nation*, but during his long lifetime (c. 673–735) he wrote treatises on such diverse subjects as spelling and cosmography, and also produced commentaries on many of the books of Scripture. He spent his entire life, after the age of seven, in the monastery. His abbot, in a letter prefixed to the *Ecclesiastical History*, said that during his last days, Bede sang the psalms and worked on a translation of the Gospel according to John into Old English. On his final day, the boy who was his scribe said to him, 'There is still one sentence, beloved master, not yet written down.' Bede said, 'Write it quickly.' After a moment the boy said, 'Now it is written.' Bede replied, 'Well have you spoken the truth. It is finished.'[1] Indeed, after saying a few more words, he died. Bede's

[1]Jn 19:30

homilies on the gospels, intended to supplement Saint Gregory the Great's homilies in providing commentaries on the passages from the gospel assigned to be read at the benedictine night office on the Sundays throughout the year, and his commentaries on Acts and the seven Catholic Epistles, have already been published in the Cistercian Studies series.[2]

Bede had already conceived the idea of borrowing excerpts from previous and orthodox exegetes. He had concluded his own commentary on the Song of Songs with verbatim excerpts from the commentary by Pope Gregory I, perhaps wishing to persuade readers of his orthodoxy by quoting excerpts from Gregory's works word for word after quoting or paraphrasing authors other than Gregory. So, when it came to composing a commentary on Saint Paul's letters, Bede did as Eugippius had done and made use of excerpts from Augustine's exegesis instead of giving his own interpretation. He undoubtedly made use of Eugippius's excerpts, but added to them, bringing the number to four hundred fifty-seven. These he arranged in the order of Saint Paul's letters as we have them now, that is, from the letter to the Romans to that to the Hebrews, then regarded as a genuine letter of Paul's.

Bede's selection of excerpts from Augustine's exegetical commentaries was of immense importance for the development of later theology. During the ninth century, Rabanus Maurus, abbot of Fulda and later archbishop of Mainz, and Florus, a deacon at Lyon, drew up a similar collection of passages from Augustine's writings. They may have used Bede as one of their sources, but some passages that Bede used are omitted, and others shortened or lengthened. Both Rabanus Maurus and Florus made use of the extracts from commentators other than Bede. Peter the Lombard, archbishop of Paris, made a collection of excerpts from commentaries on

[2]Bede the Venerable, *Homilies on the Gospels*, 2 Vols. CS 110 and 111. Translated by Lawrence T. Martin and David Hurst OSB (Kalamazoo: Cistercian Publications, 1991); Bede the Venerable, *Commentary on Acts*, CS 117. Translated by Lawrence T. Martin (Kalamazoo: Cistercian Publications, 1989); Bede the Venerable, *Commentary on the Seven Catholic Epistles*, CS 82. Translated by David Hurst OSB (Kalamazoo: Cistercian Publications, 1985); Gregory the Great, *Forty Gospel Homilies*, CS 123. Translated by David Hurst OSB (Kalamazoo: Cistercian Publications, 1990).

Saint Paul's letters similar to Bede's in the twelfth century. He later arranged these excerpts into four books, following a theological schema. This was the well-known *Book of Sentences* that was the standard handbook of theology until it was replaced by Saint Thomas Aquinas' *Summa Theologica*. Owing to the rediscovery of Aristotle's philosophical works, Thomas united reason or logical thought processes with patristic exegesis.

During the later middle ages, these compilations of material judged important for explaining the Scriptures and expanding theological thought were considerably shortened, frequently into a compact sentence or two, and employed to explain or prove doctrines by quoting a pertinent bit of Scripture. This is how theology developed and how it will undoubtedly continue to develop. But the Scriptures and the commentaries on them, must remain the basis of theological thought. This was the method used by Augustine, and followed by Eugippius, Bede and others.

Bede's compilation has never before been available in print, undoubtedly because it provided texts from the writings of Saint Augustine (or thought to be his—see §1 of the compilation) that could be found in Augustine's works, all properly identified. The present translation was made from a preliminary critical text consisting of a collation of five early manuscripts of Bede's work: St. Omer 91, Orléans 81, Orléans 84, Rouen 147, all of the ninth century, and Montecassino 178, of the eleventh century). The last of these, from Montecassino, also contains, following excerpt 394, an extraordinarily lengthy excerpt from Augustine's *On the Work of Monks*. This was probably an addition to Bede's original compilation and so it is not included here. It appears only in this manuscript, which comes from the scriptorium of a monastic house.[3]

In conformity with Cistercian Studies practice, the scriptural abbreviations used in the footnotes are those of the *New Jerusalem Bible*.[4] Psalm citations are given by the Hebrew numbers unless

---

[3]For a list of the excerpts from Augustine and a comparison of them with those chosen by Eugippius, see two articles by I. Fransen: 'Description de la collection de Bède le Vénérable sur l'Apôtre,' and 'D'Eugippius à Bède le Vénérable à propos de leurs florilèges Augustiniens.' *Revue Bénédictine* 71 (1961) 22–70, and 97 (1987) 187–94.

[4]Garden City: Doubleday & Co., 1985, p. ix.

modern versions, translated from the Hebrew, are all but unrecognizable, in which case the word 'Vulgate' follows a reference to the Vulgate number. When a text seems to reflect not a Latin version but the Septuagint Greek translation, 'LXX' follows the reference.

In translating quotations from the Bible several English versions have been consulted. When Bede prefixes a passage from Paul he usually quotes the Vulgate, but Augustine's quotations conform to no known version. In addition to our lack of a definitive text of the Latin version or versions he would have known in North Africa, the possibility remains that he is quoting from memory, and modifying the text to fit the grammar of his sentence. The translation of the Vulgate published at Douay (Old Testament, 1609) and Rheims (New Testament, 1582) often gives a helpful clue to a traditional interpretation, but when possible the translations have been brought into conformity to the *New Revised Standard Version*. Since Augustine (and Paul) were most often addressing women as well as men, their language has been silently amended to reflect this. It is no longer universally accepted that 'brothers' include sisters as well, and that 'men' means 'men and women.'

At the end of this volume the best modern edition of the text from which Bede's excerpt comes is noted for the sake of readers who desire to see it in its context. Readers should be aware that sometimes Bede's reference to his source does not agree with the modern title or number. For example, the work he knew as *On Eighty-Four Questions* is our *On Eighty-Three Questions*, and his manuscript of Augustine's homilies on John lacked homilies 20–22, which throws off all the remaining homily numbers.

The references are further complicated because Bede had a quirky way of excerpting a few words or sentences and compressing longish (and wordy) parts of Augustine into a sentence of his own. Thus this present work provides information about what Bede thought of interest and value, as well as about the state of texts earlier than the manuscripts from which the modern critical editions of Augustine's works are made.

Portsmouth Abbey David Hurst OSB

EDITOR'S NOTE

In providing an editorial review of Father David's translation I have had the assistance of the Reverend Rowan A. Greer, of the Yale Divinity School faculty, and enjoyed the hospitality of the Hermitage of the Dayspring, in Kent, Connecticut, and of the Yale Divinity School, in New Haven.

Yale Divinity School John Leinenweber

TABLE OF ABBREVIATIONS

ACW	Ancient Christian Writers
CC	Corpus Christianorum
CS	Cistercian Studies
CSEL	Corpus Scriptorum Ecclesiasticorum Latinorum
FC	Fathers of the Church
LCC	Library of Christian Classics
LCL	Loeb Classical Library
NPNF	The Nicene and Post-Nicene Fathers, series 1
Paulist	Classics of Western Spirituality: Augustine of Hippo
PL	Patrologia Latina
Works	*Works of Saint Augustine: A Translation for the 21st Century.* Translation and notes by Edmund Hill. Edited by John E. Rotelle. Brooklyn: New City Press, 1990.

Works by Saint Augustine

Ad Oros. Contra Prisc. et Orig	*Ad Orosium Contra Priscillianistas et Origenistas*
Confess.	*Confessiones*
Contra Adv. Leg. et Prohet	*Contra Adversarium Legis et Prophetarum*
Contra Duas Ep. Pelag.	*Contra Duas Epistolas Pelagianorum*
Contra Litt. Petil.	*Contra Epistolam Petiliani*
Contra Secundi. Manich.	*Contra Epistolam Secundini Manichaei*
Contra Faust. Manich.	*Contra Faustum Manichaeum*

Contra Gaud.	*Contra Gaudentium*
Contra Iul.	*Contra Iulianum*
Contra Mend.	*Contra Mendacium*
Contra Sec. Iul.	*Contra Secundam Iuliani Responsionem*
De Adulter. Coniug.	*De Adulterinis Coniugiis*
De Bapt. Contra Donat.	*De Baptismo Contra Donatistas*
De Bono Coniug.	*De Bono Coniugali*
De Civ. Dei	*De Civitate Dei*
De Cons. Ev.	*De Consensu Evangelistarum*
De Corrept. et Gratia	*De Correptione et Gratia*
De Div. Quaest. Ad Simpl.	*De Diversis Quaestionibus ad Simplicianum*
De Div. Quaest. LXXXIII	*De Diversis Quaestionibus LXXXIII*
De Doct. Christ.	*De Doctrina Christiana*
De Dono Persev.	*De Dono Perseverantiae*
De Gen. ad Litt.	*De Genesi ad Litteram*
De Gen. Contra Manich.	*De Genesi Contra Manichaeos*
De Gest. Pelag.	*De Gestibus Pelagii*
De Gratia et Lib. Arb.	*De Gratia et Libero Arbitrio*
De Mor. Eccl. Cath.	*De Moribus Ecclesiae Catholicae*
De Nat. et Orig. Animae	*De Natura et Origine Animae*
De Nupt. et Concup.	*De Nuptiis et Concupiscentia*
De Perf. Iust. Hom.	*De Perfectione Iustitiae Hominis*
De Praedest. Sanct.	*De Praedestinatione Sanctorum*
De Serm. Dom. in Monte	*De Sermone Domini in Monte*
De Trin.	*De Trinitate*
En. in Ps	*Enarrationes in Psalmos*
Enchic.	*Enchiridion*
Ep.	*Epistolae*
In Ioh. Ep.	*In Ioh. Ep.*
Quaest. Ev.	*Quaestiones Evangeliorum*
Serm.	*Sermo;*
Tract. in Ioh.	*Tract. In Ioh.*
Quodvultdeus	Quodvultdeus: *Contra Quinque Hereses*

Saint Augustine's Commentary

the Letter of Paul to the Church in Rome

PAUL, A SERVANT OF CHRIST JESUS, called to be an apostle . . . † †**Rm 1:1–3**

We must preserve this arrangement, so that even when speaking about the gospel I do not keep silent concerning the prophets. Manichaeus asserts, 'I accept neither Moses nor the prophets.' What, then, do you make of what the apostle Paul wrote at the beginning of his letter to the Romans: *Paul, a servant of Jesus Christ, called to be an apostle, set apart for the gospel of God which he had promised formerly through his prophets in the holy scriptures, about his Son, who was made for him from David's seed according to the flesh*? Do you hear that the gospel would not have come into existence if it had not been promised formerly through the prophets? Do you hear that the Son of God, according to his divine nature, became the Son of Man *from David's seed according to the flesh*?

How, indeed, are the prophets opposed to the gospel? The prophet said, 'Drop down dew, you heavens, from above, and let the clouds rain down the righteous one!' Let the angel come; let him proclaim the Word; 'let the earth be opened'; let Mary hear, give birth to God and 'bring forth the Saviour.' The prophet said, 'Behold, a virgin shall conceive in her womb and give birth to a son, and his name shall be called Emmanuel.' After quoting this, the evangelist went on to explain that this word means 'God with us.'† †Is 45:8, 7:14; Mt 1:23

Manichaeus, in vain do you attempt to oppose the prophets! See, the Apostle says *concerning his Son, who was made for him from David's seed according to the flesh.* What the prophets had foretold the apostles saw and proclaimed. He who was became . . . What was he? What did he become? He was the Word, he became flesh. He was the Son of God, he became the Son of Man. He was God, he became a human being. He took upon himself humanity, he did not lose divinity.

—from *Against Five Heresies**

---

*1. Quodvultdeus, *Serm.* 10; CC 60: 277,19–278, 43. In Bede's time this work was thought to be one of the genuine writings of Augustine. Recent scholarship has proved it to be by one of his successors in the see of Carthage, Quodvultdeus, who was bishop there A.D. 437–453. The same idea is expressed by Augustine in his *Serm.* 121.5 and 123.3 (PL 38: 680, 685). The bold face type in the notes refers to the scriptural passage being discussed.

2. *About his Son, who was made for him from David's seed according to the flesh, who was predestined Son of God in power, according to the Spirit of sanctification, by the resurrection from the dead of Jesus Christ our Lord.*† Paul said this as if he had been speaking of someone else earlier. What is the Son of God *predestined by the resurrection from the dead of Jesus Christ our Lord* if not the same Jesus Christ *who was predestined Son of God*? Therefore, when we hear in this passage the words *Son of God in the power of Jesus Christ*, or *Son of God according to the Spirit of sanctification of Jesus Christ*, or *Son of God by the resurrection from the dead of Jesus Christ*, when [Paul] could have said in the usual way 'in *his* power,' or 'according to the spirit of *his* sanctification,' or 'by the resurrection from the dead of *him*' or of his followers, we are not obliged to understand another person, but one and the same person, namely God's Son, our Lord Jesus Christ. So too, when we hear, 'God made humans in the image of God,'† although ordinarily we would say 'in *his own* image,' we are not obliged to understand another person in the Trinity, but one and the same Trinity, the one God in whose image humanity was made.

†**Rm 1:3–4**

†Gn 1:27

—from *On the Holy Trinity* 12.6*

3. *God is my witness, whom I serve in my spirit.*†

'But I say to you, Do not swear at all, either by heaven, for it is God's throne,' and so on. The righteousness of the Pharisees consisted in their not forswearing themselves.† The one who forbade all swearing confirmed this, because this is part of the righteousness of the kingdom of heaven. However since a person who calls upon God as his witness is swearing, we must consider this verse carefully or the Apostle may appear to have acted against the Lord's commandment. [Paul] often swore in this way, as when he said, 'In what I am writing to you, behold, before God, I am not lying'; and again, 'The God and Father of our Lord Jesus Christ, who is blessed for ever, knows that I am not lying.'† So too in this verse, *God is my witness, whom I serve in my spirit in the gospel of his Son, that without ceasing I make a remembrance of you always in my prayers.*†

†**Rm 1:9**

†Mt 5:34; Lv 19.12, Mt 5:33

†Ga 1:20; 2 Co 11:31

†**Rm 1:9–10**

*2. *De Trin.* 12.6.7; CC 50: 362,45/62

Someone may perhaps say that an oath requires something by which the oath is made. [Paul] then did not swear, since he did not say 'by God'; he said *God is my witness*. This supposition is ridiculous. Yet on account of those who are disputatious or very slow-witted, lest any suppose that there is a difference, they should be aware that the Apostle swore also in this manner when he said, 'I die every day, by your glory.'† †1 Co 15:31

Therefore, let those who understand that an oath is not to be employed in good but [only] in necessary matters restrain themselves as much as possible. They should not use one except out of necessity, when they see that people are slow to believe what is useful for them to believe unless it is supported by an oath. Accordingly, the following is apposite: 'Let your word be, Yes, Yes, No, No.' This is good and desirable. 'What is more than this comes from evil.'† If you †Mt 5:37
are compelled to swear, you should be aware that [an oath] is uttered out of necessity, because of the weakness of those whom you must persuade of something. This weakness is undoubtedly evil, and so we daily beg to be delivered from it when we say, 'Deliver us from evil.'† Accordingly, [our Lord] did not say, 'What is more than this †Mt 6:13
is evil,' for you are not doing something evil when you make good use of an oath. Although this is not good, it is necessary to persuade others of what you are persuading them for some useful purpose. The evil comes from them.

—from *On the Lord's Sermon on the Mount* 1*

4. *The righteousness of God is revealed in [the gospel] from faith to faith.*† **†Rm 1:17**

We can take the apostles' words to the Lord, 'Increase our faith!' as asking him to increase in themselves the faith by which what is unseen is believed. We can, however, also speak of faith in realities, when what we believe is not words but present realities themselves. This will come about when the very wisdom of God, by which all things were made, offers itself to the saints for them to contemplate

*3. *De Serm. Dom. in Monte* 1.17.51; CC 35: 57,1218/26; 1228–58,1242; 1251–59, 1264

†Lk 17:5; Jn 20:29; Heb 11:1; Ps 104:24; 2 Co 5:6

by plain sight.† Perhaps Paul the apostle meant faith in realities and in the present light when he said, *The righteousness of God is revealed in [the gospel] from faith to faith*, since he says in another place, 'But we, seeing with unveiled face the glory of the Lord, are being transformed into the same image from glory to glory, as by the Spirit

†2 Co 3:18

of the Lord.'† As he says here 'from glory to glory,' so there he says *from faith to faith*—from the glory of the gospel by which those who believe are now enlightened, to the glory of that unchangeable and obvious truth which, when they are completely changed, they will enjoy to the full; so too *from faith* in the words by which we now believe what we do not yet see, *to faith* in realities by which we will obtain what we now believe for eternity.

—from *Questions on the Gospel* 2.39*

†Rm 1:18

5. *The wrath of God is being revealed from heaven against all ungodliness.*†

Whose ungodliness, if not that of both Jews and Gentiles? People should not ask, 'Why [is it revealed] against the ungodliness of the Gentiles, when the Gentiles never received the law and

†Rm 5:20

became transgressors?† God's wrath will be rightly revealed against the Jews—the law was given to them and they chose not to observe it. It was not given to the Gentiles.'

Consider this carefully, my friends, and understand how [Paul] shows that all are guilty and all are in need of salvation and the

†Rm 3:23

mercy of God.† *The wrath of God is revealed from heaven against all the ungodliness and unrighteousness of those who in their wickedness obstruct the truth.* Notice how [Paul] did not speak of 'those who do not have the truth' but of *those who in their wickedness obstruct the truth.* He is, as it were, asking how they are able to possess the truth when they have not received the law? *What is known about God*, he says,

†Rm 1:19

is plain to them.† How could what is known about God be plain to those who did not receive the law?

[Paul] goes on, *Since the creation of the world, the invisible things of him are clearly seen, being perceived through what has been made; his*

---

*4. *Quaest. Ev.* 2.39; CC 44B: 93,2/17

everlasting power also, and divinity†—we must surely supply the words, †**Rm 1:20** 'which, being perceived, are seen.' Why would anyone look at works and not seek their maker? You look at the earth bearing fruit, the sea full of its creatures, the air filled with birds, the sky bright with stars, and all the rest, and do you not look for the maker of such great works? But you say to me, 'These things I see; him I do not see.' He has given you bodily eyes to see these things; he has given you a mind to see himself. You do not see a person's soul either, but as from the movements and management of the body you perceive the soul you do not see, so from the management of the whole universe, and from the guidance of souls themselves, perceive their creator.

But mere perception is of little use. [The Gentiles] perceived—and see what the Apostle says: *For though they knew God, they did not acknowledge his greatness or give him thanks, but they became vain in their thoughts, and their foolish hearts were darkened.* What caused this if not pride? See what follows: *Claiming to be wise*, he says, *they became fools.*† They should not have appropriated to themselves what [God] †**Rm 1:21, 22** had granted them, or boasted about what they did not possess on their own, but from him.

They were meant to attribute this to him, so that in holding to what they could see they may be healed by the one who had given them the ability to see. If they had done this they would have preserved their humility, been capable of being purified, and clung to their most blessed contemplation. But because pride was in them, a false, deceitful and proud being † insinuated himself to †Gn 3:1 ff. promise them that their souls may be purified by I do not know what techniques of pride, and he made them worshippers of demons.

From this came all the sacred rites of the pagans, which they claim are capable of purifying their souls. Listen to the Apostle saying that they received these things as a result of their pride, [and] that they did not honor God as God should be honored: *And they changed the glory of the imperishable God into the likeness of an image of a perishable human being.*† Now there are idols, things the Greeks and †**Rm 1:23** other pagan nations possess, that bear the likeness of human beings.

No greater and more superstitious form of idolatry exists than that of the Egyptians. Egypt has flooded the world with fictitious beings such as the Apostle goes on to describe when, after saying *into the likeness of an image of a perishable human being* he added *and of birds, and of four-footed animals, and of reptiles.* Have you not seen, my friends, in other temples, an idol with a dog's or a bull's head, and images of other unreasoning animals? These are the idols of the Egyptians. The Apostle includes both types [of idols] when he speaks of *the likeness of an image of a perishable human being, and of birds, and of four-footed animals, and of reptiles.*

Therefore God gave them up to impurity in the desires of their hearts,
†Rm 1:24 *so that they treated their bodies outrageously among themselves.*† These evil actions of theirs are the consequence of their ungodly pride; because these sins proceed from pride they are not only sins but also punishments. When he says that *God gave them up* [Paul means that]
†Rm 1:25 those who *changed the truth of God into a lie* † would do these things as punishment for some sin. What does *they changed the truth of God into a lie* mean? It means *into the likeness of an image of a perishable human being, and of birds, and of four-footed animals, and of reptiles.*

To keep them from saying, 'I do not worship idols, but what the idols represent,' Paul added at once, *and worshipped and served a creature instead of the Creator.* Be shrewd in how you understand this. They worship either an idol or a creature. One who worships an idol changes God's truth into a lie. The sea is a truth, while Neptune is a lie created by human beings. God's truth has been changed into a lie because God made the sea but a human being made the idol, Neptune. So too God made the sun while a human being, by making an image of the sun, changes God's truth into a lie. To keep them from saying, 'I do not worship the idol but I worship the sun,' [Paul] said that *they worshipped a creature instead of the Creator.*

— from a sermon against the pagans, on January first*

6. For you to love created things and abandon their Creator is a great mistake. They seem beautiful to you, but how much more beautiful is the One who formed them! Dear friends, be aware of

---

*5. *Serm.* 197.1; PL 38: 1021–23

this. Do not let Satan creep up on you, saying what he usually says, 'Be happy with God's creatures. Why did he make them if not for us to find happiness in them?' People are intoxicated by this, and are ruined, and forget their Creator. They are spurning their Creator when they make use of created things intemperately and greedily. Of such persons the Apostle says that *they worshiped and served the creature instead of the Creator, who is blessed forever.*† God does not forbid you to love these things; [you are] not to love them [as the source of your] happiness, but to approve and praise them so that you love their Creator. God has given you all these things. Love the one who made them! There is more that he wants to give you—[he wants to give you] himself, who made these things.

†**Rm 1:25**

—from homily two on the Letter of John*

7. It is written in the Proverbs of Solomon, 'Like the rush of water, so is a king's heart in the hand of God; he will direct it wherever he chooses'; and in the letter of the apostle Paul to the Romans, *Therefore God gave them up to impurity in the desires of their hearts.*† From these and other such testimonies in the divine scriptures I think it is clear enough that God works in the hearts of human beings to move their wills in whatever way he chooses, whether toward good, in accord with his mercy, or toward evil, in accord with their deserts. [He does this] by his judgment that is sometimes clear, sometimes hidden, yet always just. That there is no injustice on God's part ought to remain firmly and unwaveringly established in your hearts. Therefore when you read in the writings of Truth that human beings are led astray, or that their hearts are dulled or hardened by God, do not doubt that their evil deserts preceded this, and that they suffered justly. Then you will not experience what Solomon says: 'People's folly upsets their ways, and they blame God in their hearts.' Grace is not given in accord with the deserts of human beings. 'Otherwise, grace is no longer grace.'†

†Pr 21:1; **Rm 1:24**

—from *On Grace and Free Choice**

†Rm 9:14; Ex 9:12; Pr 19:3; Rm 11:6

*6. *In Ioh. Ep.* 2:11; PL 35: 1995 passim
*7. *De Gratia et Lib. Arb.* 21.42–43; PL 44: 908–09 passim

8. *Males committing shameful deeds with males, and receiving in their own*
†**Rm 1:27** *persons the due recompense for their error.*†

The Apostle was not afraid to say that those 'who served a creature instead of the Creator' would not receive *the due recompense for their error* by reluctantly suffering these shameful things but by willingly performing them. This was not the judgment of some debauched person whom such things may delight, but of the most
†Rm 1:25, 26 righteous God 'who gave them up to disgraceful passions.'† Their offenses, then, were to be requited with offenses, and the punishments of sinners are not torments but rather an increase of vices.

—from *Against the Opponent of the Law and the Prophets* 1*

†**Rm 2:1** 9. *Therefore you have no excuse, whoever you are who pass judgment . . .* †

If [Paul] says that they are without excuse who could see [God's]
†Rm 1:20 invisible things, perceiving them through what has been made,† and yet did not obey the truth but remained wicked and ungodly, how much more without excuse are those who, instructed by the law, trust that they are leaders of the blind, and while teaching others do not teach themselves; who steal as they preach against stealing; and
†Rm 2:18–23 the other things the Apostle says of them.† He tells them, *Therefore you have no excuse, whoever you are who pass judgment, for in judging another you condemn yourself, since you are doing the same things you judge.*

Human pride, as if presuming on the strength of free choice, supposes that it has an excuse when the sin seems to be committed in ignorance, not willingly. In regard to this [sort of] excuse divine Scripture says that those, whoever they may be, who are found guilty of sinning knowingly *have no excuse*. Yet the just judgment of God does not spare even those who have not heard: *Those who have*
†**Rm 2:12** *sinned apart from the law will perish apart from the law.*† And although they themselves may seem to make this excuse, [God], who knows
†Qo 7:29 that he made humans straightforward† and gave them the precept of obedience, does not accept this excuse, not even because the sin [of Adam], who used the free choice of the will badly, has passed over to remain in his descendants. Those who have not sinned are

*8. *Contra Adv. Leg. et Prophet.* 1.24.51; CC 49: 83,1459/66

not condemned, since that [sin] was passed from one to everyone, in whom all sinned† in a communal way before there were personal sins in individual cases. For this reason all sinners are without excuse, either because of the guilt [coming from] their origin or by the addition [of that coming from] their free will, whether they sin knowingly or unknowingly, whether they judge or do not judge. †Rm 5:12

The very ignorance of those unwilling to understand is without any doubt a sin, while in those unable [to understand] it is the punishment of sin. Therefore, in both instances the excuse is not just, but the condemnation is just.

—from a letter to the priest Sixtus concerning the Pelagians*

10. The excuse that people are accustomed to make on the grounds of ignorance is taken away from those who know the divine commands. But those unacquainted with God's law will not lack punishment either. *Those who have sinned apart from the law will perish apart from the law, and those who have sinned under the law will be judged by the law.*† I do not think the Apostle said this to indicate that those unacquainted with the law will suffer worse for their sins than those who know it—for perishing seems worse than being judged. Since he was speaking of Gentiles as well as of Jews—the former being apart from the law, while the latter had received the law—who can venture to say that the Jews, who sin under the law, are not going to perish since they do not believe in Christ, even while it was said of them that they *will be judged by the law*? Without faith in Christ no one can be set free, and for this reason they will be judged so as to perish. Now if the condition of those unacquainted with God's law will be worse than that of those who know it, how will what the Lord says in the gospel be true: 'The servant who does not know his master's will and does what is worthy of beating will receive few stripes, whereas the servant who knows his master's will and does what is worthy of beating will receive many stripes'?† **†Rm 2:12** †Lk 12:47–48

—from *On Grace and Free Choice**

*9. *Ep.* 194, 6.25–27; CSEL 57: 195,19/21; 196,2/9; 18–197,17
*10. *De Gratia et Lib. Arb.* 3.5; PL 44: 884

†**Rm 3:4** (Ps 116:11)

11. *God alone is true, every human being is a liar, as is written.*† Therefore, if God is true, and he alone is true while every human being is a liar, how will humans be true unless they draw near to the one who is not a liar Accordingly, this is said to humans: 'You were once darkness.' See—*every human being is a liar.* This is said to God: 'With you is the fountain of life, and in your light we shall see light.' Since *God alone is true*, because 'God is light, and in him is no darkness at all'—human beings are darkness, God is light—human beings are liars, God is true—when will a human being be true? 'Draw near to him and be enlightened.'†

†Eph 5:8; Ps 36:9; 1 Jn 1:5; Ps 34:5

Scripture intended to point out that all human beings—absolutely all, to the extent that they partake of human nature—are liars. Of themselves they are liars, and of themselves they have nothing except to be liars. This is not because they cannot be true, but because they will not be true of themselves. In order, then, that they may be true [Scripture says], 'I believed, and therefore have I spoken.'† Take from them that 'I believed'—*every human being is a liar.* When they withdraw from the truth of God they will remain in their lie, since those 'who speak a lie speak out of their own nature.'

†Ps 116:10

Ask, therefore, 'What shall I return to the Lord for everything that he has given to me?' 'In my alarm I said,' and I spoke the truth, 'every human being is a liar.'† But [God] has not given me punishment in return for my lie, but good in return for evil; by making a godless person righteous he made a truthful person out of a liar. Still, *God is true, every human being is a liar.*

†Ps 116:12, 11

—in a sermon on Psalm 115*

†Ps 116:11. Here Augustine reads *extasi*; in the preceding excerpt he read *pavore*; the Vulgate has *excessu*.

12. 'In my trance I said, Every human being is a liar.'† [The psalmist] calls his state of alarm a 'trance.' This is what human weakness suffers when persecutors threaten and suffering is imminent. We take it to have that meaning here because we hear the voice of martyrs in this psalm. 'Trance' has a different meaning when a person's mind is

*11. *En. in Ps* 115.11. This part of Augustine's explanation of Psalm 115 does not appear in the extant manuscripts or in the printed editions. The text is given by F. Dolbeau in *Revue Bénédictine* 101 (1991) 252,39–253,65.

not beside itself from alarm but is possessed by some inspiration of revelation. Terrified people have observed their own weakness and seen that they should not rely upon themselves. As far as pertains to human beings, they are liars. By God's grace they are made true lest they yield to the pressure of their enemies, and not say what they believe, but deny it. This happened to Peter when he relied upon himself. Hence Scripture says with perfect truth, 'Every human being is a liar.' They will not be liars only so far as they will not be human, since they will be gods, and children of the Most High.† †Mt 26:69–70; Ps 82:6

—in the explanation of Psalm 115*

13. *As Scripture says, 'That you may be justified in your words and prevail when you are judged.'*† †**Rm 3:4** (Ps 51:4)

What does it mean that the Judge to come is to be judged, that the Righteous One is to be judged by sinners, and will prevail in the judgment, because there is nothing in him to be judged? With foreknowledge the prophet David says to him who has no sin, 'Against you only have I sinned, and done what is evil in your sight,'† and so on. You overcome all human beings, all judges, and †Ps 51:4 those who suppose that they are righteous are unrighteous in your sight. Therefore *you prevail when you are judged*—you overcome—because you are greater than human beings, and human beings were made by you.

—in the explanation of Psalm 50*

14. *Let us do evil so that good may come.*† †**Rm 3:8**

'How unsearchable are his judgments and inscrutable his ways!'† †Rm 11:33 Wrongheaded persons who did not reflect on these unsearchable judgments and inscrutable ways, and who were inclined to be critical—being incapable of understanding them—supposed and proclaimed that the apostles were saying, *Let us do evil so that good*

*12. *En. in Ps* 115.3; CC 40: 1654,1/13; 19; 26/27
*13. *En. in Ps* 50.9; CC 38: 605–606, 2, 14/16, 30/35, 37/39

may come. Far be it from the apostles to say this! People without understanding supposed that this was being said when they heard the Apostle say, 'Law came in so that trespass may increase; but where
†Rm 5:20 trespass increased, grace abounded all the more.'† Surely grace brings it about that those who [formerly] did evil are now doing good—not that they continue in evil and consider that they are receiving good in return. Accordingly, they should not say, 'Let us do evil so that good may come,' but, 'We have done evil and good has come; let us now do good, so that we who have received good in return for evil in this age may receive good in return for good in the age to come.'

—from *On Grace and Free Choice**

15. *We have charged that all, Greeks and Jews, are under [the domination of] sin, as it is written: 'There is no one righteous, no one with understanding, no one who seeks God. All have turned aside, together they have become*
†**Rm 3:9–12** (Ps 14:3) *worthless.'*†

'All have turned aside, together they have become worthless'—that is, Jews have become just like Gentiles, of whom it was said earlier [in the psalm], 'There is not one who does good, not up to
†Ps 14:3, 1 one!'† We can take 'not up to one' [to mean] either 'including that one'—so 'no one' is understood—or, 'excepting one'—so the Lord Christ is excepted. We say, 'The field goes up to the sea,' not, of course, reckoning in the sea. The latter is the better interpretation, so that we take no one to have done good *up to* Christ, for no human being can do good unless [Christ] has shown it. This is true: until people know the one God, they cannot do good.

†**Rm 3:13** (Ps 5:9) *Their throat is an open grave.*† This either signifies the insatiability of a gaping gullet, or, in a spiritual sense, that they slay and as it were devour those they have killed when they persuade them [to follow] their own perverse ways. Like this in the opposite sense is what was
†Ac 10:13 said to Peter, 'Slaughter and eat,'† in order that he may convert the Gentiles to his own faith and good ways. *They deceived with their tongues*. Flattery is the companion of gluttony and every evil.

---

*14. *De Gratia et Lib. Arb.* 22.44; PL 44: 910

The venom of vipers is under their lips.† [The psalmist] is calling deceit 'venom,' the venom of vipers, because [the deceitful] are unwilling to listen to the commands of the law just as vipers are unwilling to listen to the words of the snake-charmer—which is said more clearly in another psalm.† *Their mouth is full of cursing and bitterness.*† This is 'the venom of vipers.' *Their feet are swift to shed blood*†—by their habit of doing evil. *Ruin and unhappiness are in their ways*†—all the ways of wicked people are full of hardship and misery. For this reason the Lord cries out, 'Come to me, all you who labor, and I will give you rest. Take my yoke upon you, and learn from me, for I am meek and humble of heart. For my yoke is easy, and my burden is light.'† *And they have not known the way of peace*†—the way, surely, that the Lord describes as an easy yoke and a light burden. *There is no fear of God before their eyes.*† Such persons do not say, 'There is no God,'† yet they do not fear God.

†**Rm 3:13** (Ps 140:3)
†Ps 58:4–5
†**Rm 3:14** (Ps 10:7)
†**Rm 3:15** (Pr 1:16; Is 59:
†**Rm 3:16**
†Mt 11:28–30
†**Rm 3:17** (Lk 1:79)
†**Rm 3:18** (Ps 36:1)
†Ps 14:1

—in the explanation of Psalm 13*

16. *We know that whatever the law says, it says to those who are subject to the law, so that every mouth may be stopped . . .* † †**Rm 3:19–20**

'Scripture has included everything under sin, so that from the faith of Jesus Christ the promise may be given to those who believe.'† Lord, merciful Lord, behave in this way—prescribe what cannot be carried out; or rather, prescribe what cannot be carried out except through your grace! Then, when human beings are unable to carry it out by their own strength, *every mouth may be stopped* and none may seem great to themselves. Let all be little children, *and let the whole world be guilty before you, because no flesh will be justified before* you *by the law.*

†Ga 3:22

—from the treatise on Psalm 118*

17. *Through the law [comes] knowledge of sin. Now the righteousness of God has been disclosed apart from the law.*† †**Rm 3:20–21**

*15. *En. in Ps* 13.2,4: CC 38: 86–87,1/4, 11/20, 4/27
*16. *En. in Ps* 118.27.3; CC 40: 1758,12/19

The Saviour's grace found everyone a transgressor, some more, some less. To the extent that the knowledge of the law was greater in each, so much less was the defense for sin, and so much more evident was the offense. It remained, then, that not their own righteousness but God's—I mean that given them by God—should come to aid them. Hence the Apostle says, *Through the law [comes] knowledge of sin*—not its removal, but knowledge of it.

Now the righteousness of God has been disclosed apart from the law, and is attested by the law and the prophets. For this reason [the psalmist]
†Ps 119:119 also added, 'Therefore I loved your testimonies,'† as if saying, 'Since the law, whether given in paradise, or implanted by nature, or promulgated in writing, has made transgressors of all the sinners on earth, therefore I loved your testimonies, which are in your law, [the result] of your grace, that not my righteousness but yours may be in me.'

The law benefits us to this end, that it sends us to grace—not only because it attests that the righteousness of God, which exists apart from the law, is to be disclosed, but also in this, that it makes us transgressors. The letter, then, kills. It compels us by fear to flee
†2 Co 3:6 to the life-giving Spirit,† who can blot out the whole of our sins and inspire a love of righteous deeds.

—from the treatise on the same psalm as above*

†**Rm 3:23** 18. *For all have sinned and lack God's glory.*†

He found all human beings sinners. He alone came without sin, he who found us sinners. This the Apostle [says]: *For all have sinned and lack God's glory*, that [Christ]—not you—may set [you] free. Because you cannot free yourself, you need someone to set you free. What have you to boast about? What allows you to rely on the law and on righteousness? See, then; pay attention to the one who says, 'I delight in the law of God in my inmost self,' and so on, to where he says, 'Who will deliver me from this body of death? The
†Rm 7:22–25 grace of God through Jesus Christ our Lord!'† Why grace? Because

---

*17. *En. in Ps* 118.25.5; CC 40: 1750,7/27

it is given gratuitously. Why is it given gratuitously? Because your own merits have not preceded it, but the kindnesses of God have anticipated you. Glory then be to him who sets us free! *For all have sinned and lack God's glory.*

—from the treatise on Psalm 30*

19. *Where then is your boasting? It is excluded . . .*† †**Rm 3:27**

'Take from me the path of iniquity,' [the psalmist] says. And because a law of actions has come in to increase trespass he goes on, 'And out of your law have mercy on me.' Out of what law if not the law of faith? Listen to the Apostle: *Where then is your boasting? It is excluded. By what law? That of actions? No, by the law of faith.* This is *the law of faith*, that we believe and pray that we be granted by grace to carry out what we are unable to fulfill by ourselves; otherwise, being unaware of the righteousness that comes from God and wanting to establish our own, we may fail to submit to God's righteousness.† †Ps 119:29; Rm 5:20; Rm 10:3 Accordingly, the righteousness of the God who gives commands lies in *the law of actions*, whereas the mercy of the God who comes to our assistance lies in *the law of faith.*

—from the treatise on Psalm 118*

20. We *consider that a person is justified by faith apart from works of the law.*† †**Rm 3:28**

'Abraham believed God, and it was reckoned to him as righteousness, and he was called the friend of God.'† †Jm 2:23 That [Abraham] believed God deep in his heart is the result solely of faith; that he led out his son to be sacrificed, that undaunted he took a knife in his right hand, that he would have struck at that moment had he not been stopped by a voice, is surely [an indication of] great faith as well as [being] a great work. And God praised this very work when he said, 'Because you have listened to my voice.'† †Gn 22:18

*18. *En. in Ps* 30.2.6; CC 38: 195,25/27, 28/30, 37/46
*19. *En. in Ps* 118.5; CC 40: 1694,4/13

Why then does the apostle Paul say, *We consider that a person is justified by faith apart from works of the law,* and in another place speaks
†Ga 5:6 of 'faith that works through love'?† How does faith work through love and how is a person justified by faith apart from works of the law? A person believes, receives the sacraments of the faith—and is dead. He had no time in which to perform works. What shall we say—that he was not justified? Of course we say that one who
†Rm 4:5 believes 'in him who justifies the godless'† was justified! Therefore, he was justified and he performed no works. The Apostle's statement is borne out where he says, *We consider that a person is justified by faith apart from works of the law.* The thief who was crucified with the Lord believed with his heart unto righteousness and confessed with his
†Lk 23:39–43; Rm 10:10 mouth unto salvation.†

The faith that works through love, even though lacking an opportunity to work externally, is yet kept burning in the heart. Some persons under the law boasted of works of the law, works they may have done not out of love but out of fear. They wanted to regard themselves as righteous and to be considered better then the nations that did not do the works of the law. The Apostle, who was preaching the faith to the nations, observed that those drawing near to the Lord were justified by faith, with the result that they were doing good works because they had already believed, not that they deserved to believe because they did good works. Therefore he spoke up confidently and said that a person can be justified by faith apart from works of the law. Those who were doing what they did out of fear were not righteous, since faith works in the heart through love, even if it has no external outlet in a work.

—from the sermon concerning Abraham when he sacrificed his son Isaac to God*

21. *What then shall we say that Abraham, our father according to the flesh,*
†Rm 4:1–2 *found?*†

*20. *Ser.* 2.8; PL 38: 31–32 passim. Bede discusses the seeming discrepancy between Paul (Romans 3:28) and James (2:23) at length in his *Exp. In Ep. VII Cath.* (CC 121: 198, 194–200, 254; Eng. trans. in CS 82: 30–32), the first part of which is a quotation from Augustine's *De Div. Quaest. LXXXIII* 76.1 (CC 44A: 218,4–219,27).

The apostle Paul bore witness that this psalm has to do with the grace by virtue of which we are Christians. When commending the righteousness that comes from faith against those who boast of the righteousness that comes from works, he says, *What then shall we say that Abraham, our father according to the flesh, found? For if Abraham was justified by works he has something to boast about, but not before God.* Many people boast about their works and you find many pagans who for this reason are unwilling to become Christians. They are quite satisfied with their good lives. They say, 'I lead a good life—why do I need to have Christ teach me? I do not commit murder, theft or violence. I do not covet other people's possessions. I am not defiled by adultery. If you find anything in my life to blame, let the one who blames me make [me] a Christian.' This person has something to boast about—but not to God.

Our father Abraham was not like this. What does Scripture say justified Abraham? *Abraham believed God, and it was credited to him for righteousness.*† And so Abraham was justified by faith. But you may say, 'You see that Abraham was not justified because of his works but by faith. Therefore, I will do whatever I want, because, even though I may not have good works and only believe in God, that is credited to me for righteousness.' I answer concerning Abraham what we find in another apostle's letter.† Wishing to correct certain persons who had misunderstood the apostle [Paul] because they were unwilling to perform good works and relied on their faith alone, [James] commended the works of this same Abraham whose faith Paul commended. [James] was speaking about a work well known to everyone, that Abraham offered his son to God to be sacrificed. If Abraham had done this without the right sort of faith, it would have been of no avail to him, however good that work may have been. Again, if Abraham's faith was such that when God commanded him to offer his son to him as a sacrifice he said to himself, 'I will not do it—yet I believe that God will deliver me even though I scorn his orders,' his faith without works would be dead; it would remain barren and dry, like a root without fruit.

—from the prologue to [the explanation of] Psalm 31*

†**Rm 4:3**=Jm 2:23 (Gn 15:6)

†Jm 2:21

*21. *En. in Ps* 31.2–4; CC 38: 225,1/8; 226,10/19, 28/31, 2/5, 9/16, 19–227,26

†**Rm 4:7**
(Ps 32:1)

22. *Happy are those whose iniquities are forgiven and whose sins are covered.*†

Everything is imputed to his grace, not to our merits. Therefore sins are covered over completely, covered so as to be blotted out, not in those in whom no sins are found but [in those] *whose sins are covered.* Why does [the psalmist] say that sins are covered? In order that they may not be seen. What is it for God to see sins except to punish them? And that you may know that for God to see sins is for him to punish them, what do we say to him?
†Ps 51:9 'Turn away your face from my sins.'† Let him not see your sins, so that he may see you; then [your sins] will not obstruct the eyes of God's mercy.

—[from the explanation of Psalm 31]*

†**Rm 4:14–15** 23. *If those of the law are heirs, faith is worthless . . .*†

The promise [made to Abraham] would be destroyed if anyone were made righteous by the law. *If those of the law are heirs, faith is worthless and the promise goes for nothing; for the law produces wrath.* Surely we need grace for this reason, to avoid God's wrath.

—from the second book against Julian*

24. Why, I ask, do you not notice that there are no heirs as a result of the law because *the law produces wrath? Where there is no*
†**Rm 4:15** *law, neither is there transgression.*† So then, [heirs] are the result of the promise [made to Abraham], because God does what he has promised. Those who suppose that they are fulfilling the commands of the law by a decision of their own free will wish to establish their
†Rm 10:3 own righteousness † apart from the spirit of grace, not to receive God's righteousness.

—from the same book*

---

*22. *En. in Ps* 31.9; CC 38: 232,40/44, 50/56
*23. *Contra Sec. Iul. Resp.* 160; CSEL 85,1: 282,10/13. The usual title given to this work is *Against the Second Reply of Julian, [bishop of Eclanum], An Incomplete Work.*
*24. *Contra Sec. Iul. Resp.* 158; CSEL 85,1: 280,18/24

25. God's predestination in a good person is the preparation for grace, and grace is the consequence of that predestination. When God promised Abraham that the faith of the nations would exist in all his descendants, saying 'I have made you the father of many nations'—whence the Apostle says, *For this reason it depends on faith, so that the promise may be established for all his descendants*†—[God] made this promise depend not upon the power of our wills but upon his predestination. He promised what he was going to bring about, not what humans would do. Although humans perform the good deeds that are an essential part of their worship of God, he himself brings about their doing what he has commanded. They do not make him do what he has promised. Otherwise, that God's promises are carried out would depend not on the power of God but of humans, and what the Lord promised would be bestowed on Abraham by them.

†Gn 17:5 (Rm 4:17); **Rm 4:16**

This is not how Abraham believed God. *He grew strong in faith as he gave glory to God, knowing full well that what he promised he is also able to do.*† [Paul] did not say 'to foretell,' he did not say 'to foreknow,' for [God] is able to foretell and foreknow the deeds of others too; he said *is also able to do*—not the deeds of others but his own. He promised children to Abraham—which they cannot be unless they have faith; therefore, he himself bestows faith. Indeed, since the Apostle says, *For this reason it depends on faith, so that the promise may be established,* I wonder why human beings prefer to rely on their own infirmity, rather than on the firmness of God's promise?

†**Rm 4:20–21**

—from *To Prosper and Hilary**

26. . . . *who gives life to the dead, and calls those things that are not as those that are.*†

†**Rm 4:17**

'And let your mercy come upon me, Lord.' If we ask what that mercy is, let us listen to what follows: 'your salvation follows upon your word.'† He promised this, *who calls those things that are not as*

†Ps 119:41

*25. *De Praedest. Sanct.* 10.19–11.21; PL 44: 975–76 passim

those that are. Those to whom the promise was made were not yet in existence lest any of them glory in their own merits. Even those who were to receive the promise [i.e., the elect] were themselves promised. Thus the whole body of Christ may say, 'By the grace of
†1 Co 15:10 God I am what I am!'†

—from the treatise on Psalm 118*

27. *He was handed over for our trespasses and rose again for our justi-*
†Rm 4:25 *fication.*†

As we are sown by his death, so do we germinate in his resurrection. His death signifies the destruction of our old life, and his resurrection signifies the newness of our life. Concerning this the Apostle says, 'We have been buried together with him by baptism into death, so that, just as Christ rose from the dead, so we too may
†Col 3:9–10; Rm 6:4 walk in newness of life.'† [Paul] did not say, 'He was handed over for our justification and rose again for our trespasses.' Trespass is implied in his handing over; righteousness is implied in his resurrection. Let trespass die, then, and righteousness rise!

—from a sermon on the gospel reading for the Tuesday after Easter*

†Rm 5:8–9 28. *God proves his love for us . . .*†

People had to be persuaded of how much God loves us, and what kind of people he loves; of how much, to keep us from despair; what kind, to keep us from pride. The Apostle explains this crucial point here: *God proves his love for us in that while we were still sinners Christ died for us. Much more, now that we have been justified by his blood, will we be saved through him from [God's] wrath.*

—from *On the Trinity* 4.1*

*26. *En. in Ps* 118.13.1; CC 40: 1705,22/29
*27. *Serm.* 236.1; PL 38: 1120 passim
*28. *De Trin.* 4.1.2; CC 50: 161,23–162,30

29. *Justified by his blood,*† [Paul] says—*justified* clearly by the fact that we have been freed from all sin—freed from all sin because God's Son, who had no sin,† was slain for us. Therefore *we will be saved through [Christ] from [God's] wrath*—clearly from the wrath which is nothing else than just punishment.† God's wrath is not like human agitation. His wrath is the wrath of one to whom holy Scripture says in another place, 'You, Lord of might, judge with tranquillity.'†

†**Rm 5:9**
†2 Co 5:21; 1 P 2:22
†Rv 16:7, 19:2
†Ws 12:18

If the just divine punishment has been described in such a way, then, God's reconciliation too, when properly understood, [comes] only when wrath of this sort is brought to an end. We were not God's enemies except to the extent that sins are enemies of righteousness. When these have been forgiven, enmities of this kind are brought to an end, and those he justifies are reconciled to the Just One. Yet surely he even loved these enemies since 'he did not spare his own Son, but handed him over for all of us'† when we were still enemies. Therefore the Apostle rightly went on, *For if while we were enemies we were reconciled to God by the death of his Son*—by which forgiveness of sins was brought about—*much more, having been reconciled, will we be saved in his life* †—we who were reconciled by death are saved in life! Who can doubt that he will give his life to his friends, for whom, when they were enemies, he gave his death?

†Rm 8:32
†**Rm 5:10**

—from *On the Trinity* 13.16*

30. *For if while we were enemies we were reconciled to God by the death of his Son, much more, having been reconciled, will we be saved in his life.*†

†**Rm 5:10**

Christ died for the wicked, and Christ is God. How great will be the life of the righteous, found in the life of God, when the wicked were even sought by the death of God, so that they would not perish! We will be saved in God's life because we would have perished in our own life. When we hear 'God's life' and 'God's death' let us distinguish the origin of each. He brought life to us,

*29. *De Trin.* 13.16.21; CC 50A: 410,52–411,72

but received death from us—not because he deserved it, but for our sake.

—from a sermon on the passion*

31. 'We were by nature children of wrath,' [Paul] says, 'like everyone
†Eph 2:3 else.'† Human beings were [subject to] this wrath because of original sin—and more seriously and calamitously as they had added greater additional sins to it. Therefore they needed a mediator—that is, one who would bring about reconciliation—to appease this wrath by the offering of a unique sacrifice, of which all the sacrifices of the law and prophets were prefigurations. Hence the Apostle says, *For if while we were enemies we were reconciled to God by the death of his Son, much more now, being reconciled, will we be saved from the wrath*
†**Rm 5:10 and 9** conflated *through [Christ].*†

When God is said to be angry, no agitation on his part, like that in the mind of an angry person, is intended. We use this expression, transferred from human emotions, analogously, so that
†Rv 16:7, 19:2 his punishment—which is nothing if not just†—receives the name *wrath*. That we are reconciled to God by a mediator, and receive the Holy Spirit—so that from having been enemies we become children ('as many as are led by the Spirit of God, these are children
†Rm 8:14 of God')†—this comes about by the grace of God through Jesus Christ our Lord.

—from *Enchiridion* 33*

32. *Not only that,* [Paul] says, *but we even boast in God through our Lord*
†**Rm 5:11** *Jesus Christ, through whom we have received reconciliation.*†

Not only will we be saved, he says, *but we even boast*—not in ourselves but *in God*, not through ourselves but *through our Lord Jesus*

*30. *Serm.* This sermon is quoted by Bede but is not to be found in the printed editions of Augustine's authentic sermons. But see PL 39: 1723.

*31. *Enchir.* 10.33; CC 46: 68,10/25. This is a handbook or manual of theological questions.

Christ, through whom we have received reconciliation, in the way that was discussed earlier.

Then the Apostle adds, *Therefore, as sin entered into this world through one man, and through sin death,*† and so on. In this passage he discusses two people at some length. One is the same 'first Adam' by whose sin and death his descendants were bound as if by hereditary evils. The other, the 'second Adam,' is not only a human but also God. When he paid for us a debt he did not owe, we were set free from our debts, both ancestral and those incurred by ourselves. Hence, since on account of that *one man* [Adam] the devil held [captive] all who were generated through his corrupted carnal desire, it is just that on account of this one man [Christ], [God] should forgive all who have been regenerated through his untainted grace. †**Rm 5:12**

—from *On the Trinity* 13.16*

33. If the Apostle had wanted us to understand [that sin *spread to all people*]† by imitation [of Adam] he would have said that sin entered the world through the devil. It is written of the devil, 'They imitate him who are on his side.'† [Paul] said *through one man*, the one from whom generation of the human race began, to teach that original sin [comes] through generation. †**Ibid.** †Ws 2:24 (25)

—to Count Valerius*

34. *Therefore, just as sin entered into this world through one man, and through sin death, so too [death] spread to all people—in [Adam] all sinned.*† †**Rm 5:12**

As [they are] from that *one man* [Adam], so infants cannot be free from the same sin except when they are released from its

*32. *De Trin.* 13.16.21; CC 50A: 411,72–412,90

*33. *De Nupt. et Concup.* 2.45; CSEL 42: 299,10–17 passim. Count Valerius was an acquaintance of Augustine's who lived at Ravenna. Augustine addressed the treatise *On Marriage and Concupiscence* to him.

guilt by Christ's baptism. *Sin was in the world until the law*—it is not said that thereafter it was not in anyone, but that it could not be taken away by the letter of the law because it could only [be taken away] by the Spirit of grace. Therefore, lest any trust in the strength—I do not say of their wills, but rather of their vanity—and suppose that they could satisfy the law by free choice and scorn the grace of Christ, the Apostle says, *Sin was in the world*
†Rm 5:13 *until the law, but sin was not reckoned when there was no law.*† He did not say 'did not exist' but *was not reckoned* because the law did not exist. By maintaining this the point is proven, whether [he was referring to] the law of reason in children or the written law among ordinary people.

Yet death reigned from Adam until Moses, [Paul] says, because not even the law given by Moses could take away the reign of death, which only Christ's grace has taken away. But see in whom it reigned: he says *even over those who did not sin after the pattern of*
†Rm 5:14 *the trespass of Adam.*† It reigned, then, *even over those who did not sin.* He adds the reason why it reigned when he says *after the pattern of the trespass of Adam.* This is the better interpretation of these words, so that when he had said that *death reigned even over those who did not sin*, as if to explain to us why it reigned over those who did not sin he added, *after the pattern of the trespass of Adam*—that is, because *the pattern of the trespass of Adam* was present in their [bodily] members.

We can also take it this way: *death reigned from Adam until Moses, even over those who did not sin after the pattern of the trespass of Adam*, because at the time of their birth they would not yet have in themselves the use of the reason which [Adam] used when he sinned, nor would they have received the precept which [Adam] transgressed; only the original fault by which the reign of death would draw them to condemnation would hold them bound. Only in those who have been reborn by Christ's grace and who belong to his reign does this reign of death not exist. Although temporal death was passed on as a result of the original fault, in their case it puts an end to their bodies but does not draw their souls to punishment—which is how he wished us to understand death's reign.

In order that a soul renewed by grace should not now die in Gehenna—that is, in order that it not be alienated or separated from the life of God—temporal death remains for the time being, even for those redeemed by Christ's death, as a test for their faith and a contest of our present struggle—in which the martyrs too have striven—but this too will be done away with in the restoration of the body which the resurrection promises. Then death, whose reign Christ's grace now takes away, will be entirely swallowed up in victory† lest it drag down souls that belong to him to the punishments of the underworld. †1 Co 15:54

Neither should we interpret what [Paul] added concerning Adam, *who is an image of the one who was to come*,† in only one way. **†Rm 5:14** We can take [Adam] to be *an image* of Christ by being his opposite, so that 'as in [Adam] all die, so also in Christ all will be made alive,'† †1 Co 15:22 and as through [Adam's] disobedience many were made sinners, so through the obedience of Christ many may be made righteous; or [we can say that] he called [Adam] *an image of the one who was to come* because he imposed the image of death on his descendants. The former is the better interpretation, so that we believe that he is *an image* [of Christ] by being his opposite, which the Apostle highly commends.

Then, so that we will not take the opposite to be the equal of the image, [Paul] adds, *But the free gift is not like the trespass; for if many died on account of one person's trespass, much more have God's grace and the gift in the grace of the one person, Jesus Christ, abounded for many.*† We should not take *much more* as said of persons, since **†Rm 5:15** the wicked who will be condemned are much more numerous, but that [grace] has abounded more. In those redeemed by Christ the image of death from Adam will prevail for a time, but the image of life through Christ will prevail for ever. Although [Paul] says that Adam *is an image of the one who was to come* by being his opposite, yet Christ benefits those who are regenerated more than [Adam] harmed those he generated.

—from a letter in reply to the queries of Hilary,
a monk at Syracuse*

*34. *Ep.* 157.18–20; CSEL 44: 466,19–468,16; 469,1/21

35. We are not discussing some sinner who sinned at one time or another, but the one through whom sin entered into the world. If we seek a model for imitation we find the devil. If [we seek] the source of contamination in generation [we find] Adam. Hence when the Apostle said, *Sin entered into the world through one man,*† he wanted us to understand the sin of generation. The sin of imitation did not enter into the world through one man but through the devil.

†**Rm 5:12**

—from the second book against Julian*

36. Do sinners not imitate Eve? Does the sin of the human race not take its beginning from her? 'From a woman sin had its beginning, and because of her,' Scripture says, 'we all die.'† Why do you choose not to notice that the Apostle chose to say that *sin entered into the world through one man*† because he wanted us to understand not imitation but generation? As the beginning of sin was from a woman, so the beginning of generation is from a man; first the man inseminates so that the woman may give birth. So *sin entered into the world through one man* because it entered through the seed of generation; receiving it from the man, the woman conceived. In this way he who alone was born without sin chose to be born of a woman.†

†Si 25:24

†**Rm 5:12**

†2 Co 5:21; 1 P 2:22; Ga 4:4

—from the same book*

37. In the place where [Paul] said that *sin entered into the world through one man, and through sin death, and so spread to all people,*† whether sin, or death, or both *spread to all people* seems unclear. The subject itself, however, shows clearly which of these it is. If sin had not spread, we would not all be born with the law of sin that dwells in our members.† If death had not spread, we would not all die, insofar as that belongs to the condition of mortal beings. The Apostle says *in whom all have sinned*†—we must understand *in whom* only as 'in

†**Rm 5:12**. The second *mors* of the Vulgate is missing in Augustine's text.

†Rm 7:23

†**Rm 5:12**

*35. *Contra Sec. Iul. Resp.* 49; CSEL 85,1: 198,21–199,28
*36. *Ibid.* 56; CSEL 85,1: 204,40–205,52

Adam'—in whom, [Paul] says, [all] die as well, since to pass down punishment was not just unless there was a guilty action.

What else do the Apostle's words which follow indicate? When he had said this he added, *Sin was in the world until the law*—that is, because the law was unable to take away sin, *sin was not reckoned when there was no law.* [Sin] existed, then, but it was not reckoned, since what could be reckoned was not evident. As [Paul] says elsewhere, 'Through the law [comes] knowledge of sin.' *Yet death reigned*, [Paul] says, *from Adam until Moses*.† This is what he †**Rm 5:13**, 3:20,
had said previously—*until the law*, not *until Moses*—so that [he did **5:14**
not mean that] thenceforth there would be no sin, but that the law given through Moses could not take away the reign of death—which surely does not reign except through sin. Furthermore, [death's] reign is that it casts a mortal person into a second death as well, a death which is everlasting.

Death reigned—in whom? *Even over those*, [Paul] says, *who did not sin after the pattern of the trespass of Adam, who is an image of the one who was to come*.† Of what *one who was to come* if not Christ, and what †**Rm 5:14**
kind of image if not the opposite? [Paul] also says this elsewhere: 'As in Adam all die, so also in Christ all will be made alive.'† As in †1 Co 15:22
the former, that [is the case], so in the latter this [will be the case]. [Adam] is the image—but this image is not in every way identical. Hence here the Apostle adds, *But the free gift is not like the trespass; for if many died on account of one person's trespass, much more have God's grace and gift in the grace of the one person, Jesus Christ, abounded for many*.† †**Rm 5:15**
What does *much more have* they *abounded* mean? That all who are set free by Christ die temporarily because of Adam, but because of Christ they will be victorious forever.

And after an interval:† The Apostle's words, *Sin was in the world* †Bede's addition.
until the law, he wants us to understand not only of original sin but of all sin, and therefore it existed *until the law* because the law could not take away sin. He said *until the law* so that this statement could also include the law, just as the gospel says, 'All the generations from Abraham until David are fourteen [generations]'†—David was not †Mt 1:17
excluded, but this number is fulfilled by counting him too.

So the law is not separate from the persistence of sin because sin is said to have existed *until* [*the law*], and as a result of this no one takes

†Rm 7:12 away sin. The law, although holy and just and good,† was unable to take it away. Only the one of whom it was said, 'Behold, the Lamb of God, who takes away the sins of the world,' [was able to take it
†Jn 1:29 away].† He takes sin away by forgiving what has been committed—including original [sin]; by providing aid—so that [sins] may not be committed; and by leading the way to the life where [sins] are altogether impossible.

—from the same book*

38. What the Apostle says is true and, therefore, what you say is false. As to what you earlier said that the Apostle had carefully insisted on—*much more have God's grace and gift of the one person, Jesus*
†Rm 5:15 *Christ, abounded for* the majority,† wanting it understood that 'the majority' were spoken of because God's grace reached even infants, with whom we do not associate imitation of the first man—either a faulty text misled you, or you yourself were being misleading, or you were deluded by someone deceiving [you], whether by deceit or forgetfulness. The Apostle did not say 'the majority' but *many*.† Turn to the Greek text and you will find *many*, not 'the majority'. [The Apostle] said that grace abounded much more *for many*, not 'for many more'—that is, not for the majority, as I have already shown. If he had spoken of 'the majority' because of infants whom grace possesses—since imitation of the first man does not possess them—he would have been speaking falsely, and would have been like you. If all who imitate Christ after his incarnation, including regenerated infants, should be joined with sinners, all of whom you want to associate with the imitation of the first man on account of their freedom of choice, clearly those who sin willingly from [the time of] Adam up until the end of the world are in the majority, so that you are refuted by your own deceitfulness.

†*plures* (lit. 'more') and *multos*; Augustine read *multos*, Julian and the Vulgate *plures*.

And the gift is not like the trespass; for the judgment following one
†Rm 5:16 *[brought] condemnation.*† *Following one* what if not trespass? For there follows, *The grace following many trespasses [brought] justification.* Let

*37. *Ibid.* 64–84; CSEL 85,1: 210,30/41; 213,3–214,28; 221,15–222,22; 27/34 them say how *following one trespass [comes] condemnation* unless even one original sin, which is passed on to all people, is sufficient for condemnation. *The grace following many trespasses [brought] justification,* then, because it not only did away with that one [trespass] that we take in by reason of our origin, but also with the other [trespasses] that are added in the case of each person by the action of each one's will.

—from the same book*

39. *If because of one man's trespass death reigned through that one man, much more will those who receive the abundance of grace and righteousness reign in life through the one man, Jesus Christ.*† †Rm 5:17

If because of one man's trespass death reigned through that one man, from whose trespass infants are purified by baptism, *much more will those who receive the abundance of grace and righteousness reign in life through the one man, Jesus Christ*—much more, surely, will they reign in life, because it will be the reign of eternal life; death overtakes them temporarily, [but] it will not overtake them for ever.

—from a letter in reply to the queries of Hilary of Syracuse*

40. *Therefore as one man's trespass led to condemnation for everyone, so too one man's act of righteousness led to justification for life for everyone.*† Let †Rm 5:18 them still maintain their superficial understanding, and say that one man did not draw his descendants [after him] but [only] provided an example of sin. How then did *one man's trespass lead to condemnation for everyone,* and not rather his many trespasses, unless that one alone is capable of leading to condemnation even without the addition of any others, just as it leads infants born of Adam, who die unless they are reborn in Christ?

In that these two positions appear to you to be contradictory, so that everyone proceeds to condemnation because of Adam and

*38. *Ibid.* 148,103; CSEL 85,1: 271,18/37; 233,1–234,12
*39. *Ep.* 157.13; CSEL 44: 460,12/18

everyone proceeds to justification because of Christ, you are entirely mistaken. Except through Adam no member of the human race is led to the condemnation from which people are set free by the bath of rebirth, and except through Christ no member of the human race is set free from this condemnation. Therefore in both instances [Paul] said *everyone*, because no one [incurs] condemnation [as a result] of generation except through the former, and no one [comes] to the life of regeneration except through the latter. The universality of the one part does not exclude a place for the other, because Christ brings to life those whom he chooses from among those who universally die in Adam. On this account he too is said to set *everyone* free, since no one but he sets anyone free—just as he is said to enlighten
†Jn 1:9 everyone† since no one but he enlightens anyone.

—from the second book against Julian*

41. Further on [Paul] calls the same people *many* as well as 'everyone' when he adds, *As by the one man's disobedience many were made sinners,*
†**Rm 5:19** *so by the one man's obedience many will be made righteous.*† See how he calls to our attention *one* and *one*, that is, Adam and Christ; the former for condemnation, the latter for justification, since Christ came in the flesh so long after Adam in order that we may know that even the righteous of old, as many as could be so, were set free by the same faith by which we also are set free—faith of course in the incarnation of Christ, which was foretold to them just as it is proclaimed to us.

In this place, then, he refers to Christ as a human being, although he is also God. He did not want anyone to presume that those righteous persons of old could have been set free by Christ as
†Jn 1:1 God only—that is, by the Word that was in the beginning†—and not also by faith in his incarnation, because of which Christ is also said to be a human being.

What [Paul] adds, saying, *But law came in so that trespass may*
†**Rm 5:20** *increase,*† does not pertain to the trespass derived from Adam, of

*40. *Contra Sec. Iul. Resp.* 104, 135–36; CSEL 85,1: 234,15/26; 261,28/39; 262,7/10

which he said earlier that 'death reigned through one man.'† We †Rm 5:17
should understand [him to mean] either the natural law which
appears in people at the age when they are able to make use of their
reason, or the written law given through Moses, which was unable
to bring life and liberation from the law of sin and of death † which †Rm 8:2
derived from Adam, but rather added increase to the transgression.
'Where there is no law, neither is their transgression.'† After the †Rm 4:15
transgression of the law given in paradise, humans were born from
Adam with 'the law of sin and death,' of which [Paul] says, 'I see in
my members another law at war with the law of my mind,'† and so †Rm 7:23
on. Yet unless this law is later strengthened by bad habit it is fairly
easily overcome—though not without God's grace.

By transgression of the other law, the one that exists in the use of reason by the rational soul at the time when a human being makes use of reason, all the sinners on earth become transgressors. After transgression of the law given by Moses as well, trespass increased all the more. *Law*, therefore, *came in so that trespass may increase*, either when humans neglect what God commands, or when they presume on their own strength, failing to ask for the help of grace and adding pride to their weakness. When by divine inspiration they understand to whom they must utter their groans, and they call on him in whom they rightly believe, saying, 'Have mercy on me, God, according to your great compassion,' and, 'I said, Lord have mercy
upon me; heal my soul, for I have sinned against you'†—when, then, †Ps 51:1, 41:4
a human being reaches out to him and groans thus, the following
words will be realized: *Where trespass increased, grace abounded all the more*, and, 'Many sins are forgiven her because she has loved much,'
and, 'God's love is poured out in the heart.'† †**Rm 5:20**;
Lk 7:47; Rm 5:5

From this comes 'the fulfillment of the law'—not through the
power of choice that is in us, but 'through the Holy Spirit that has
been given to us,'† so that *just as sin reigned in death, so grace may also* †Rm 13:10; 5:5
reign through righteousness unto eternal life, through Jesus Christ our Lord.† †**Rm 5:21**
When he says now, *just as sin reigned in death*, he does not say 'through one man' or 'through the first man' or 'through Adam,' since he has already said that *law came in so that trespass may increase.* This increase does not pertain to the descendants of the first man, but to the transgression proceeding from human conduct, which has now, in

mature years, been added to that trespass, the only one, by which alone infants are held bound, out of the abundance of iniquity.

Since our Saviour's grace is capable of doing away with the whole [mass of sin], even that which does not pertain to the origin in the one man's trespass, when he said *so grace may also reign through righteousness unto eternal life* he added *through Jesus Christ our Lord*. Accordingly, no one's arguments against these apostolic words should keep infants from the salvation that is in Jesus Christ our Lord. The less capable they are of speaking on their own behalf, the more must we speak for them.

—from a letter in reply to the queries of Hilary*

42. When [Paul] had spoken of the punishment [that came] through one man and the grace [that came] through one man, he next commended the sublime mystery of holy baptism in the cross of Christ in such a way that we can understand that Christ's baptism is nothing else than a likeness to Christ's death, and that Christ's death upon the cross is nothing else than a likeness to the pardon of sin. Just as in him, then, a real death took place, so in us a real remission of sins; and as in him a true resurrection, so in us a real justification.

[Paul] asks, *What then shall we say? Shall we continue in sin so that grace may abound?*† He had said earlier, 'Where sin increased, grace abounded all the more,'† and therefore he asked himself whether we should continue in sin for the sake of producing an abundance of grace. He answered, *By no means!* and he added, *If we are dead to sin, how can we live in it?*†

—from *Enchiridion* 52*

†**Rm 6:1**

†Rm 5:20. Here Augustine read *peccatum*; in the preceding excerpt he read *delictum* as does the Vulgate.

†**Rm 6:2**

43. Nothing shorter and better could be said. What does God's grace bestow upon us in this present corrupt age more useful than that we die to sin? And for this reason the person who chooses to

*41. *Ep.* 157.13–18; CSEL 44: 461,1/17; 462,18–463,3; 13/23; 464,14/21; 465,5/11; 23–466,16

*42. *Enchir.* 14.52; CC 46: 76,46–77,61

live in sin by means of that grace by which we die to sin will be found ungrateful for this grace.

—from a letter to the monk Valentine*

44. Then, to show that we are dead to sin [Paul] says, *Do you not know that we who have been baptized into Christ Jesus have been baptized in his death?*† If that *we have been baptized in his death* shows that we †**Rm 6:3**
are dead to sin, unquestionably even the infants who are baptized in Christ die to sin, since they are baptized in his death. No one was excepted when he said that *we who have been baptized into Christ Jesus have been baptized in his death.* He said this to prove that we are dead to sin. But to what sin do infants die by being reborn except to one they contracted by being born? Therefore what follows also applies to them: *For we have been buried together with him by baptism into death, so that, just as Christ rose from the dead by the glory of the Father, so we too may walk in newness of life*, and so on to the place where he says, *In that he died to sin, he died once; in that he lives, he lives for God. So you also must consider that you are dead to sin and alive to God in Christ Jesus.*† It was from this point that [Paul] began to prove that we are †**Rm 6:4–11**
not to continue in sin so that grace may abound, and asked, 'If we are dead to sin, how can we live in it?'† And to show that we are †Rm 6:2
dead to sin he added, *Do you not know that we who have been baptized into Christ Jesus have been baptized in his death?* Thus he concludes this entire passage just as he began it.

He introduced the death of Christ in this way in order to say that he too is dead to sin. To what sin [did he die] if not to the flesh—in which there was no sin, but a likeness of sin, and so it was called 'sin'. Accordingly, to those who have been baptized in the death of Christ—in which not only adults but infants too are baptized—he says, *So you also*—that is, just like Christ—*so you also must consider that you are dead to sin and alive to God in Christ Jesus.*

Thus whatever happened on Christ's cross, in his burial, in his resurrection on the third day, in his ascension into heaven, and in his being seated at the right hand of the Father, happened in such a

*43. *Ep.* 215.8: CSEL 57: 395,12/16

way that the Christian life happening here and now may conform to these things, things not only spoken of mystically but that really happened. Because of his cross [Paul] said, 'Those who belong to Jesus Christ have crucified their flesh with its passions and cravings'; because of his burial, *we have been buried with Christ by baptism into death*; because of his resurrection, *that just as Christ rose from the dead by the glory of the Father, so we too may walk in newness of life*; and because of his ascension into heaven and his being seated at the right hand of the Father, 'If you have risen with Christ, seek the things that are above, where Christ is seated at the right hand of God. Set your minds on things that are above, not on things on earth, for you have died, and your life is hidden with Christ in God.'†

†Ga 5:24; **Rm 6:4**; Col 3:1–3

—from *Enchiridion* 52*

45. [Christ] gave out that cry, intended to express the death of our soul, as a mysterious reference to our inner self. Not only in the psalm but also on the cross [he cried out], 'My God, my God, why have you forsaken me?'† The Apostle concurred with this cry when he said, *We know that our old self was crucified with him so that the body of sin may be destroyed, and that we may no longer be enslaved to sin.*† We should take the crucifixion of our inner self to mean penitential sorrow and a kind of salutary torment [that results from] self-discipline; by this death the death of ungodliness—in which God does not abandon us—is done away with. Therefore by such a cross is *the body of sin* destroyed so that we may no longer present our members to sin as weapons of wickedness. Also, if our inner nature is surely being renewed from day to day, clearly it is old before being renewed. This is done inwardly, as the same apostle says: 'Strip off your old self.' This he subsequently explains, 'So then, putting away lying, speak the truth.' Where is lying put away except inwardly, so that people who speak the truth in their hearts may dwell on God's holy mountain?†

†Ps 22:1; Mt 27:46

†**Rm 6:6**

†Rm 6:13; 2 Co 4:16; Eph 4:22, 25; Ps 15:2, 1

—from *On the Holy Trinity* 4.3*

*44. *Enchir.* 14.52–53; CC 46: 77,61–78,111
*45. *De Trin.* 4.3.6; CC 50: 167,58–168,75

46. *In that he died to sin, he died once; in that he lives, he lives to God. So you also must consider that you are dead to sin and alive to God in Christ Jesus.*† This is a mystery, in which those who are baptized experience the end of their old life and begin entering into a new one. Hence [Paul] says, *We have been buried together with him by baptism into death, so that, just as Christ rose from the dead by the glory of the Father, so we too may walk in newness of life.*† Therefore let us recognize that through this mystery we are both dead to sin with Christ and alive to righteousness in Christ. In his cross is the sorrow of those who confess, in his burial is the repose of those who have been absolved, in his resurrection is the life of the righteous.

†**Rm 6:10–11**

†Rm 6:4

—from a sermon on the Lord's resurrection*

47. *Therefore, do not let sin reign in your mortal body to make you obey its desires, nor present your members to sin as weapons of wickedness.*†

†**Rm 6:12–13**

[Paul] does not say, 'Do not let [sin] exist,' but, *do not let [sin] reign*. Although sin necessarily exists in your members, at least do away with its reign; do not do what it commands. Does anger arise? Do not give over your tongue to anger for cursing, or your hand or foot for doing violence. Irrational anger would not arise if sin did not exist in your members. Take away its reign, do not let it have weapons for fighting against you—it learns not to arise when it begins to find no weapons. *Do not present your members to sin as weapons of wickedness* Otherwise you will be completely its captive, and you will be unable to say, 'With my mind I serve the law of God.'†

†Rm 7:25

—from homily thirty-eight on the Gospel of John*

*46. *Serm.* This sermon is not to be found in the printed editions of Augustine's authentic sermons but both Bede and Florus of Lyon give it in their collections. See PL 39: 1724.

*47. *Tract in Ioh.* 41.12; CC 36: 364,2/13. The difference in chapter numbers in Augustine's homilies on John as given by Bede and in the modern printed editions is quite possibly due to the absence of homilies 20–22 from Bede's manuscript. See the article by D.F. Wright, 'Tractatus 20–22 of St. Augustine's In Iohannem,' *Journal of Theological Studies* 15 (1964) 321.

†Rm 6:20 48. *When you were slaves of sin, you were free of righteousness.*†

A sinner's freedom of choice has not disappeared to such an extent that everyone—especially those who sin with enjoyment and love of sin—sins by choice, and they are pleased because they like it. Hence the Apostle says, *When you were slaves of sin, you were free of righteousness.* See how he shows that they were altogether unable to serve sin except by another [kind of] freedom. Therefore, they are not free from righteousness except by a choice of freedom, while they do not become free from sin except by our Saviour's grace.

For this reason our estimable teacher has distinguished these very words: *When you were slaves of sin,* he says, *you were free of righteousness. But what return did you then derive from those things of which you are now ashamed? The end of those things is death. Now that you have been freed from sin and enslaved to God, the return you derive is*
†Rm 6:20–22 *sanctification, and its end is eternal life.*† [Paul] said *free of righteousness,* not 'freed'—but not 'free of sin' lest they attribute this to themselves. He preferred to say, with great care, *freed [from sin],* connecting this to our Lord's statement, 'If the Son makes you free, then you are
†Jn 8:36 truly free.'† And a little later:† But this inclination that is free in evil
†Bede's addition. things, because it takes pleasure in evils, is therefore not free in good things, because it has not been freed. A person cannot choose to do anything good unless aided by him who is unable to choose evil.

—from *Against Julian* 1*

49. We describe as free to perform works of godliness those to whom the Apostle says, *Now that you have been freed from sin and enslaved to*
†Rm 6:22 *God, the return you derive is sanctification, and its end is eternal life.*†
This return, sanctification—a return which is doubtless love and its works—we can in no way possess on our own, but we possess it through the Holy Spirit that has been given to us. God, our master,

*48. *Contra Duas Ep. Pelag.* 1.2.5; 3.7; CSEL 60: 426,4/22; 428,24–429,3. There appears to be a discrepancy in the title of this excerpt. It is not from either the book against Julian of Eclanum, or from one of the six books against that same Pelagian bishop, but from a work entitled *Against Two Letters of the Pelagians.*

was speaking of this return when he told the branches who remain in him, 'Apart from me you can do nothing.'† †Rm 5:5; Jn 15:5

—from the same book*

50. Hence the Apostle calls even eternal life itself, which is surely the reward for good works, *the gift of God*. He says, *The wages of sin is death, but the gift of God is eternal life in Christ Jesus our Lord*.† †Rm 6:23 *Wages* is the pay due in return for a service; it is not a gift. [Paul] said that *the wages of sin is death* to show that death is not paid sin undeservedly, but is owed it. Unless a gift is gratuitous it is not a gift.† †Rm 4:4, 11:6 We must understand, then, that even a person's good deserts are presents from God. When eternal life is paid in return for them, what is paid but grace in return for grace?† †Jn 1:16. In this excerpt both 'gift' and 'grace' translate the Latin *gratia*.

—from *Enchiridion* 110*

51. *Do you not know, brothers and sisters—for I am speaking to those who know the law—that the law has jurisdiction over a person only so long as that person is alive? . . .*† **†Rm 7:1–5**

In this analogy the Apostle is speaking of a husband and wife, and since a wife is bound to her husband by law [Paul] is suggesting three subjects for us to consider: the wife; the husband; and the law. A wife, who is subject to her husband by the bond of law, is freed from this bond by her husband's death so that she may marry whom she chooses. This is what he says: *A married woman is bound by law to her living husband; but if her husband dies, she is released from the law of the husband. Accordingly, she will be called an adulteress if she lives with another man while her husband is alive. But if her husband dies, she is freed from the law so that if she lives with another man she is not an adulteress.*

Thus far the analogy. Then [Paul] begins to speak of the reality that he brought in the analogy to explain and prove. Here too three subjects are brought to our attention: human beings; sin; and the

---

*49. *Contra Sec. Iul. Resp.* 86; CSEL 85,1: 98,5–99,13
*50. *Enchir.* 28.107; CC 46: 107,48/57

law. He says that humans are under the law as long as they live to sin—just as a wife is legally bound to her husband as long as he is alive. We must take 'sin' here as what has resulted from the law. He says that this sin is 'beyond measure' since it comes to be sin on its appearance and yet is augmented by further transgression. 'Where there is no law, neither is there transgression.'† And this is what he means when he says, 'So that the sinner, or the sin, may grow beyond measure through the commandment.'†

†Rm 4:15

†Rm 7:13. Owing to a misreading of the Greek text Augustine read *peccator aut peccatum* rather than *peccans peccatum* with the Vulgate.

And [Augustine writes] a little further on: Therefore although we see three particular things in the analogy—the wife, the husband and the law—and three again in the reality on account of which the analogy is employed—the soul, sin and the law—there is here only this difference, that in the analogy the husband dies with the result that the wife may marry whom she chooses and is released from the law of the husband, whereas here the soul dies to sin, with the result that it may marry Christ; when it dies to sin, it also dies to the law of sin.

And so, my brothers and sisters, [Paul] says, *you yourselves have died to the law through the body of Christ, so that you may belong to another, who rose from the dead in order that we may bear fruit for God. For when we were in the flesh,* [Paul] says—that is, when we were held in bondage to physical desires—*our sinful passions, aroused by the law, were at work in our members to bear fruit for death.* When the law forbids the covetousness that increased where there was no faith, and added the offense of transgression to the accumulation of sins—because 'where there is no law, neither is there transgression'—[Paul] calls these the *passions* which are *aroused by the law,* [passions] *at work in our members to bear fruit for death.* Before grace came, through faith, the soul acted under the influence of those passions as if in subjection to a husband. Those who now serve the law of God with the mind die to these passions, although the passions themselves are not yet dead as long as they serve the law of sin with the flesh.†

†Rm 7:25

—from *On Eighty-Four Questions* 66*

*51. *De Div. Quaest. LXXXIII* 66,1–2; CC 44A: 150,2–151,26; 152,60–153,80. Augustine's work has eighty-three questions concerning various scriptural passages, but Bede's copy contained eighty-four questions.

52. Why have we *died to the law through the body of Christ* if the law is good?† Because we have died to the law's domination we have been set free from the disposition that the law punishes and condemns. We most commonly call 'law' something that threatens, causes alarm and punishes. Accordingly, the same commandment is a law for those who fear, and a grace for those who love—hence this [verse] in the gospel: 'The law was given through Moses; grace and truth came through Jesus Christ.'† Indeed the very law that was given through Moses to produce dread became the grace and truth through Jesus Christ to bring it to fulfillment. So Scripture says, *You have died to the law*, as if saying, You have died to the punishment [threatened by] the law *through the body of Christ*, through which trespasses, which normally would have been subject to legitimate punishment, were forgiven.

†**Rm 7:4**; 1 Tm 1:8

†Jn 1:17

—from *To Simplician, Bishop**

53. What does *when we were in the flesh*† mean if not 'when we were relying on the flesh,' that is, 'when we made our own decisions'? Scripture said to a human being about human beings, 'All flesh shall see the salvation of God.'† What does 'all flesh shall see' mean if not that every human will see? Therefore, *when we were in the flesh*—that is, when we were involved in the cravings of the flesh, and putting all our hope there, as if in ourselves—the *sinful passions aroused by the law* were increased by the law. By prohibiting [certain deeds] they produced a transgressor of the law, because one who has become a transgressor does not have God as a helper. Therefore, *[sinful passions] were at work in our members to bear fruit*—for what, if not *for death*? Do not, then, be *in the flesh*. Be in the Spirit! What does 'be in the Spirit' mean? Put your hope in God!

†**Rm 7:5**

†Lk 3:6 (Is 40:5)

—from a sermon on the letter to the Romans*

54. [Why are we *released from the law* if the law is good?]† Because the law is [a mere] letter for those who do not fulfill it in the spirit

†**Rm 7:6;** 1 Tm 1:8

*52. *De Div. Quaest. Ad Simpl.* 1.1.17; CC 44: 22,336/47. Simplician was bishop of Milan in succession to Saint Ambrose.

*53. *Serm.* 153.6,8–7,9; PL 38: 829–30 passim

of love—which pertains to the new covenant. Accordingly, those dead to sin are free from the letter which holds captive those who do not fulfill what is written. What else is the law but a mere letter for those who know how to read it and are unable to fulfill it? It is not unknown to those for whom it was written; but since they know it only insofar as they read what is written, and not insofar as they perform what they love, for such people it is nothing but a letter. This letter is not a help for those who read, but a witness against those who sin.

Those renewed by the Spirit are freed from its sentence of condemnation. They are no longer bound to the letter for punishment, but are united to its meaning by righteousness. That is why 'the
†2 Co 3:6 letter kills, but the Spirit gives life.'† And since [Paul] had said, *We are released from the law of death which held us captive, so that we may serve in newness of spirit and not in the oldness of the letter*—and may by these words seem to have found fault with the law—he added at once, *What then should we say? That the law is sin? By no means! Yet I did not know sin except through the law, and I was ignorant of covetousness*
†**Rm 7:6–7** (Ex 20:17; Dt 5:21) *except that the law said, 'You shall not covet.'*†

Here [Paul] shocks us again: if the law is not sin, but the inseminator of sin, even so he is finding fault with it in these words. Therefore we should understand that the law was not given to implant or to eradicate sin, but simply to make it known—to make the human soul, as something secure in its innocence, conscious of its guilt by making sin known. Then, since sin cannot be overcome without God's grace, anxiety over its guilt may turn the soul toward accepting grace. Accordingly, [Paul] did not say, 'I did not commit sin except through the law,' but, *I did not know sin except through the law.* Hence it is apparent that the law did not implant covetousness but [only] made it known. The result, however, was that, since it had not yet received grace, [the human soul] could offer no resistance to covetousness—in fact, covetousness even increased. When the fault of transgression is added, covetousness has even greater strength; [it is stronger] when it acts against the law than if no law prohibited it.

Accordingly [Paul] adds, *Sin, seizing an opportunity in the com-*
†**Rm 7:8** *mandment, produced in me every kind of covetousness.*† Sin also existed

before [the law], but not *every kind* when the fault of transgression was still lacking. Hence [Paul] says in another place, 'Where there is no law, neither is there transgression.'† As to what he adds, *Apart from the law sin is dead,* he sets this down as if he means, '[Apart from the law sin] lies hidden,' that is, is presumed to be dead. †Rm 4:15

He is going to say this more clearly further on: *I was once alive apart from the law*—that is, death from sin did not alarm me, since [sin] was not apparent when there was no law. When *the commandment came, sin revived*—that is, it became apparent. *I died*†—that is, I realized that I was dead, because the guilt of transgression was threatened by the sure punishment of death. **†Rm 7:9–10**

That he says *sin revived* is sufficient evidence that sin was once alive in this way. I mean that it was known, as I believe, in the transgression of the first human being, because he too had received a commandment. Only what was once alive can revive. But [sin] had died, that is, had been concealed, when humans, born mortal, lived apart from the commandment of the law, following the desires of the flesh without any realization [of sin] because without any prohibition.

I was once alive apart from the law, [Paul] says, showing that he is not speaking in his own person, but in a general way, as a member of the human race. *The commandment that was for life was found to be death for me.* If the commandment is obeyed, surely it is life; but it *was found to be death* when he acted against the commandment. He not only committed sin—which he did even before the commandment [was given]—but [he did this] more frequently and disastrously, now that he sinned knowingly and as a transgression.

Sin, [Paul] says, *seizing an opportunity in the commandment, deceived me and through it killed me.*† Sin, unlawfully using the law meant as a prohibition, became more attractive once desire had increased, and thus deceived him. Attractiveness which is followed by more numerous and more severe punishments is deceitful. Since people who have not yet received spiritual grace find more pleasure in allowing what is forbidden, sin deceives [them] by a false attraction; and because it also brings upon [them] the guilt of transgression, it kills. **†Rm 7:11**

*So then the law is holy, and the commandment is holy and righteous
†**Rm 7:12** *and good.*† It commands what must be commanded, and prohibits what must be prohibited. The defect is in those who use it badly—not in the commandment itself, which is good, because 'the law is
†1 Tm 1:8 good, if one uses it lawfully.'† They use it badly who do not subject themselves to God with devoted humility so as to fulfill the law through grace.

—from *To Simplician, Bishop*★

55. Can we not praise [the law] more highly? A little earlier, with the words, 'By no means!' Paul had defended it against an accusation; he had not yet praised it. Now [he says], *The law is holy, and the*
†**Rm 7:12** *commandment is holy and righteous and good.*†

Did what is good, then, become death for me? By no means, because death is not good. *Sin, that it may appear as sin, worked death in me*
†**Rm 7:13** *through what is good.*† The law is not death, but sin is death. *Sin,* [Paul] says, *that it may appear as sin.* He did not say, 'that it may be [sin]', because it was [sin] even when it did not *appear [as sin].* What does *that it may appear as sin* mean? 'I was ignorant of covetousness except that
†Rm 7:7 (Ex 20:17; Dt 5:21) the law said, You shall not covet.'† [Paul] did not say, 'I did not possess covetousness,' but, 'I was ignorant of covetousness.' So here too he does not say, 'that it may be sin,' but, *that it may appear as sin, sin worked death in me through what is good.* What death? *That the sinner, or the sin,*
†**Rm 7:13**.★★ *may grow beyond measure through the commandment.*† Why *beyond measure*? Because now it is also a transgression. 'Where there is no law, neither is there transgression.' See then, my brothers and sisters, see that the human race has descended from the first death of that first man. 'Sin entered into this world from the first man, and through
†Rm 4:15; 5:12. Here Augustine reads *a primo homine* rather than *per unum hominem* as above, section 34. sin death, and so it passed to all people, in whom all have sinned.'†

—again, the sermon as above★

★54. *De Div. Quaest. Ad Simpl.* 1.1.17; 1.1.1–1.1.6; CC 44: 23,356/68; 8,21–11,94 passim. This passage follows almost immediately on section 52, hence the opening sentence is grammatically incomplete. It is an answer to the question as to why we, as Christians, have been freed from the Mosaic law, even though that law was good.
★★Owing to a misreading of the Greek text Augustine read *peccator aut peccatum* rather than *peccans peccatum* with the Vulgate.
★55. *Serm.* 153.10.12–11.14; PL 38: 831–32 passim

56. Next, [Paul] adds the reason why this should be so. *We know*, he says, *that the law is spiritual, but I am carnal.*† In saying this he shows well enough that the law cannot be fulfilled except by those who are spiritual, who do not become so except through grace. The more in accord with the spiritual law people become—that is, the more they rise to a spiritual disposition—the more do they fulfill it, because so much more do they delight in it. Now they are not afflicted in its name, but they flourish in its light, since 'the commandment of the Lord is clear, enlightening the eyes,' and 'the law of the Lord is unspotted, converting souls.'† Grace forgives sins and pours out the spirit of love, making righteousness not burdensome but even delightful.

†**Rm 7:14**

†Ps 19:8, 7

What I do, [Paul] says, *I do not understand.*† He does not say *I do not understand* as if he does not know that he sins. This would be the opposite of his words, 'Sin, that it may appear as sin, worked death in me through what is good,' and his earlier words, 'I did not know sin except through the law.' How does sin not appear, or how does he know what he does not understand? He said this as the Lord will tell the wicked, 'I do not know you.' Nothing escapes God's notice, since 'the Lord's face is against evildoers, to destroy their remembrance from the earth.'†

†**Rm 7:15**

—again, from *To Simplician, Bishop* *

†Rm 7:13, 7; Mt 25:12; Ps 34:16

57. If the Apostle says of himself, *we know that the law is spiritual, but I am carnal*, we should understand him to mean spiritual in mind and carnal in body. When will he be entirely spiritual? When what 'is sown a natural body will rise a spiritual body.' Now, while the struggle with death is strong, *I do not do what I want.*† Being partly spiritual, partly carnal, I am still in conflict, I have not yet conquered. For me not to be conquered is a great thing. *I do not do what I want, but what I hate, this I do*. Why do you do it? Because I covet. Although I do not consent to covetousness, although I do not go after the things I covet, yet still I covet.

†**Rm 7:14**; 1 Co 15:44; **Rm 7:15**

*56. *De Div. Quaest. ad Simpl.* 1.1.7–1.1.8; CC 44: 12,109/119; 13,137–14,145

†**Rm 7:16** *Now if I do what I do not want, I agree that the law is good.*† When you do what the law hates, how are you agreeing to the law? Precisely, *if I do what I do not want, I agree that the law is good.* In what way? Because the law commands, 'You shall not covet.'† My weakness does not fulfill the law, but my will consents to the law. *But now it is no longer I who do it.*† What does *but now* mean? I, who was earlier 'sold under sin,' have now been redeemed. Now I have received the grace of the Saviour, so that in my mind 'I delight in the law of God,'† *it is no longer I who do it.* The mind is free, the flesh is a prisoner.

†Rm 7:7 (Ex 20:17; Dt 5:21)

†**Rm 7:17**

†Rm 7:14, 22

—again, from the second sermon on this reading*

58. Our good works are only brought to perfection when the flesh is in such agreement with the spirit that its cravings are not opposed to it.† This is what we will when we desire the perfection of righteousness, an objective we ought to will without any respite. But since we cannot do this perfectly in this perishable flesh, [Paul] said, *The willing is ready at hand, but I do not find a way of doing good perfectly,*† or, as the Greek manuscripts have it, *The willing is ready at hand, but bringing it to perfection is not.* He means that doing good perfectly is ready at hand, because doing good means not going after your lusts,† while *doing good perfectly* means not lusting.

†Ga 5:17

†**Rm 7:18**

†Si 18:30

—from *Against Julian* 4*

†**Rm 7:19** 59. *I do not do the good I want, but the evil I do not want is what I do.*†

†Not Ambrose but Ambrosiaster.

If, as Ambrose† has well perceived, the Apostle is saying this too about himself, and the righteous have no great amount of freedom to make their own choices for accomplishing good in this life, how much [freedom] will exist in that other life, where no one will say, 'I do not do what I want'!

—from *Against Julian* 1*

*57. *Serm.* 154.6.8 & 10; PL 38: 836–38 passim
*58. *Contra Iul.* 3.62; PL 44: 734
*59. *Contra Sec. Iul. Resp.* 1.99; CSEL 85,1: 117,21/24 (Ambrosiaster, *Ad Rom.* 7.15–20; CSEL 81,1: 236,4–239,24 passim)

60. How did you walk in the ways of the Lord if you did the evil you did not want since the holy psalm proclaims, 'Those who work iniquity have not walked in his ways'?† Listen to [Paul] answering in the next sentence: *If I do what I do not want, it is no longer I who do it, but sin that dwells in me.*† See how those who walk in the ways of the Lord do not commit sin and yet are not without sin—they no longer do it themselves, but the sin that dwells in them.

†Ps 118:1, 3 Vulgate

†**Rm 7:20**

At this point someone will ask, 'How did he do the evil he did not want, and how did he not do it, but the sin that dwells in him?' [Paul] said both 'I do not do what I want' and *It is not I who do it, but sin that dwells in me*. From this we ought to understand that when the sin that dwells in us works in us we do not do it ourselves—when our will in no way agrees to it, and even controls the members of our body so that they do not obey its desires. What produces sin against our will if not solely unlawful desires? If we do not give the consent of the will to them, some affect is moved, but they have no effect. Moreover, we are said to be responsible for the impulse of an unlawful desire—by not obeying it we do not *do it*—for this reason, that it is not the influence of some external force but inertia on our part. We will be completely freed from this inertia when we have become immortal both in mind and in body.

All the guilt of this inertia and weakness, whence unlawful desires arise—which the Apostle calls *sin*—is washed away by the sacrament of baptism, together with all that we have done, said or thought disobediently. Our inertia would not henceforth be against us, although still in us, if we never yielded any obedience to its unlawful desires, whether by deed, by word, or by tacit consent, until even this is healed.

—from the treatise on Psalm 118*

61. *I delight in the law of God in my inmost self, but I see in my members another law at war with the law of my mind, making me captive to the law of*

*60. *En. in Ps* 118.2.2–3; 3.1–2; CC 40: 1670,32/33; 1671,15/24; 33–1672,37; 6/13. Augustine is concerned here about whether the elect are still able to sin. He considers baptism rather the medicine than the cure.

†Rm 7:22–23 *sin that dwells in my members.*† *Making me captive*—in the flesh; *making me captive*—in part. The mind is at war, and it delights in the law of God. It has its own inner delights that are in no way comparable to the delights of the flesh. If it does not consent, and there is in me something dead and something alive, death still dissents, but my living mind does not consent.

†Rm 7:24 What have I to hope for from there? *Wretched man that I am,*† with sin tickling me, exciting me, enticing me, if my mind does not consent! *Wretched man*, even if not in mind, yet in the flesh. *Who will deliver me from this body of death?* The day is coming when 'all who are in the tombs will hear his voice and will come out, those who have done good to the resurrection of life'—see them delivered from *this body of death*—'but those who have done evil, to
†Jn 5:28–29 the resurrection of judgment'†—see them returned to *this body of death*. This body of death returns to the ungodly, who will never be released from it. Then it will not be eternal life, but eternal death, because eternal punishment.

But you, O Christian, ask as strongly as you can, cry out and say, *Who will deliver me from this body of death?* so that you may hear the
†Rm 7:25 answer, *The grace of God through Jesus Christ our Lord!*† You will not be delivered from *this body of death* in such a way that you will not have this body; you will have it, but no longer as a *body of death*. You will be delivered from *this body of death* so that this mortal [body] may be clothed with immortality and this corruptible [body] may
†1 Co 15:53 be clothed with incorruptibility.† By what? Through whom? *The grace of God through Jesus Christ our Lord!*

—from the second sermon cited earlier on this reading*

62. *Thus I myself serve the law of God with my mind, but with my flesh*
†Rm 7:25 *I serve the law of sin.*†

In this conclusion [Paul] showed why he said what he had said
†Rm 7:20 earlier, 'It is no longer I who do it, but sin that dwells in me.'† He did not do it with his mind, by consenting, but with his flesh,

*61. *Serm.* 154.10,14–12,17; PL 38: 839–40 passim

by coveting. This he calls *sin*—from it arise all sins, that is, from carnal covetousness. Whatever sins there are, in actions, in words, in thoughts, do not arise except from evil desire. They do not arise except from unlawful pleasure.

When, then, he had said, *I serve the law of God with my mind, but with my flesh I serve the law of sin*—not by permitting his members to commit evil actions, but only by coveting—and not even by giving a hand to unlawful covetousness—he added, *There is therefore now no condemnation for those who are in Christ Jesus.*† There is condemnation †**Rm 8:1** for those who are in the flesh, but no condemnation for those who are in Christ Jesus. And lest you should think that this will come later, he added *now*. Expect afterward not to have any covetousness in yourself for you to struggle against.

There is therefore now no condemnation for those who are in Christ Jesus. They should not be concerned if they are tickled by unlawful covetousness. They should not be concerned because there still seems to be a law in their members at war with the law of their minds. *There is now no condemnation!* But for whom is this true? *Those who are in Christ Jesus*. Where then is that law about which he said a little earlier, 'I see in my members another law at war with the law of my mind, making me captive to the law of sin that dwells in my members'?† He was talking about 'me,' [meaning what comes] †Rm 7:22–23 from the body, not from the mind.

Where then is that law if *there is no condemnation for those who are in Christ Jesus*? *For*, he says, *the law of the spirit of life in Christ Jesus*—not *the law* given in writing on Mount Sinai—not *the law* in 'the obsolete letter'—but *the law of the spirit of life in Christ Jesus has freed you from the law of sin and death,* so that you may delight in the law of God in your inmost self.† How would you have this unless *the law* †Ga 4:24–25; Rm 7:6; **Rm 8:2;** Rm 7:22 *of the spirit of life in Christ Jesus* freed you *from the law of sin and death*?

Therefore, O human mind, do not attribute to yourself the fact that you do not consent to the desires of the flesh, that the law of sin does not fling you down from the summit. *The law of the spirit of life in Christ Jesus has freed you from the law of sin and death.*

—again, from the third sermon on the same letter*

*62. *Serm.* 155.1,1–3,3; PL 38: 841–42 passim

†**Rm 8:2** 63. It is not called *the law of sin*† because the law itself is sinful, but because it is imposed on sinners. So too [it is called] 'the law of death' because 'the wages of sin is death.' 'The sting of death is sin,
†Rm 6:23; 1 Co 15:56 and the power of sin is the law.'† By sinning we slip down into death. We sin far more grievously when the law forbids [what we do] than if no law forbids it. With the onset of grace we carry out, not as a burden but with great gladness, the very thing the law had enjoined as a burden. *The law of sin and death*—that is, [the law] imposed on those who sin and die—only commands us not to covet. Yet we do covet. The law of the spirit of life, which concerns grace and delivers us from *the law of sin and death,* brings it about that we do not covet and that we fulfill the commands of the law. We are no longer slaves of the law through fear, but friends [of God] through love, and slaves of the righteousness which is the source of the law.

—from *On Eighty-Four Questions* 66*

†**Rm 8:3** 64. *What was impossible for the law, in that it was weakened by the flesh.*† The law charged, but did not discharge, because where grace was absent the flesh invincibly resisted. The law *was weakened by the flesh*
†Rm 7:14 because 'the law is spiritual but I am carnal.'† How then was the law to relieve me when it gave commands through the letter without giving grace? *It was weakened by the flesh.*

†**Rm 8:3** *God sent his own Son in the likeness of sinful flesh*†—that is, to be flesh, real flesh. And what is the source of *the likeness of sinful flesh*? Death from sin is present in all sinful flesh, of course. The Apostle
†Rm 6:6 says of it, 'that the body of sin may be destroyed.'† Death, then, exists in all sinful flesh—each is there, death and sin, death *in the likeness of sinful flesh*, but not sin. What [Jesus] did with regard to the
†Mt 17:24–26 tribute money† he did with regard to death—as he paid the tribute money he did not owe, so he paid off death. He owed nothing and yet he paid. Unless he restored what he did not owe he would never have delivered us from what we owed.

†**Rm 8:3** *And from sin he condemned sin in the flesh.*† How was he without sin if he condemned sin from sin? In the law a sacrifice for sin was

*63. *De Div. Quaest. LXXXIII* 66.1; CC 44A: 152,39/52

called 'sin'. Christ was that kind of sin. Listen to what the Apostle says, speaking of him: 'Him who knew no sin [God] made sin for us.'† God the Father made him, Christ, who knew no sin, to be sin for our sake *so that the righteousness of the law may be fulfilled in us.*† It was not fulfilled by itself, it was fulfilled by Christ. He did not come to abolish the law but to fulfill it.† But why is God's *righteousness* fulfilled *in us*, and in which of us? [It is fulfilled in those] *who walk not according to the flesh but according to the Spirit.*† What does walking *according to the flesh* mean? It means consenting to the desires of the flesh. What does walking *according to the Spirit* mean? It means being helped inwardly by the Spirit and not obeying the desires of the flesh.

†2 Co 5:21 †**Rm 8:4** †Mt 5:17 †**Rm 8:4**

—again, from the second sermon on this reading*

65. *God sent his own Son in the likeness of sinful flesh, so that from sin he may condemn sin in the flesh.*† †**Rm 8:3**

His was not *sinful flesh* since he had not come into Mary['s womb] with the transmission of mortality by a male. Yet because death exists *from sin*, this flesh was mortal even though it came from a virgin, and from the fact that it was mortal it possessed the likeness of sinful flesh. [Paul] calls this too *sin*, saying in the words that follow, *so that from sin he may condemn sin in the flesh.* He also asserts in another place, 'For our sake he made him to be sin who knew no sin, so that we may be the righteousness of God in him.'† †2 Co 5:21

—from *Against Faustus* 14*

66. *For the concern of the flesh is hostility toward God; it does not submit to the law of God for it cannot.*† †**Rm 8:7**

What does *for it cannot* mean? Not that a human being *cannot*, not that a soul *cannot*, moreover not that flesh itself, because it is God's creature, *cannot*, but that *the concern of the flesh cannot*—the

*64. *Serm.* 155.7–9; PL 38: 844–46 passim
*65. *Contra Faust. Manich.* 14.5; CSEL 25: 406,18/28. Faustus of Milevis was a noted African Manichaean of Augustine's day.

vice, not the nature, *cannot*. You could say, 'Limping cannot submit to walking correctly, for it cannot.' The foot can, but limping cannot. Take away the limping and you will see correct walking. Therefore, do not interpret the words, *the concern of the flesh is hostility toward God,* as if this hostility could injure God. It is hostile in that it resists [God], not in that it harms [him]. It harms the one in whom *the concern of the flesh* exists.

Those who are in the flesh—that is, those whose confidence is
in the flesh, who pursue their lusts, who live in them, who are
entertained by the pleasures they offer, who consider that a happy
and blissful life comes from enjoying them—these people are *in the*
†**Rm 8:8** *flesh*, they *cannot please God*.† *Those who are in the flesh cannot please*
God is not said as if it meant, 'In this life, since they are human they
cannot please God.'

You, however, are not in the flesh, but in the spirit, if only the Spirit
†**Rm 8:9** *of God dwells in you*.† *You are not in the flesh* because you do not do
the works of the flesh by consenting to the lusts of the flesh. You
are in the spirit, because you take delight in the law of God in your
†Rm 7:22 inmost self.† But this is so *if only the Spirit of God dwells in you*. If you
rely on your own spirit you are still *in the flesh*. Therefore use your
freedom of choice to appeal for help.

If anyone does not have the Spirit of Christ, that person does not
†**Rm 8:9** *belong to him*.† So this needy and faulty nature must not think too
highly of itself, not vaunt itself, not claim its own strength. *If anyone*
does not have the Spirit of Christ—let us not deceive ourselves—
that person does not belong to him. See how we do have the Spirit
of Christ with the aid of his mercy. We know that the Spirit
of God is present within us by our delight in righteousness, our
integral faith, our catholic peace. But what of that mortal flesh?
What of the law in our members at war with the law of our
mind? What of our sigh of complaint, 'Wretched man that I
†Rm 7:23–24 am?'† Listen: *If Christ is in you, the body is dead because of sin*.†
†**Rm 8:10** This is why [Paul] asked, 'Who will deliver me from this body
†Rm 7:24 of death?'†

—again, from the second sermon cited earlier on this reading*

*66. *Serm.* 155.10–14; PL 38: 846–49 passim

67. The body is not only said to be going to die because of the soul's withdrawal, which lies ahead, but it is even called dead because of the great weakness of flesh and blood. The Apostle says, *The body is dead because of sin, but the spirit is life because of righteousness.*† This life comes about through faith, since 'one who is righteous through faith is alive.'†

†**Rm 8:10**

†Rm 1:17; Ga 3:11; Heb 10:38 (Hab 2:4)

—from *On the Trinity* 4.3*

68. [Paul] does not say, 'The body is going to die', but *The body is dead.*† Actually our bodies still possess life—and yet, compared to that body which will be like the bodies of angels, the human body is found to be dead, even though it still possesses a soul.

†**Rm 8:10**

—from the treatise on Psalm 85*

69. Must we now despair of the body, dead because of sin? Is there no hope? Will it sleep so as never to rise again?† You were already saying, to comfort yourself, 'I wish my body was alive, but since it cannot be, let at least my spirit, let at least my soul, be alive!' Wait—do not be anxious. *If the Spirit of the one who raised Jesus from the dead dwells in you, the one who raised Jesus Christ from the dead will give life to your mortal bodies also.*† What are you afraid of? Why are you anxious even concerning your flesh? 'Not a hair on your head will be destroyed!'† By sinning Adam condemned your bodies to death; but God, if his Spirit is in you, *will give life to your mortal bodies also.* So you will be delivered 'from this body of death'† not by being without a body, or by having a different one, but by not dying any more. *He will give life to your mortal bodies also through his Spirit that dwells in you,*† not because you deserve it, but on account of his favor.

†Ps 41:8/9

†**Rm 8:11**

†Lk 21:18

†Rm 7:24

†**Rm 8:11**

—from the third sermon on the letter to the Romans*

---

*67. *De Trin.* 4.3.6; CC 50: 166,39/45
*68. *En. in Ps* 85.17; CC 39: 1190,29/33
*69. *Serm.* 155.14–15; PL 38: 848–49 passim

70. *So then, brothers and sisters*, having received assistance, having had divine help—the Lord's arm—extended to us from above—and this arm of the Lord extended for our help is the Holy Spirit—*we are not debtors to the flesh, to walk according to the flesh*, since faith can only
†**Rm 8:12**; Ga 5:6 work well through love.† To have love, and to be able to work well as a result of it—can we give this to ourselves, when it is written, 'God's love has been poured out in our hearts through the Holy
†Rm 5:5 Spirit that has been given to us'?†

For if you live according to the flesh you will die. [Paul] had already
†**Rm 8:13**, 6 said earlier, 'The concern of the flesh is death,'† not because the flesh is something evil, but because to live according to the flesh is evil.

But if by the Spirit you put to death the actions of the flesh you will
†**Rm 8:13** *live.*† This is our task in this life, daily to *put to death the actions of the flesh by the Spirit*, to weaken them, diminish them, check them, destroy them. How many things that used to delight those who are making progress do so no longer! When something used to give delight, and you did not consent, you were putting it to death; because it does not produce delight now, it has been put to death.

Since the Apostle said, *But if by the Spirit you put to death the actions of the flesh you will live*—meaning those desires of the flesh, to withhold consent from which is praiseworthy, and to be without which is perfection—we must here be apprehensive lest some rely on their own spirits again for putting to death the actions of the flesh. Therefore to keep this human spirit from priding itself, and boasting that it is apt and strong for this work, [Paul] adds, *For as*
†**Rm 8:14** *many as are led by the Spirit of God, these are children of God.*† Not those who live according to their flesh, not those who live according to their own spirit, not those led by the satisfaction of the flesh, not those led by their own spirit, but *as many as are led by the Spirit of God, these are children of God.*

Someone will say to me, 'And so we are led, we do not lead.' I answer, 'No, you both lead and are led, and you lead well if you are led by good. God's Spirit, which leads you, is your support when you lead; he appoints for you the name 'support' because you yourself lead something too.

For as many as are led by the Spirit of God, these are children of God—[led] not by the letter but by the Spirit, not by a law that commands, threatens and promises, but by the Spirit who exhorts, enlightens and helps. Perhaps you were about to say, 'But the law is enough for us.' The law produced fear. See what the Apostle has added, since those who are led by the Spirit of God are led by love—'God's love has been poured out in our hearts through the Holy Spirit that has been given to us'—as he continues: *For you did not receive a spirit of slavery again in fear.*† †**Rm 8:15**

What does *again* mean? The way a very demanding schoolmaster makes you afraid.† What does *again* mean? As you received *a spirit of slavery* on Mount Sinai.† Some may say, 'The spirit of slavery is one thing and the spirit of freedom is another.' If it was a different [spirit] the Apostle would not have said *again*. Therefore the spirit is the same, but [given] on tablets of stone in fear and on tablets of the heart in love.† You have heard how the voices, the fire and the smoke on the mountain terrified the people who were a long way off, while the Holy Spirit rested on each of the disciples in tongues of fire†—not in fear, now, but in love, so that we may not be slaves but children. Those who are still doing right because they fear punishment, and do not love God, are not yet counted among the children. Yet I would have them at least fear punishment! Fear is a slave, love is free. At least act out of fear of punishment if you cannot yet act out of love of righteousness. The lady [love] will come, and the slave will depart, because 'love perfected casts out fear.'†

†See Augustine's *Confessions* 1. 9 and 12.
†Ga 4:24–25
†2 Co 3:3 (Dt 4:13, 5:22; Ezk 11:19)
†Ex 20:18; Ac 2:2–3
†1 Jn 4:18

But you received a spirit of adoption of children in which we cry out, 'Abba! Father!'† We fear a master, we love a father. This is a cry of the heart, not of the throat or the lips. It sounds inside, in God's ears. The mouth is closed, the lips do not move. Susanna cried out with such a voice. Let the heart cry out, 'Our Father in heaven!'†

†**Rm 8:15**
†Dn 13:42–43 Vulg.; Mt 6:9

Why not simply *Father*? What does *Abba Father* mean? If you ask what *Abba* means you will be told *Father*, for *Abba* is the Hebrew† word for *Father*. Why did the Apostle choose to give both? Because he saw the cornerstone that the builders rejected, and that became the head of the corner.† This was called a corner[stone] for a reason—it accepted in a kiss both walls, one coming from each direction†—the circumcision from one side, the uncircumcision from the other—hence *Abba*, hence *Father*—a union of the walls, the glory of the corner.

†Actually Aramaic, a Hebrew dialect.
†Is 28:16; Ps 118:22; Mt 21:42; Mk 12:10; Lk 20:17; Ac 4:11; 1 P 2:7
†Eph 2:14–16

The Spirit himself bears witness to our spirit that we are children of
†Rm 8:16 *God.*† Our own spirit does not bear witness *to our spirit* that we are children of God, but God's Spirit, the pledge, *bears witness* in favor of what has been promised us.

†Rm 8:17 *And if children, then heirs.*† We are not children for nothing. Our recompense is an inheritance, but not like an inheritance from human parents. Human parents leave it to their children, they do not possess it along with their children—yet they consider themselves generous, and desire to be thanked because they have chosen to give what they cannot take with them. God's heirs are such that God himself is our inheritance. To him the psalmist says, 'The Lord is
†Ps 16:5 the portion of my inheritance.'† *Heirs, indeed, of God.* If that is too little for you, listen to what may cause you greater joy: *and joint heirs with Christ.*

—from the fourth sermon on the same letter*

71. *I consider that the sufferings of this [present] time are not worthy [to be compared] with the future glory that will be revealed in us.* This is clear. [Paul] had said previously, 'If by the Spirit you put to death the deeds of the flesh,' which you cannot do without the vexation for which patience is necessary. Connected with this is what he had just said, 'If only we suffer with [Christ] so that we may also be glorified
†Rm 8:18, 13, 17 with him.'†

Accordingly, I take his words, *The expectation of creation is awaiting*
†Rm 8:19 *the revelation of the children of God,*† to mean, 'What suffers pain in us when we put to death the deeds of the flesh—that is, when we hunger and thirst through abstinence, when we restrain sexual pleasure through chastity, when we put up with the wounds of injustice and the stings of slander through patience, when we work for the good of our mother the Church, disregarding and rejecting our own selfish pleasures—whatever in us suffers pain in these and other kinds of tribulation is *creation.*' The body suffers pain along with the soul—which undoubtedly is *creation*—and awaits *the*

*70. *Serm.* 156.5,5–15,17; PL 38: 852–59 passim

revelation of the children of God; that is, it awaits the time when what has been called will appear in that glory to which it has been called. Since the only-begotten Son of God cannot be called *creation* (since all things whatsoever that God made were made through him),† clearly it is we who are called *creation* before that manifestation of glory; and clearly it is we who are called *children of God*, although we merit this only by adoption, for the Only-begotten is a child by nature.

†Jn 1:3

Therefore, *the expectation of creation*—that is, our expectation—*is awaiting the revelation of the children of God*—that is, awaits the time when what has been promised will appear, the time when the reality we now are in hope will be manifest. For 'we are God's children, and what we will be has not yet appeared; we know that when it appears we will be like him, because we will see him as he is.'† This is *the revelation of the children of God* which *the expectation of creation is* now *awaiting*—not because *creation is awaiting* the revelation of another nature which may not be *creation*, but [*creation*] as it now is awaits a time when it will be what it is to be. He may be saying, 'When a painter is at work, with his colors at hand and ready for his use, the expectation of colors is awaiting the manifestation of the picture, not because they will then be different, or will no longer be colors, but only because they will have another value.'

†1 Jn 3:2

Creation, [Paul] says, *was subjected to vanity*.† This is the same as, 'Vanity of vanities, and all is vanity. What more do human beings have for all the toil at which they toil under the sun?' They were told, 'In toil you shall eat bread.'† Therefore *creation was subjected to vanity, not of its own accord*. The addition of *not of its own accord* is proper. Humanity sinned of its own accord, but was not condemned of its own accord. The voluntary sin was to act contrary to the commandment of the Truth, while the punishment for the sin was to be subjected to deception. *Not of its own accord*, then, *was creation subjected to vanity, but because of the one who subjected it in hope*—that is, because of the righteousness and loving-kindness of the one who neither left sin unpunished nor willed that the sinner remain without remedy.

†**Rm 8:20**

†Qo 1:2–3; Gn 3:19

Because even creation itself—that is, humanity itself, since with the sign of the image already lost on account of sin† it remained

†See note to section 71.

only *creation*—that is, what is not yet called the perfect expression of children but is only called *creation*—*will be delivered from the slavery of destruction*.† When [Paul] says *even it will be delivered* he means *even it*, just like ourselves. In other words, even those who are not yet called children of God, but only *creation*, because they have not yet believed, are not to despair of themselves, because they too will believe and be delivered *from the slavery of destruction*, just like ourselves who already are children of God—although what we will be is not yet revealed. *[Creation itself] will be delivered from the slavery of destruction into the freedom of the glory of the children of God*. They will be free after having been slaves, and glorious after having been dead, in the perfect life which the children of God will possess.

†**Rm 8:21**

We know that the whole creation is groaning together and in pain until now.† *The whole creation* is summed up in humanity, not because all the angels and supereminent virtues and powers, and heaven and earth and the sea and everything that is in them,† are included in it, but because *the whole creation* is part spirit, part soul and part body. And a little further on:† *The whole creation* is in humanity because humans understand by their spirit, perceive by their soul, and move about spatially by their bodies. And a bit further on:† [Paul] rightly said *until now* because, even if some people are already 'in Abraham's bosom,' and the thief settled with the Lord 'in paradise' left his pain behind on the very day he believed,† nevertheless *until now the whole creation is groaning together and in pain* because, on account of being spirit, soul and body, *the whole [creation]* is in those things that have not yet been delivered.

†**Rm 8:22**. Augustine reads *congemescit* here and *congemescimus* in 8:23.
†Ps 146:6
†Bede's addition.
†Ibid.
†Lk 16:22, 23:43

And not only, [Paul] says, *is the whole creation groaning together and in pain, but we ourselves also*—that is, not only are the body, soul and spirit in humanity in pain together as a result of troubles of the body—*but we ourselves also*—apart from our bodies—*groan together within ourselves*.† Well did he say, *having [our] spirits as the first fruits*.† He means that our spirits have already been offered as a sacrifice to God and seized by the divine fire of love. They are the first fruits of humanity because the Truth first takes hold of our spirit in order to seize the rest through it. The one who says, 'I serve the law of God with my mind, but with my flesh [I serve] the law of sin,' and who says, 'God, whom I serve in my spirit,' and of whom it is said, 'The

†**Rm 8:23**
†Ibid. Augustine takes *spiritus* as objective plural, in apposition with *primitias*, rather than as possessive singular ('of the Spirit').

spirit indeed is willing, but the flesh is weak,'† already possesses the first fruits offered to God. But since he is still saying, 'Wretched man that I am, who will deliver me from this body of death?'—and 'He will give life to your mortal bodies also through the Spirit that dwells in you'† is still being said to such people—he is not yet a whole burnt offering. This he will be when death is swallowed up in victory, when [death] is told, 'Where, O death, is your strife? Where, O death, is your sting?'†

†Rm 7:25, 1:9; Mt 26:41

†Rm 7:24, 8:11

†1 Co 15:54–55. See notes to sections 218 and 219.

Now, therefore, [Paul] says, *not only* the whole creation—that is, embodied [creation]—*but we ourselves also, having [our] spirits as first fruits*—that is, we souls, who have even offered our minds to God as first fruits—*groan together within ourselves*—that is, apart from the body—*awaiting adoption, the redemption of our body*—that is, so that even the body itself, receiving the privilege of adoption as children by which we have been called, may show that, with all troubles over, we have been wholly delivered to be children of God in every respect.

By hope we have been saved, but hope that is seen is not hope.† When what we will be appears, then will the reality which is now hope exist—that is, [we will be] like him, 'because we will see him as he is.'†

†Rm 8:24

†1 Jn 3:2

—from *On Eighty-Four Questions* 67*

72. [Creation] loves vanity† of its own accord when it abandons firm truth and adopts conjectures, that is, changeable views. When it pays the punishment it deserves for this it is not subjected to vanity of it own accord as it was subjected in sinful humanity. The Apostle said that the whole *creation was subjected to vanity, not of its own accord*† because all [creation] exists in humanity. There is in humanity both something invisible, as attested by the soul, and something visible, as attested by the body. The whole creation is in part visible and in part

†Ps 4:2/3

†Rm 8:20

*71. *De Div. Quaest. LXXXIII* 67,2–5; CC 44A: 165,19–168,86; 169,102/105; 170,115–172,149. In his *Retractions* (1.26; PL 32: 628) Augustine explained that we must not take his words 'with the sign of the image already lost on account of sin' to mean that humanity has competely lost the image.

invisible—though not all is in beasts, which lack an understanding mind. [Paul] says that [creation] was *subjected in hope* on account of the mercy of the one who delivers it through the forgiveness of sins and the adoption of grace.

—again, from *Against the Letter of the Manichaean, Secundinus**

†**Rm 8:26**

73. *We do not know what to pray for as we should.*† Why do we suppose [Paul] said this, if not that temporal troubles and tribulations are frequently advantageous, either to reduce the swelling of pride or to test and exercise patience? A brighter and richer reward is reserved for [patience so] tested and exercised. Being unaware of the good they may do us, we desire to be freed from every tribulation. The Apostle shows that he was not a stranger to this ignorance. To keep him from being too elated he was given a thorn in the flesh. Three times he asked the Lord to take it from him, and he heard why it was not expedient that this be done.†

†2 Co 12:7–9

—to Proba, on praying to God*

74. Lest we leap to the conclusion that merits precede prayer—in such a way that grace would not be given gratuitously—indeed would not even be grace, because it would be the repayment of a debt—we find even [prayer] among the gifts of grace. *We do not know what to pray for as we should,* says the teacher of the Gentiles, *but the Spirit himself intercedes for us with inexpressible groanings.*† What does *intercedes* mean if not that [the Spirit] prompts us to intercede? Interceding with groans is evidence that a person is in need. We are not to believe that the Holy Spirit is in need of anything. He is said to intercede because he prompts us to intercede, and inspires in us

†1 Tm 2:7; **Rm 8:26**

*72. *Contra Secund. Manich.* 8; CSEL 25: 916,10/21. Nothing more is known of Secundinus than that he was a Manichaean opponent of Augustine. See also section 365.

*73. *Ep.* 130.14.25; CSEL 44: 68,12–69,10 passim. Proba was a noble Roman lady who took refuge in Africa after the sack of Rome in 410 with a retinue of other women. See also section 139 and361.

a disposition to intercede and to groan—as in the gospel, 'It is not you who speak, but the Spirit of your Father who speaks in you.'† †Mt 10:20

And yet this does not happen to us as if we do nothing. The help of the Holy Spirit is expressed in such a way that he himself is said to do what he prompts us to do. The Apostle shows well enough that we ought not to take *intercedes with inexpressible groanings* as said of our own spirit but of the Holy Spirit, by whom our weakness is helped. Hence he begins by saying, *The Spirit helps our weakness*, and then he adds, *for we do not know what to pray for as we should, but the Spirit himself asks for us.*† †**Rm 8:26**. In this reprise Augustine reads *postulat* (with the Vulgate) instead of *interpellat* as he did earlier.

—from a letter to the priest Sextus*

75. *We know that all things work together for good for those who love God.*† †**Rm 8:28**

Without the Lord's working that we may will, or working together [with us] when we will, we are incapable of any good works of religion. Of his working, that we may will, it has been said that 'God is the one who works in you even to will . . .'† Of his working together [with us] when we already will, and act by willing, [Paul] says, *We know that all things work together for good for those who love God*. What does *all things* mean if not even terrible and cruel sufferings? The burden that is heavy for weakness becomes light for love. The Lord told people such as Peter was when he suffered for Christ, not as he was when he denied Christ, that their burden is light.† †Ph 2:13 †Mt 26:75, 11:30

—from *On Grace and Free Choice**

76. The restlessness of heretics awakens my industry, as from the sleep of sloth, to examine the Scriptures more thoroughly. In this way I can oppose them so that they do not harm Christ's flock. By the manifold grace of the Saviour, God is turning even what the

*74. *Ep.* 194.4.16–17; CSEL 57: 188,11–189,20 passim. Sixtus was a Roman presbyter who became Pope Sixtus III.
*75. *De Grat. et Lib. Arb.* 17.33; PL 44: 901

enemy contrived for destruction into help, because *all things work*
†**Rm 8:28** *together for good for those who love* him.†

—from a letter to the priest Sixtus concerning the Pelagians*

77. *Those he foreknew he also predestined to be conformed to the image of*
†**Rm 8:29** *his Son.*†

Predestination cannot exist without foreknowledge, but foreknowledge can exist without predestination. By predestination God foreknew the things he himself was going to do. Hence it was
†Is 45:11 LXX said, 'He does what is going to be.'† He can also foreknow even what he himself does not do, for instance every kind of sin, since although some are sinful in such a way as also to be punishments for sins—hence it was said, 'God handed them over to a debased
†Rm 1:28 mind, to do what should not be done'†—the sin in this case is not God's, but the judgment is. Therefore God's predestination for good is the preparation for grace, and grace is the consequence of that predestination.

—from *To Prosper and Hilary**

78. The passage in which [Paul] says that the predestined *are con-*
†**Rm 8:29** *formed to the image of* God's *Son*† can also be understood of the inner self. Hence he tells us in another place, 'Do not be conformed to
†Rm 12:2 this world, but be reformed in the newness of your mind.'† When we are reformed so that we are not conformed to this world, we are conformed to God's Son. We can also take it that just as he was conformed to us by mortality, so we may be conformed to him by immortality—which is indeed connected to the resurrection of bodies.

—from *City of God* 22.16*

*76. *Ep.* 194.10.47; CSEL 57: 213,21–214,6
*77. *De Praedest. Sanct.* 10; PL 44: 975. Hilary and Prosper of Aquitane were correspondents of Augustine.
*78. *De Civ. Dei* 22.16; CC 48: 835,1/8

79. *So that he may be the first-born among many brothers*—'first-born from the dead,' surely, as the same apostle says. By this death his flesh was sown in dishonor but rose in glory. As to this image of the Son to whom we are conformed in body through immortality, we even strive for what the same apostle also says, 'As we have borne the image of the earthly one, let us also bear the image of the one who is from heaven'†—in order, of course, that when we have been made firm by true faith and certain hope, we who were mortal, as was Adam, may hold fast [to the conviction] that we are going to be immortal, as is Christ. At present we are able to bear the same image, not yet in vision but in faith, not yet in reality but in hope.

—from *On the Trinity* 14.18*

†**Rm 8:29**; Col 1:19; 1 Co 15:43, 49

80. To whomsoever God gives these gifts of his, without any doubt he foreknew that he would give them, and in his foreknowledge he prepared them. Therefore *those whom he predestined he also called*, with that call of which it is said, 'The gifts and the call of God are irrevocable.'† For [God] in his foreknowledge, which cannot be deceived or changed, to dispose his future works is entirely and nothing else than to predestine.

—from *On the Gift of Perseverance**

†**Rm 8:30**, 11:29

81. *And those he called he also justified.*†

†**Rm 8:30**

Here we must supply some words: *those he called* according to his purpose *he also justified* according to his purpose. Others were called, but not chosen.†

—[from a letter] to Paul[inus of Nola]*

†Mt 20:16, 22:14

82. *What then shall we say to this? If God is for us, who is against us?*†

†**Rm 8:31**

*79. *De Trin.* 14.18.24; CC 50A: 456,12/23
*80. *De Dono Persev.* 17.41; PL 45: 1018–19
*81. *Ep.* 186.7.25; CSEL 57: 65,11/14

The cry of all good and faithful Christians, and especially of the most glorious martyrs, is *If God is for us, who is against us?* The world raged against them, peoples plotted in vain, rulers gathered
†Ps 2:1–2 together,† new kinds of torture were contrived and their ingenious cruelty found incredible ways of inflicting pain; [the martyrs] were overwhelmed with scurrilous insults, charged with false crimes, shut up in unbearable conditions, gouged with hooks, slain with swords, tossed by wild beasts, burned with fire—and they said, *If God is for us, who is against us?*

The entire world is against you and you ask, *Who is against us?* The [martyrs] would answer you: 'And what is the entire world, when we are dying for the one through whom the world was made? They can not only slaughter your body, but also tear it to pieces—and what will they accomplish?' 'Behold, God is my helper, and the
†Jn 1:10; Ps 54:4 Lord is the upholder of my soul.'† 'What harm is done me when the Lord is the upholder of my soul, because the world is the slayer of my body? Since he is the upholder of my soul, he is also the restorer of my body.'

How do you prove this, O blessed and glorious martyr? How do you prove to me what you are saying: *If God is for us, who is against us?* [Paul] immediately brought forth irrefutable proof. He immediately introduced the martyr of martyrs, the witness of witnesses, *his own Son* whom the Father *did not spare,* whom he *handed over for us all.* This is how [Paul] proved the truth of what he said: *If God is for us, who is against us? He did not spare his own Son, but handed him over for*
†**Rm 8:31–32** *us all. How has he not also given us everything along with him?*† When he gave us everything along with him, he also gave us him. Does the world's rage terrify you, to whom the world's Maker has been given? Let us rejoice that Christ has been given to us, and in this age fear no enemies of Christ!

—from a sermon on the birthday of the martyrs*

83. *For I am sure that neither death, nor life, nor angels, nor principalities, nor things present, nor things to come, nor virtue, nor height, nor depth, nor*

---

*82. *Serm.* 334.1–2; PL 38: 1467–68 passim

any other creature will be able to separate us from the love of God in Christ Jesus our Lord.† †Rm 8:38–39

If then nothing separates us from his love, what can be not just better, but even more certain, than this blessing? No one separates us from it by threatening us with death. The very thing we love, God, cannot die—unless one for whom not loving God is death fails to love God, which is nothing else than loving and obeying something else instead of him. No one separates us from it by promising life, for no one separates us from the spring by promising water. An angel does not separate us—an angel is not more powerful than our mind when we cling to God. Virtue does not separate us—if the virtue referred to here possesses some power in this world, the mind that clings to God is far more sublime than the whole world; if, however, the virtue spoken of is the perfectly upright state of our mind, this in another person favors our union with God, and in us is the very thing that unites us [to God]. Present troubles do not separate us—we feel them less the closer we cling to him from whom they are trying to separate us. The promise of things to come does not separate us—God's promise of whatever good is to come is sure, and nothing is better than God himself, who unquestionably is already present to those who truly cling to him.

—from *On the Practices of the Catholic Church*★

84. *The word of God cannot fail. Not all who are of Israel are Israelites, nor are all Abraham's descendants his children, but 'in Isaac shall your descendants be called.'*† †Rm 9:6–7 (Gn 21:12)

God had said to Abraham, when he was unwilling to carry out the will of his wife regarding the dismissal of the slave woman and her son, 'In Isaac shall your descendants be called.' And these words certainly follow: 'And I will make him, the son of this slave woman, into a great nation, because he is your descendant.'† How, then, was it said, 'In Isaac shall your descendants be called,' when God also called Ishmael his descendant? Explaining this the Apostle says, '*In Isaac shall your descendants be called.' This means that it is not the children* †Gn 21:12–13

★83. *De Mor. Eccl. Cath.* 1.11.18–19; PL 32: 1319

of the flesh who are the children of God, but the children of the promise are
†Rm 9:7–8 *counted as descendants.*† In order that *the children of the promise* may be the descendants of Abraham they are called *in Isaac*—that is, they are gathered together in Christ by the call of grace.

—from *On the City of God* 22.16*

85. The great Apostle, who distinguished the allegorical significance of the two covenants as a slave woman and a free woman, attributing the children of the flesh to the old [covenant] and the children of
†Ga 4:22–24 the promise to the new,† was not unaware of what he was saying. *It is not the children of the flesh,* he said, *who are the children of God,*
†Rm 9:8 *but the children of the promise are counted as descendants.*† The *children of the flesh* belong to the earthly Jerusalem, who is in slavery with her children, while the *children of the promise* belong to her who
†Ga 4:25–26 is above, free, our mother, eternal in the heavens.† From this we easily see who belongs to the earthly kingdom and who to the kingdom of heaven. Those who understood this difference by the grace of God even at that time became *children of the promise.* They were accounted heirs of the new covenant under the hidden plan of God, even though they suitably administered the old covenant that had been divinely given, in accord with the division of times, to the people of old.

—from *On the Actions of Pelagius**

86. Blessed Paul, therefore, wanting to show that God is capable also of doing what he promised (especially where grace, whose enemies you are, is commended) and that God's fulfilling what he promised is not in the power of humans but rather in the power of the one who promised it—wanting to show this he said, *The word of God cannot fail. For not all who are of Israel are Israelites, nor are all Abraham's descendants his children, but 'in Isaac shall your descendants*

---

*84. *De Civ. Dei* 16.32; CC 48: 536,14/25
*85. *De Gest. Pelag.* 5.14; CSEL 42: 66,21–67,8

be called.' This means that it is not the children of the flesh who are the children of God, but the children of the promise are counted as descendants. For this is the wording of the promise, 'At this time I will come, and Sarah shall have a son.'† Keep the *children of the promise* in mind, since the one who made the promise is capable also of carrying it out.

†**Rm 9:6–9** (Gn 21:12; 18:10)

—from *Against Julian* 1*

87. You are speaking against God when you say, 'We are doing what he promised he would do.' Those who make themselves righteous were not prefigured in Isaac, the son promised to Abraham, but those whom God himself was going to make so. Hence he says to the whole Church through the prophet, 'I am the Lord who creates you.'† Hence they are also called *children of the promise.*

†Is 45:8 LXX

—from the second book against the same person*

88. *Not only that,* [Paul] says; Isaac was promised in the words, *'At this time I will come, and Sarah shall have a son.'* No meritorious works had gained from God for Isaac the promise that he would be born, and that *in Isaac* would Abraham's *descendants be called.*† In other words, those who would understand that they are the children of the promise, not being proud because of their own merits, but attributing to the grace of the call that they were to be joint heirs with Christ—these were to belong to the inheritance of the saints† in Christ. When the promise was made they did not yet exist, and of course merited nothing.

†**Rm 9:10, 9, 7** (Gn 21:12)

†Col 1:12

But also Rebecca, having conceived by one act of intercourse, of our father Isaac . . . † [Paul] specifies that *by one act of intercourse* twins were conceived, lest it be attributed to the father's merits if someone were to say, 'A son of such a kind was born because his father was so influenced at the time when he implanted his

†**Rm 9:10**

*86. *Contra Sec. Iul. Resp.* 1.141; CSEL 85,1: 158,26–159,37
*87. *Ibid.* 2.153; CSEL 85,1: 276,19–277,25

seed in the mother's womb,' or, 'His mother was so influenced when she conceived him.' Both were conceived together, at the same time.

—from *To Simplician, Bishop*★

89. We must thoroughly examine the Apostle's purpose as to why, in order to emphasize grace, [God] did not choose that the one of whom it was said, *Jacob I loved*, should glory except in the Lord.†

†**Rm 9:13** (Mal 1:3); 1 Co 1:31

[Jacob and Esau] were from the same father and the same mother, by one act of intercourse—and before they had done anything good or evil, God loved one and hated the other. This was so that Jacob would realize that he was from the lump of original iniquity when he saw that his brother, with whom he had a common origin, in justice deserved to be condemned, and that he could be distinguished only through grace. For, [Paul] says, *even before they were born or had done anything good or bad—in order that God's purpose of election might continue, not by works but by his call—[Rebecca] was told, 'The elder shall serve the younger.'*†

†**Rm 9:11–12** (Gn 25:23)

The same apostle also clearly asserts in another passage that the election brought about by grace comes from no antecedent merits proceeding from works: 'So too at this time a remnant has been saved through the election of grace. But if by grace, it is no longer because of works; otherwise grace is no longer grace.' Going on, he appropriates the prophet's testimony concerning this grace: *As it is written, 'Jacob I loved but Esau I hated,'* and then, *What then are we to say? Is there injustice on God's part? By no means!*†

†**Rm** 11:5–6, **9:13–14**

Why [did he say] *By no means*? Was it because he foresaw the future works of both [Esau and Jacob]? Again, by no means! *For he says to Moses, 'I will show mercy to whom I will show mercy, and have pity on whom I will have pity.' So it depends not on the one who wills or runs, but on God, who shows mercy.*†

†**Rm 9:15–16** (Ex 33:19)

—from a letter to the priest Sixtus concerning the Pelagians★

★88. *De Div. Quaest. Ad Simpl.* 1.2.3; CC 44: 26,54/68
★89. *Ep.* 194.8.38–39; CSEL 57: 206,12–207,15

90. As to the words, *The elder shall serve the younger,*† scarcely anyone among us has taken this to mean anything else than that the elder people of the Jews was going to serve the younger Christian people. And in fact, this might seem to have been fulfilled in the nation of the Idumeans, which sprang from the elder (who had two names—he was called both Esau and Edom, hence 'Idumeans') because later it was to be overcome by the people descended from the younger—that is, by the Israelites—and would be subjected to them. Yet we do better to believe that something more was intended by the prophetic statement that 'one people shall overcome the other, and the elder shall serve the younger.'† And what is this, except what is manifestly fulfilled in the Jews and Christians?

†**Rm 9:12** (Gn 25:23)

†Gn 25:23

—from *On the City of God* 16.35*

91. And [Paul] goes on, *What then are we to say? Is there injustice on God's part? By no means!*† Why [did he say] *By no means*? Was it because he foresaw the future works of both [Esau and Jacob]? No—and again, by no means! *For he says to Moses, 'I will show mercy to whom I will show mercy, and have pity on whom I will have pity.' So it depends not on the one who wills or runs, but on God, who shows mercy.*†

—[from a letter to the priest Sixtus concerning the Pelagians]*

†**Rm 9:14**

†**Rm 9:15–16** (Ex 33:19)

92. If you paid careful attention, you would not extol the merits of the will against grace when you hear that *it depends not on the one who wills or runs, but on God, who shows mercy.*† Therefore, God did not show mercy because Jacob willed and ran, but Jacob willed and ran because God showed mercy. 'The will is prepared by the Lord,' and 'A person's steps are directed by the Lord, and he will choose his way.'†

†**Rm 9:16**

†Pr 8:35 LXX; Ps 37:23

Then, because the general statement, *It depends not on the one who wills or runs, but on God, who shows mercy,* was made on account

*90. *De Civ. Dei* 16.35; CC 48: 540,17/28
*91. *Ep.* 194.8.39; CSEL 57: 207,8/15

of Jacob, he also gives the example of Pharaoh, on account of the
words, 'But Esau I hated.' [Paul] adds, *For Scripture says to Pharaoh,
'This is why I have raised you up, to show my power through you, and that
my name may be proclaimed throughout the earth.'* After this, he sums
up both: *Consequently he shows mercy to whom he wills, and hardens*
†**Rm 9:13** *whom he wills.*† Surely, however, he shows mercy in accord with
(Mal 1:3), **17–18** (Ex 9:16) grace, which is given freely and not in return for merits, whereas
he hardens in accord with a judgment which is in return for merits.
To make from a condemned lump a vessel for honorable use is a
manifestation of grace, while to make from it a vessel for ignoble
†Rm 9:21; 2 Tm 2:20 use is a just judgment.†

—from *Against Julian* 1*

93. [Paul] said, *It depends not on the one who wills or runs, but on God,*
†**Rm 9:16** *who shows mercy,*† not, 'It depends not on the one who wills or
scorns, but on God, who hardens.' Hence, since further on he sets
down both [ideas]—*Consequently he shows mercy to whom he wills, and*
†**Rm 9:18** *he hardens whom he wills*†—we are given to understand an agreement
with the former statement, so that God's hardness is an unwillingness to show mercy. Thus [God] is not imposing something to
make a person worse, but only not imposing something to make a
person better.

If [God] makes no distinction in merits, who would not burst
out with the words that the Apostle put to himself: *You say to*
†**Rm 9:19** *me, then, 'Why does he still find fault? For who can oppose his will?'*†
God frequently finds fault with humans—countless passages in the
Scriptures show this—because they are unwilling to believe and to
live upright lives. Hence those who are faithful, and who do his
will, are said to live faultless lives since Scripture finds no fault in
them. *Why does he still find fault?* you ask. *Who can oppose his will*
when *he shows mercy to whom he wills and he hardens whom he wills?*

The Apostle dulls the brazenness of the question as follows: *Who*
†**Rm 9:20** *are you, O human, to talk back to God?*† A person talks back to God
when displeased because God finds fault with sinners—as if God

*92. *Contra Sec. Iul. Resp.* 1.141; CSEL 85,1: 159,51–160,68

compels anyone to sin! [God] compels no one to sin, but merely does not bestow the mercy of his righteousness on certain sinners. He is said to harden certain sinners because he does not show them mercy, not because he forces them to sin. He does not show mercy to those to whom—by his most secret impartiality, which is far beyond human comprehension—he judges that mercy is not to be granted.

And if you are disturbed because no one resists his will—since he assists whom he wills, and abandons whom he wills, when both the one he assists and the one he abandons are from the same lump of sinners—and although each deserves punishment, it is taken from one and given to the other—if you are disturbed, *Who are you, O human, to talk back to God?* I think that *human* has here the same significance as when he asks, 'Are you not carnal, and behaving in a purely human way?'† †1 Co 3:3

—from *To Simplician, Bishop**

94. *Does what is formed say to the one who formed it, 'Why did you make me thus?' Does not the potter have power over the clay, to make from the same lump one vessel for honor and another for shame?*† †**Rm 9:20–21**

When the entire lump has been rightly condemned, justice pays it deserved shame, and grace gives it undeserved honor. This is not as a sign of merit, not as required by fate, not by accident of fortune, but because of the depth of the riches of the wisdom and knowledge of God. The Apostle does not explain it, but marvels at it unexplained, crying out, 'O the depth of the riches of the wisdom and knowledge of God! How unfathomable are his judgments and unsearchable his ways!'† †Rm 11:33

—from the letter cited above to Sixtus, the priest*

95. *If God, wishing to show his wrath and demonstrate his power, produced with much patience vessels of wrath fit for destruction*—supply the words,

---

*93. *De Div. Quaest. Ad Simpl.* 1.2.15–17; CC 44: 40,424–41,440; 42,475/85; 43,492/98

*94. *Ep.* 194.2.5; CSEL 57: 179,18–180,4

†Rm 9:22, 20 *Who are you, to talk back to God?*† Connecting this statement with the earlier one, then, this must be the meaning: *If God, wishing to show his wrath, produced vessels of wrath, who are you, to talk back to God?*

And not only *wishing to show his power,* but also what follows, *to make known the riches of his glory to the vessels of mercy which he has prepared for glory.*† What advantage is it for the vessels completed for destruction that God endures them patiently, so as regularly to annihilate them, and use them for the salvation of those to whom he shows mercy? But surely it is to the advantage of those for whose salvation he uses this means, as is written, 'Let the righteous wash their hands in the blood of sinners!'†—in other words, let them be cleansed of evil deeds by fear of God when they see the punishments of sinners.

†Rm 9:23

†Ps 58:10

Even us, whom he has called, not only from the Jews, but also from the Gentiles. From Adam comes one lump of sinners and ungodly persons, in which [Jews] and Gentiles, without God's grace, belong to the one dough.†

†Rm 9:24; 1 Co 5:7

—from *To Simplician, Bishop*, cited above*

96. To mercy, given freely and not as an obligation, belongs the preparation of vessels for glory out of the condemned lump, *not only from the Jews*, as [Paul] says, *but also from the Gentiles.* For this reason he sets down the testimony of the prophet Hosea, *I called those who were not my people 'my people,'* and of Isaiah, *Concerning Israel, a remnant will be saved.*†

†Rm 9:24, 25 (Ho 2:24); 9:27 (Is 10:22)

—from *Against Julian* 1*

97. *Decisively and quickly will the Lord bring his word to pass*—that is, he will save believers by grace, using the short way of faith, and not by the innumerable observances by which the vast number [of Jews]

*95. *De Div. Quaest. Ad Simpl.* 1.2.18–19; CC 44: 46,589–47,605; 617/18; 48,620/23

*96. *Contra Sec. Iul. Resp.* 1.141; CSEL 85,1: 161,87/92

was burdened and oppressed. By grace is his word *decisively* spoken for us. 'My yoke is easy, and my burden is light.'† †**Rm 9:28**; Mt 11:30

—from *To Simplician, Bishop**

98. That God's grace brought the remnant into being [Paul] teaches by the following testimony from the same prophet. [Isaiah] said, *Unless the Lord of hosts had left us descendants, we would have become like Sodom.* Then he shows that the Gentiles attained righteousness on the basis of faith, but Israel did not attain it because [they sought it] *not on the basis of faith, but as if it were based on works.*† [The Gentiles] had faith, since he says a little later that 'everyone who calls on the name of the Lord will be saved.'† This salvation requires that good works and righteousness come to us from God, not from ourselves. Therefore [it is taken] from those [who sought it] *not on the basis of faith, but as if it were based on works. They stumbled over the stumbling stone.* [Paul] goes on to say, *Brothers and sisters, my heart's desire and prayer to God for them is for salvation. I testify to them that they have zeal for God, but not in accord with knowledge,*† and so on.

†**Rm 9:29** (Is 1:9); **9:32**

†Rm 10:13 (Jl 2:32)

†**Rm 9:32, 10:1–2**

—from the book against Julian cited above*

99. *They stumbled over the stumbling stone, as it is written, 'See I am laying in Zion a stumbling stone and a rock of scandal; and everyone who believes in him will not be put to shame.'*† †**Rm 9:32–33** (Is 28:16); 1 P 2:6–8

The Jewish people were expecting that Christ would come, but because he came in a lowly state they did not recognize him. Because the stone was small they stumbled over him and were broken. But the stone grew in size 'and became a great mountain.' And what does Scripture say? 'Whoever stumbles over that stone will be shattered, and that stone will crush the one on whom it comes.'† †Dn 2:35; Lk 20:18

We must consider the different words. [Jesus] said that the one who stumbles is shattered, and the one on whom he comes is

*97. *De Div. Quaest. Ad Simpl.* 1.2.19; CC 44: 49,645/51
*98. *Contra Sec. Iul. Resp.* 1.141; CSEL 85,1: 161,92/105

crushed. At first, because he came in a lowly state people stumbled over him; because he is to come in an exalted state for judgment he will crush the one on whom he comes. But when he comes he will not crush the one he did not shatter when he came. Anyone who does not stumble over him in a lowly state will not be afraid of him when he has been exalted. Christ is a stumbling stone for all the wicked; whatever Christ says is bitter to them.

—from homily three on the Letter of John*

†**Rm 9:33** 100. *And everyone who believes in him will not be put to shame.*†

Everyone who waits for him in faith will rejoice when he comes. Those who are without faith will feel shame when what they do not now see comes. Their shame will not last for a day and pass, as those caught in some misdeed and taunted by other people are accustomed to feeling shame. This shame will bring those who are ashamed to [Christ's] left hand, to hear, 'Go into the eternal fire
†Mt 25:41 that has been prepared for the devil and his angels.'† Let us abide in his words, then, so that we may *not be put to shame* when he comes.

—from homily four on the Letter of John*

101. *Being ignorant of God's righteousness, and seeking to establish their*
†**Rm 10:3** *own, they have not submitted to God's righteousness.*†

Being ignorant of God's righteousness—that is, [the righteousness]
†Rm 4:5 that God 'who justifies the ungodly'† bestows—*and* wanting *to establish their own*—as if accomplished by the strength of their own wills—*they have not submitted to God's righteousness.*

—from *To Hilary**

102. This is exactly what you do—you want to establish your own
†Rm 10:3 righteousness,† for which God can give back grace in accord with

---

*99. *In Ioh. Ep.* 3.6; PL 35: 2000
*100. *In Ioh. Ep.* 4.2; PL 35: 2006
*101. *Ep.* 157.1.2.6; CSEL 44: 452,18/21

your merits. You do not want God's grace to come first, to cause you to possess righteousness.

Then, bringing his thoughts together, [Paul] arrives at the place where he says, *I ask, then, has God rejected his people? By no means! . . . But if by grace, it is no longer because of works; otherwise grace is no longer grace.* Then, see what he adds: *What then?* he asks; *what Israel was seeking it did not obtain; but the election obtained it.*† †**Rm 11:1–6, 7**

Look back at the kind of election he meant: *A remnant was saved by the election of grace; but if by grace, it is no longer because of works.*† And this is connected with the statement from which this chain of thought began: 'even before they were born or had done anything good or bad—in order that God's purpose of election might continue, not by works . . .'† This is the election of grace, 'not by works'. Vessels are made 'for honor' so that they can perform good works. Good works follow grace, and do not precede it. God's grace causes us to perform them so that we may not establish our own righteousness but that God's righteousness may be in us—that is, [the righteousness] that God bestows on us. †**Rm 11:5–6** †Rm 9:11–12

The rest were blinded. This is the judgment by which vessels are made for shame. Because of this judgment it was said, 'Esau I hated.' Because of this judgment it was said to Pharaoh, 'This is why I have raised you up.'† †**Rm 11:7**, 9:13, 17

—from *Against Julian* 1*

103. *Everyone who calls upon the name of the Lord will be saved.*† †**Rm 10:13**

The human race was oppressed by great misery as a result of sin, and was in need of divine mercy. Therefore the prophet, foretelling the time of God's grace, said, 'It shall come to pass that everyone who calls upon the name of the Lord will be saved.'† For this reason prayer exists. But the Apostle, when he had recalled the prophetic testimony in order to commend this grace, immediately added, *But how will they call on one in whom they have not believed?*† For this reason the creed† exists. Behold three things in two: faith believes, hope and love pray. Apart from faith [hope and love] cannot exist, and †Jl 3:5 (2:32 Vulgate) †**Rm 10:14** †*symbolum*

*102. *Contra Sec. Iul. Resp.* 1.141; CSEL 85,1: 161,106–163,136

through them faith too prays. That is why [Paul] asked, *How will they call on one in whom they have not believed?*

—from *Enchiridion* 7*

104. What the Apostle said to the Romans, *How will they call on one in whom they have not believed, and how will they believe one of whom*
†**Rm 10:14** *they have not heard?*† He said of the nations, not of the Jews, as this person foolishly imagines. The teacher of the Gentiles wanted to refute those who supposed that the gospel was to be preached solely to the nation of the Jews and not also to the uncircumcised nations. Wanting to show that it belonged not to Jews only, but to all nations, he first set down the testimony from the prophet, 'It shall come to pass that everyone who calls upon the name of the Lord will be saved,' and then after he had asked, *How will they call on one in whom they have not believed, and how will they believe one of whom they have not heard?* he immediately added, *How will they hear without someone*
†Jl 3:5 (2:32 Vulgate); **Rm 10:14–15** *to preach, and how will they preach unless they are sent?*† In this way he refuted those who denied that Christ's preachers were to be sent to the uncircumcised nations.

—from *Against the Opponent of the Law and the Prophets* 2*

†**Rm 11:1** 105. *I ask then, has God rejected his people? By no means!*† In order to say this the Apostle had just recalled the prophetic testimony about the future unbelief of the people of Israel which had been foretold: 'All day long I stretched out my hands to a people that did not believe and
†Is 65:2 (Rm 10:21) that opposed me.'† Not wanting anyone to misunderstand and suppose that the entire people was condemned for the offense of unbelief and opposition, he immediately added, *I ask then, has God rejected his people? By no means! I too am an Israelite, of the race of Israel and the tribe of Benjamin.* He is indicating which people he means, the former people, of course, [the Jews]. If God had rejected and condemned

*103. *Enchir.* 2.7; CC 46: 51,3–13
*104. *Contra Adv. Leg. et Prophet.* 2.3.11; CC 49: 98,352/65

them all completely, surely [Paul] would not have been an apostle of Christ, *an Israelite, from the seed of Abraham and the tribe of Benjamin.*† **†Rm 11:1**. Augustine has just given this sentence in a somewhat different form.

He employs an especially needed testimony when he asks, *Do you not know what the Scripture says about Elijah, how he pleads with God against Israel? 'Lord, they have slain your prophets.' . . . So too at this time a remnant has been saved through the election of grace.*† This remnant was a portion of that race of God's inheritance, not of those of whom he says a little later, *the rest were blinded.*† **†Rm 11:2–5** **†Rm 11:7**

—An explanation of Psalm 78*

106. 'For this reason they could not believe, because again Isaiah said, He has blinded their eyes and hardened their heart . . .'† Then what shall we answer concerning another testimony from this same prophet? The Apostle quotes it, saying, *What Israel was seeking it did not obtain, but the election obtained it; the rest were blinded, as it is written: 'God gave them a spirit of remorse, eyes that they should not see and ears that they should not hear, even to this very day.'*† †Jn 12:39–40 (Is 6:9–10) **†Rm 11:7–8** (Is 6:10, 29:10; Dt 29:4)

Brothers and sisters, you have heard the question that this raises, and you perceive its depth. I will respond as well as I can. [The Jews] 'could not believe' because the prophet Isaiah foretold it. The prophet foretold it because God knew beforehand that this would come about. If I am asked why they 'could not' I immediately answer that they were unwilling. God foresaw their ill will, and the one from whom the future cannot be concealed foretold it through the prophet.

But, you say, the prophet offers another reason than that of their will. What reason does the prophet give? That *God gave them a spirit of remorse, eyes that they should not see and ears that they should not hear,* and 'blinded their eyes and hardened their heart.' This too, I answer, their will deserved. God blinds and hardens by withdrawing and not giving his help. He is able to do this by a hidden judgment, but not by an unjust one.

—from homily fifty on the Gospel of John*

---

*105. *En. in Ps* 78.2; CC 39: 1099,44; 52–1100,73

*106. *Tract. In. Ioh.* 53.5–6; CC 36: 454,10/11; 20/15

107. *And David says, 'Let their table be a snare and a trap, a stumbling block and a recompense for them . . .'*†

†**Rm 11:9** (Ps 69:22)

I was thirsty, and I received vinegar—that is, I longed for faith from them, and I found oldness. 'Let their table be a snare before them.' Let there be for them a snare like the one they set for me by giving me such a drink. Why, then, 'before them'? 'Let their table be a snare' would be enough. These are such persons as recognize their wickedness and persevere in it obstinately. It becomes 'a snare before them'. These are the ones who 'go down alive into hell.'†

†Ps 69:21–22, 55:15

'Let their eyes be darkened so that they cannot see'† follows here. Thus, since they have seen without good reason, let them not see. 'Let their table be a snare before them,' then. This is not from one who wants this, but from one prophesying—not that something *may* happen, but because it *will* happen. I have often brought this up, and you ought to remember it, so that what the prophetic mind says in the Spirit of God it may not seem to be asking for out of ill will.

†Ps 69:23 (**Rm 11:10**)

'And keep their backs forever bent.'† This is a natural result. In the case of those whose eyes are darkened so that they do not see, it follows that their backs are bent. Why is this so? Since they have ceased to inquire into what is above, they must reflect on what is below. Those who listen well have hearts on high, not bent backs. They await with upright posture the hope laid up for them in heaven, especially if they send their treasure on ahead, where their hearts may follow.† On the other hand, those who do not understand the hope of the life to come are already blinded and reflect on what is below. This is to have a bent back—the affliction from which the Lord freed the woman [in the gospel]. Satan had held her bound for eighteen years, and [Jesus] raised her who was bent.†

†Ibid.

†Col 1:5; Mt 6:21

†Lk 13:11–16

—from the treatise on Psalm 68*

108. *In regard to the gospel, they are enemies [of God] for your sake . . .*†

†**Rm 11:28–29**

What does *In regard to the gospel, they are enemies [of God] for your sake* mean if not that their enmity, by which they killed Christ, is

*107. *En. In Ps* 68.2.6–8; CC 39: 922,37–923,7; 17/24; 1/12

without any doubt an advantage to the gospel, even as we see? *In regard to the election they are beloved for their ancestors' sake. Enemies* and *beloved* are not the same. When we hear, 'Israel did not obtain' [and] 'the rest were blinded,' we are to understand *enemies*. When we hear, 'the election obtained it,'† we are to understand *beloved for their ancestors' sake*, to whom these things were promised. 'The promises were made to Abraham': *The gifts of God are irrevocable*†—that is, they are firmly established and changeless.

†Rm 11:7

†Ga 3:16; **Rm 11:29**

—from *To Prosper and Hilary**

109. *Just as once you did not believe in God but have now obtained mercy . . . For God included all things in unbelief, that he may be merciful to all.*†

†**Rm 11:30–32**

This does not mean that [God] will condemn no one, but the meaning appears in what [Paul said] earlier. When the Apostle was speaking to the Gentiles—to whom, as doubtless already believing, he was writing his letters—about the Jews who would later believe, he said, *Just as once you did not believe in God but now have obtained mercy on account of their unbelief, so for the present they too have not believed in the mercy shown you in order that they too might obtain mercy*. He then added the reason they delude themselves in their error: *God included all people in faithlessness, that he may be merciful to all.*† Who are *all people* if not those of whom he was speaking, just as if he was saying, 'both you and them'? *God*, then, *included in faithlessness all people*, both Gentiles and Jews, 'whom he foreknew and predestined to be conformed to the image of his Son,'† so that from the bitterness of their own faithlessness they might by repenting be confounded, and by believing be converted to the sweetness of God's mercy, and cry out in the words of the psalm, 'How great is the abundance of your goodness, Lord, that you have hidden from those who fear you, and perfected for those who hope' not in themselves but 'in you!'† [God] has mercy, then, on all the vessels of mercy. What does 'all' mean? Both those from the Gentiles, and those from the Jews,

†**Rm 11:32**. Augustine read *omnes in infidelitate* where the Vulgate, quoted by Bede at the beginning of this excerpt, reads *omnia in incredulitatem*.

†Rm 8:29

†Ps 31:19

*108 De Praedest. Sanct. 16.33; PL 44: 984–85 passim

†Rm 8:30 whom he predestined, called, justified and glorified.† [He does not mean] 'all people,' but that he will condemn none of all the saints.

—from *On the City of God* 21*

110. *O the depth of the riches of the wisdom and knowledge of God! . . .*
†Rm 11:33–36 *to him be glory for ages of ages.*†

Those ignorant of [God's] righteousness, who want to establish
†Rm 10:3 their own,† are unwilling that his be the glory in making the ungodly righteous by his freely-given gift. [They are unwilling] even when constrained by the voices of religious and devout persons who call out together for them to confess that they are divinely assisted in possessing or bringing about righteousness—so that something precedes their own merit. They are like people who want to be first to give, so that recompense may be made them by the one of whom it is said, *Who has first given to him, and recompense will be made him?* They suppose that their own merits go ahead of them to the one of whom they hear—or rather are unwilling to hear—*For from him and through him and in him are all things.* Of his riches is the depth of his wisdom and knowledge, [and] from these are 'the riches of his glory in the vessels of mercy' that he calls to adoption. These riches he chooses to make known even through 'the vessels of wrath' that
†Rm 9:23, 22 are destined 'for destruction.'†

And what are the *unsearchable ways* if not those chanted in the psalm: 'All the ways of the Lord are mercy and truth'? His mercy and truth are *unsearchable* when 'he shows mercy to whom he wills,' not by righteousness but by the mercy of grace, and 'hardens whom he wills,' not by injustice but by the truth of punishment. Nevertheless,
†Ps 25:10; Rm 9:18; Ps 85:10 mercy and truth meet—as is written, 'Mercy and truth meet'†—in such a way that mercy does not stand in the way of the truth by which the deserving are punished, nor does truth stand in the way of the mercy by which the undeserving are set free.

—from a letter to the priest Sixtus*

---

*109. *De Civ. Dei* 21.24; CC 48: 793,164/85
*110. *Ep.* 194.3.6; CSEL 57: 180,1–181,7

111. I am asking of whom [Paul] says, *For from him and through him and in him are all things. To him be glory for ages of ages.*† If [he is speaking] of the Father and the Son and the Holy Spirit, assigning one [phrase] to each person—*from him*, from the Father; *through him*, through the Son; *in him*, in the Holy Spirit—clearly Father, Son and Holy Spirit are one God, since he concluded in the singular, *To him be glory for ages of ages.* When he began this thought he did not say, *O the depth of the riches of the wisdom and knowledge* of the Father and of the Son and of the Holy Spirit, but *of the wisdom and knowledge of God! How unsearchable are his judgments . . .* †**Rm 11:36**

If they want this understood of the Father alone, how are *all things* through the Father, as is said here, and *all things* through the Son as well—as [Paul] says to the Corinthians, 'and one Lord, Jesus Christ, through whom are all things,' and as [we find] in John's gospel that 'all things came to be through him'?† If some things [came to be] through the Father and some things through the Son, *all things* did not come to be through the Father nor *all things* through the Son. If *all things* [came to be] through the Father and *all things* through the Son, the same things [came to be] through the Father as through the Son. Therefore, the Son is equal to the Father, and the working of the Father and Son is indivisible. †1 Co 8:6; Jn 1:3

—from *On the Trinity* 1.6*

112. *And do not be conformed to this world.*† †**Rm 12:2**

Those who, on being reminded, turn to the Lord† from the deformity by which they were conformed to this world through their worldly desires, are reformed by him when they hear the Apostle saying, *Do not be conformed to this world, but be reformed in the newness of your mind.* Thus the image begins to be reformed by him by whom it was [originally] formed. It cannot reform itself, as it could deform itself. †Ps 22:27

—from *On the Trinity* 14.16*

---

*111. *De Trin.* 1.6.12; CC 50: 41,78–42,99
*112. *De Trin.* 14.16.22; CC 50A: 451,1/7

113. Behold, O Lord our God, our Creator, when the passions by which we were dying by living wickedly have been restrained from love of this world, and the soul by living rightly begins to be alive, and your word which you spoke by your apostle has been fulfilled—*Do not be conformed to this world*—what you immediately added will follow—*but be reformed in the newness of your mind.*† This will no longer be 'according to our kind,' as if in imitation of someone before us, or as living by the example of someone better. You did not say, 'Let a human being be made according to its kind,' but, 'Let us make a human being in our own image and likeness,' that we may *verify what is* your *will.*†

†**Rm 12:2**

†Gn 1:3, 21, 26; **Rm 12:2**

For this reason your steward, who begets children through the gospel, did not want them always to be infants whom he would have to nourish with milk and care for as a nurse.† *Be reformed,* he said, *in the newness of your mind, to verify what is God's will, what is good and pleasing and perfect.* Therefore you do not say, 'Let a human being be made,' but, 'Let us make [a human being],' and you do not say 'according to its kind' but 'in our own image and likeness.' [Humans], being renewed in mind, and discerning and understanding your truth, do not need another human to show them how to imitate their kind. With you to show them, they *verify what is* your *will, what is good and pleasing and perfect.*

†1 Co 4:1, 15; 3:1–2; Heb 5:12; 1 Th 2:7

—from *Confessions* 13, speaking of the beginning of Genesis, where a living soul is created according to its kind†*

†Gn 2:7

114. *Do not be high-minded, but associated with the humble.*†

†**Rm 12:16**

'If we say we have no sin, we deceive ourselves, and the truth is not in us,'† and so on. Let us experience these things as we say them. Humility will be genuine when we do not exhibit it only in speech, but are, in the Apostle's words, *not high-minded, but associated with the humble.* This is not done by the mouth but by the heart. Hypocrite, if you say you have sin when you believe you have none, outwardly

†1 Jn 1:8

*113. *Confess.* 13.22 (32); CC 27: 260,1/20

you are feigning humility while inwardly you are embracing vanity. You have the truth neither in your mouth nor in your heart. What do you gain if what you say appears humble to people while God sees that you are high-minded?

—from the treatise on Psalm 118*

115. 'All who exalt themselves will be humbled, and all who humble themselves will be exalted.' Therefore, since the Apostle advises us *not to be high-minded, but associated with the humble,*† let them, if they †Lk 14:11; 18:14; **Rm 12:16**
can, consider the high precipice of pride they are borne to if they do not associate with the humble God, and how calamitous it must be for humans to bear with impatience what the just Lord wills, if God bore with patience what an unjust enemy willed.

—again, from a sermon on the Lord's passion*

116. *Do not vindicate yourselves, beloved.*† †**Rm 12:19** (Dt 32:35)

Scripture says, 'The just will rejoice to see vengeance on the wicked, and will wash their hands in the blood of the sinner.'† The †Ps 58:10
Apostle says, *Do not vindicate yourselves, beloved, but leave room for the wrath; for it is written, 'Vengeance is mine, and I will repay,' says the Lord.* He does not prohibit them from wishing to be avenged, but tells them that by not avenging themselves they leave room for the wrath of the God who said, *Vengeance is mine, and I will repay.* In the gospel, too, the Lord related the parable of the widow. Desiring to be avenged, she importuned an unjust judge and at length he listened to her; he was not guided by righteousness, but overcome by weariness. The Lord related this to show that much more will the just God quickly give judgment for his chosen ones who cry out to him day and night.† †Lk 18:1–8

*114. *En. In Ps* 118.2.1; CC 40: 1669,39/51 passim
*115. *Serm.* Guelferb. 3.4 (*Serm. Post. Maurinos Reperti*, ed. G. Morin, *Miscellanea Agostiniana* I, 455,2–8; cf. PL 39: 1723).

†Mt 5:44; **Rm 12:17**

How [do you read] these texts, 'Love your enemies,' and, *Do not repay anyone evil for evil?*† Those persons repay by an evil desire who, even if they themselves do not take vengeance, yet wait and long for God to punish their enemy. Therefore, since both righteous and evil persons want to be avenged against their enemies by the Lord, how are we to distinguish them if not that the righteous want their enemies reformed rather than punished? When they see vengeance taken against them by the Lord, they take no pleasure in their punishment, because they do not hate them, but in divine righteousness, because they love God.

Moreover, if in this age vengeance is taken against them, they either rejoice for them if they are reformed, or for others, that they may be afraid to imitate them. They themselves are also improved, not by nourishing their hatred at the chastisement of another, but by correcting their own mistakes. Thus from good will, and not from malice, do the just rejoice to see vengeance on the wicked, and wash their hands—that is, accomplish purer works—in the blood—that is, in the destruction—of the sinner. From this they do not derive joy in another's misfortune, but an example of divine counsel.

—from the treatise on Psalm 78*

†**Rm 12:20** (Pr 25:21–22)

117. *If your enemies are hungry, feed them . . .* †

In figurative speech we will observe a rule of this kind: we will carefully and long mull over what we read until we draw its interpretation into the realm of love. If its meaning is immediately clear, we will not suppose it to be figurative. If the speech is preceptive—either forbidding a shameful or wicked action, or commanding a useful or kind one—it is not figurative. If, however, it seems to be ordering something shameful or wicked, or forbidding something useful or kind, it is figurative.

Scripture says, *If your enemies are hungry, feed them; if they are thirsty, give them something to drink.* This, no one can doubt, commands a kindness. But what follows—*for by doing this you will heap burning coals*

---

*116. *En. in Ps* 78.14; CC 39: 1107,7–1108,42 passim

on their heads—you may suppose orders a wicked act of malevolence. Therefore, you should not doubt that it was said figuratively. And since it can be taken in two ways, one harmful, the other helpful, let love recall you to kindness. Then you will take the *burning coals* to be the scorching groans of repentance that heal the pride of those who grieve that they are enemies of the persons who come to help them in their misery.

—from *On Christian Doctrine* 3*

118. The Apostle has carefully added, *Do not be overcome by evil, but overcome evil with good.*† How can those who are apparently good but really evil, indulgent in act but furious in heart, gentle in power but cruel in intent, *overcome evil with good*? In the guise of someone asking it in this psalm, [the psalmist] prophesies future vengeance on the ungodly.† This will enable us to grasp that God's holy ones loved their enemies and desired nothing but good for anyone. This is godliness in this age, [and] everlasting life in the age to come. In the punishments of the wicked they found no pleasure in their punishments, but in God's good judgments. Wherever in the holy Scriptures we read of their hatred for people, this was hatred of vices, which all must hate even in themselves, if they love themselves.

†**Rm 12:21**

†Ps 79:10

—in the explanation of Psalm 78*

119. If you are no longer evil yourself, desire for the evil that they be good. Why are you enraged at the evil? 'Because they are evil,' you say. By being enraged at them you add yourself to their number. I give you some advice: Is the evil person offensive to you? Do not let there be two of you! You object to them, but you join them. You increase the number of those you condemn as evil. Do you want to overcome evil with evil, to overcome malice with malice?

---

*117. *De Doct. Christ.* 3.15.23–16.24; CC 32: 91,3–92,4; 9/18
*118. *En. in Ps* 78.14; CC 39: 1108,65/76

There will be two malices, both needing to be overcome. Do not you hear your Lord's advice through the Apostle: *Do not be overcome*
†Rm 12:21 *by evil, but overcome evil with good*?† Perhaps the other person is worse. Still, when you are evil, two are evil. I would like at least one to be good.

—from a sermon on the birthday of Saint Lawrence, martyr*

120. *Do you want to have no fear of authority? Do good, and you will*
†Rm 13:3 *receive praise from it.*†

Someone may ask, 'What evil had Saint Lawrence done that he was killed by authority? How was *Do good, and you will receive praise from it* fulfilled in his case, when by doing good he earned such great suffering from it?' If the holy martyr Lawrence did not receive praise from it, he would not be honored today, would not be proclaimed by me, would not receive praise in such a great celebration. Therefore he is receiving *praise from it*, even if [authority] is unwilling.

What did the Apostle say? *Do good*, and authority itself will praise you. All the apostles and martyrs did good, and instead of praising them the authorities killed them. Therefore, if [Paul] said, '*Do good*, and it will praise you,' he deceived you. But he has qualified his words, he has been circumspect, he has measured his words, restrained them, made them succinct. Analyze what you have heard: *Do good, and you will receive praise from it.* If authority is just, *you will receive praise from it*, with [authority] itself giving praise. If it is unjust, when you have died for your faith, for righteousness' sake, for the truth, *you will receive praise from it*, even if it is in a rage. *You will receive [praise] from it*, not with [authority] itself giving praise, but with [authority] providing you with an occasion of praise.

—from a sermon on the birthday of Saint Lawrence, martyr*

---

*119. *Serm.* 302.11.10; PL 38: 1389
*120. *Ibid.* 12.11–13.12; PL 38: 1389–90

121. *Those who eat must not despise those who do not eat . . .* † †**Rm 14:3**

Concerning kinds of food, because every kind of human food can be taken indiscriminately, with a good intention and a guileless heart, and without the vice of concupiscence, the Apostle prohibits those who eat meat and drink wine from being judged by those who hold back from those kinds of nourishment. He says, *Those who eat must not despise those who do not eat, and those who do not eat must not pass judgment on those who eat.* Concerning such things, which may be done with a good and guileless and generous intention—although they can also be done with a bad intention—these people, although only human, want to pass sentence on secrets of the heart that God alone judges.

—from *On the Lord's Sermon on the Mount* 2*

122. *For the kingdom of God is not food and drink, but righteousness and peace and joy in the Holy Spirit.*† †**Rm 14:17**

What is more important, then, is not the kind and quality of nourishment people take, in accord with human nature in general and individually, and the requirements of each one's health, but the readiness and tranquillity of mind with which they do without, when doing without is appropriate or necessary. This is so that the Apostle's words may be fulfilled in Christians: 'I know what having little is, and I know what having plenty is; everywhere and in everything I am instructed';† and this too, *For the kingdom of God* †Ph 4:12
is not food and drink, but righteousness and peace and joy. And, since human beings are used to finding pleasure in fleshly feasting, he added, *in the Holy Spirit.*

—from *Questions on the Gospel* 11*

123. *For Christ did not please himself, but, as it is written, 'The reproaches of those who reproached you fell on me.'*† †**Rm 15:3** (Ps 69:10)

*121. *De Serm. Dom. in Monte* 2.18.59; CC 35: 155,1360/71 passim
*122. *Quaest. Ev.* 2.11; CC 44B: 54,25–55,31,33/36

The Apostle called these words Christ's: 'The taunts of those who taunted you fell on me.' Why 'you'? Is the Father taunted, and not Christ himself? Why is it that 'the taunts of those who taunted you fell on me'? Because 'the one who has known me has known the Father too'; because no one has taunted Christ without taunting God; because no one honors the Father except the one who honors the Son as well.† (†Ps 69:9; Jn 14:9, 5:23)

—from the treatise on Psalm 68*

124. *For I say that Christ Jesus was a minister of the circumcision.*† (†**Rm 15:8**)

Christ, then, is king of the Jews. Even the Gentiles are sent under his light yoke† (†Mt 11:30) to salvation because this was granted them by an act of even greater mercy. The Apostle shows this more clearly when he says, *For I say that Christ Jesus was a minister of the circumcision on behalf of the truth of God, to confirm the promises made to our ancestors, while the Gentiles glorify God for his mercy*. It was not right 'to take the children's bread and throw it to the dogs' unless the dogs have been humbled enough to gather the crumbs they saw fall 'from the table of their masters.'† (†Mt 15:26–27) Raised up, then, by this very act of humility, and become human, they would deserve to come to the table.

—from a sermon on the passion*

125. *For I say that Christ Jesus was a minister of the circumcision . . .* † (†**Rm 15:8**)

The Lord who said, 'I was sent only to the sheep that are lost of the house of Israel,' was showing them the fulfillment of the promise of his presence, yet he said in another place, 'I have other sheep that do not belong to this fold,' and so on.† (†Mt 15:24; Jn 10:16) Hence the Apostle too says, *I say that Christ was a minister of the circumcision on behalf of the truth of God, to confirm the promises made to our ancestors*. This explains, 'I was sent only to the sheep that are lost of the house of Israel.' Then

---

*123. *En. in Ps* 68.1.13; CC 39: 913,24/30

*124. *Serm.* See PL 39: 1723. Augustine refers to the yoke of crossed spears beneath which vanquished soldiers had to pass in token of submission.

the Apostle adds, *while the Gentiles glorify God for his mercy*. This explains, 'I have other sheep that do not belong to this fold; I must bring them also, that there may be one flock and one shepherd.' Both things are succinctly said in what the Apostle quotes from the prophet: *Rejoice, O Gentiles, with his people!*† **†Rm 15:10** (Dt 32:43 LXX)

—from the treatise on Psalm 78*

*125. *En. in Ps* 78.3; CC 39: 1100,26–1101,45

Saint Augustine's Commentary

the First Letter of Paul to the Church at Corinth

PAUL, CALLED TO BE AN APOSTLE of Christ Jesus by the will of God.† † Co 1:1

Jesus and *Christ* have different meanings, although there is one Jesus Christ, our Saviour. *Jesus* is his proper name. As Moses, Elijah and Abraham are called by their proper names, so the Lord's proper name is *Jesus*. *Christ* is the name of his sacramental character.† †*sacramentum nomen* As we call someone a prophet or a priest, so we commend one *Christ*, in whom was the redemption of the entire people of Israel.

—from homily three on the Letter of John*

127. *With all those who call on the name of our Lord Jesus Christ.*† †1 Co 1:2

My faith calls on you, Lord, [the faith] you gave me, that you breathed into me through the humanity of your Son and the ministry of your preacher.† †Probably Saint Ambrose, bishop of Milan. And how shall I call on my Lord and God? Surely when I call on him I am calling him into me.

—from *Confessions* 1*

128. *Was Paul crucified for you?*† †1 Co 1:13

'I am writing to you, little children, because your sins are forgiven you through his name.'† †1 Jn 2:12 [I call you] 'little children' because the forgiveness of sins is a birth. But through whose name are sins forgiven? Is it Augustine's? Therefore, not through Donatus' name either. See who Augustine is, who Donatus is! Not through Paul's name, or Peter's name either. There are people dividing the Church for their own purposes, and trying to fracture its unity. Toward them the Apostle's love is a mother bringing forth small children—she shows her heart, she tears her breasts, so to speak, by her words, she weeps over the children she sees being borne away; she calls back to the one name those who want to make for themselves many names; she turns love away from herself so that they may love Christ, and she asks, *Was Paul crucified for you?*

---

*126. *In Ioh. Ep.* 3.6; PL 35: 2000
*127. *Confess.* 1.1–2; CC 27: 1,16–2,2

Were you baptized in the name of Paul? What is she saying? 'I do not want you to belong *to* me so that you can be *with* me. Be with me. We all belong to the one who died for us, who was crucified for us.'

—from homily two on the Letter of Saint John*

129. *I will destroy the wisdom of the wise, and the discernment of the*
†**1 Co 1:19** (Is 29:14) *discerning I will reject.*†

He does not destroy and reject in them his own wisdom, which he himself gave them, but the wisdom that those who have none of their own claim for themselves. Hence, after recalling the prophet's testimony [Paul] goes on and asks, *Where is the one who is wise? Where is the scribe? Where is the debater of this age? Has not God made foolish the wisdom of this world? . . . But we preach Christ crucified, a stumbling block to Jews and foolishness to Gentiles, but to those who are called, both Jews and Greeks, Christ the power of God and the wisdom of God. For God's foolishness is wiser than humans, and God's weakness is*
†**1 Co 1:20–25** *stronger than humans.*† Those who are, as they think, wise and strong because of their own strength despise this as foolish and weak. But this is the grace that heals the weak—not those proudly boasting of their own false blessedness, but rather those humbly confessing their true wretchedness.

—from *On the City of God* 10*

†Ps 69:5 130. 'O God, you know my folly.'† What folly is there in Christ? Is he not *the power of God and the wisdom of God*? By his 'folly' does [Christ] mean that of which the Apostle says that *God's foolishness*
†**1 Co 1:24–25** *is wiser than humans*?† 'My folly—the very quality that those who seem to themselves to be wise ridiculed in me! You knew why it happened; you knew what my folly was.'

What is so like folly as for the one who was able by a word
†Jn 18:6 to throw his persecutors to the ground† to allow himself to be

*128. *In Ioh. Ep.* 2.4; PL 35: 1992
*129. *De Civ. Dei* 10.28; CC 47: 304,27/43

arrested, scourged, spat upon, struck, crowned with thorns, nailed to the cross? It is like folly, it seems foolish. But this folly triumphs over all the wise.

—from the treatise on Psalm 68*

131. *But to those who are called, both Jews and Greeks, Christ the power of God and the wisdom of God.*† †**1 Co 1:24**

What the Jews said—'Where did this man get this wisdom and power?'—[refers to] the wisdom in what he said and the power in what he did. The Apostle too, when he said *Christ the power of God and the wisdom of God*, was referring *power* to 'signs' for the sake of the Jews, and *wisdom* to teaching for the sake of the Greeks,† that is, of the Gentiles. †Mt 13:54; 1 Co 1:22

—from *Questions on the Gospel* 1*

132. *Consider your call, brothers and sisters. Not many of you were wise by human standards, not many were powerful, not many were of noble birth. But God chose what is foolish in the world to confound the wise.*† †**1 Co 1:26–27**

Why did the Lord first choose people of low birth, who were few in number, uneducated, unpolished, when he had before his eyes a great crowd? They were indeed few in comparison to the poor, but many of his race were wealthy, of noble birth, learned and wise; later he also included them. The Apostle explains the mystery: *God chose what is weak in this world to confound the strong, God chose what is foolish in this world to confound the wise, and God chose what is base in this world and what is not*—that is, what counts for nothing—*that what is may be made nothing.*† †**1 Co 1:27–28**

[Christ] had come to teach humility and to make war on pride; the humble God had by no means come to seek those of high station first. He had come in such a humble manner that at the beginning he chose to be born of a woman who had been espoused to a carpenter. He chose no important ancestors so that the nobility

*130. *En. in Ps* 68.1.10; CC 39: 910,1/12 passim
*131. *Quaest. Ev.* 1.14; CC 44B: 15,2/6

on this earth would not become proud. He did not even choose to be born in an important city, but 'he was born in Bethlehem of Judea,'† which is not even called a city. Today the inhabitants of the place call it a village—it is so small, and so insignificant that it would be almost nothing if it not been ennobled by the ancient birth of Christ, the Lord.

†Lk 1:27; Mt 1:18, 13:55, 2:1; Lk 2:4–7

He chose people who were weak, poor and unlearned, not because he abandoned the strong, wealthy, wise and noble—if he had chosen these people first they may have thought they were chosen on account of their wealth, their possessions or their high birth. Puffed up because of these things, they may not have accepted the salvation brought about by humility. Without this no one can return to that life from which they would not have fallen away except through pride.

—from a sermon on the three types (of disciples)*

133. But someone may possibly say, 'Even though he himself was born in humble circumstances, [Jesus] wanted to boast of the high birth of his disciples.' He did not choose kings or senators or philosophers or orators; instead he chose persons from the lower class, people poor and unlettered, fishermen. Peter was a fisherman,† Cyprian an orator—if the fisherman had not gone first in faith, the orator would not have followed in humility. The abject must not lose hope for themselves; let them hold on to Christ, and their hope will not prove illusory.

†Mt 4:18

—from a sermon against the pagans, on January first*

†**1 Co 1:29**

134. *So that no flesh may glory in his sight.*†

See how he has taken glory from us so that he may bestow glory! He has taken our glory to bestow his own, he has taken empty glory

*132. *Serm.* PL 39; 1731–32. See sections 332, 388. Bede calls the source of these excerpts *Sermo de tribus virgis*, a phrase not readily comprehensible.
*133. *Serm.* 197.2; PL 38: 1023

to bestow full, he has taken faltering glory to bestow firm. You must not glory in yourselves, then; the Truth has forbidden it. What the Apostle says, the Truth has commanded: *Let the one who glories, glory in the Lord.*† †**1 Co 1:31** (Jr 9:24)

—from the treatise on Psalm 65*

135. *He is the source of your life in Christ Jesus, who became for us wisdom from God, and righteousness and sanctification and redemption.*† †**1 Co 1:30**

The Son *became for us wisdom from God, and righteousness and sanctification*, because we turn to him in time—that is, at some point in time—that we may abide with him for ever. At a certain point in time he too, the Word, became flesh and lived among us.† †Jn 1:14

—from *On the Trinity* 7.3*

136. The righteousness, furthermore, that has life in itself is undoubtedly God, and lives without change. Because life exists in itself, it also becomes life for us when we are enabled in some way to share in it. In the same way, because righteousness exists in itself, it also becomes righteousness for us when we live by adhering to it. We are righteous to the degree that we adhere to it. Hence, it is written of God's only-begotten Son, that as he is the wisdom and righteousness of the Father, and always exists in himself, *he became for us wisdom and righteousness and sanctification and redemption, in order that, as it is written, 'The one who glories may glory in the Lord.'*† The supreme God is true righteousness, and the true God is supreme righteousness, that for which we ought to hunger and thirst. This is our righteousness during this pilgrimage, and as it is our full righteousness in eternity, it is that with which we will be filled hereafter.† †**1 Co 1:30–31** (Jr 9:24) †Mt 5:6

—from a letter to Consentius on the Trinity*

*134. *En. in Ps* 65.4; CC 39: 841,54–842,61 passim
*135. *De Trin.* 7.3.4; CC 50: 252,46/49
*136. *Ep.* 120.3.19; CSEL 34: 720,26–721,15 passim. Consentius was a Catholic layman of Augustine's time.

†1 Co 1:31 137. Thus *let those who glory glory in* no one but *the Lord*† when they realize that their existence is not their own doing but his; their well-being, too, is from no one but him, from whom they have their existence.

—from the *Literal Commentary on Genesis* 11*

†1 Co 2:8 138. *If they had known, they would never have crucified the Lord of glory.*†

Unless the same one who is Son of God because of the 'form of God' in which he existed was Son of Man because of the 'form
†Ph 2:6–7 of a servant that he assumed† the Apostle would not have said of the rulers of this age, *If they had known, they would never have crucified the Lord of glory*. He was crucified in the 'form of a servant—and yet the *Lord of glory* was crucified! Such was the nature of that assumption that it made God a human and a human God. With God's help a prudent and careful reader will discern what is said 'for the sake of' something and what is said 'in accord with' something. You know that I said that 'in accord with' his being God he glorifies his own—'in accord,' of course, with his being the *Lord of glory*. And yet the *Lord of glory* was crucified, because we can correctly say even that God was crucified, owing not to the power of the divinity but to
†*De Trin.* 1.12.24; 2 Co 13:4 the weakness of the flesh.†

—from *On the Holy Trinity* 1.13*

139. *But, as it is written, 'What eye has not seen, nor ear heard, neither*
†1 Co 2:9 (Is 64:4, 65:17 Vulgate) *has it ascended into the human heart.'*†

What eye has not seen, because it is not color, *nor ear heard*, because it is not sound, *neither has it ascended into the human heart*, because the human heart must ascend to it.

—from *To Proba, On Praying to God**

*137. *De Gen. ad Litt.* 11.8; CSEL 28,1: 341,23/26
*138. *De Trin.* 1.13.28; 1.12.24; CC 50: 69,1/14; 63,42/43. Augustine is expressing the principle of *communicatio idiomatorum*.
*139. *Ep.* 130.8.17; CC 44: 59,19–60,3

140. *For the Spirit scrutinizes everything, even the depths of God*†—not, surely, to find out what is unknown, but because nothing at all remains unknown to the Spirit. †**1 Co 2:10**

—from the treatise on Psalm 118*

141. *What human being knows what is truly human except the human spirit that is within?*† †**1 Co 2:11**

Scripture calls the rational power of the human soul that distinguishes humans from beasts, and dominates them by a law of nature, *the human spirit.* Of this the Apostle says that no one *knows what is truly human except the human spirit that is within.*

—from *On Genesis, Against the Manichaeans* 2*

142. *No one knows what goes on in a human being except the human spirit that is within*† until the Lord comes and brings to light what is hidden in darkness—and he will disclose the thoughts of the heart,† so that all people will see not only their own [thoughts] but also those of others. In this sense the Apostle said that *no one knows what goes on in a human being except the human spirit that is within,* in accord with what we see in ourselves. In accord with what we believe but do not see, we are aware both that many believers exist, and that we are known to many. †**1 Co 2:11**. Augustine quotes two somewhat different versions of this text. †1 Co 4:5

—from *To Paulina, On Seeing God**

143. *We have not received the spirit of this world . . .* † †**1 Co 2:12**

Let us be aware, beloved, of what our Master is doing for us so that we can be his friends. He, 'and not we ourselves,'† makes us not only human, but also righteous. And who but he makes us aware †Ps 100:3

---

*140. *En. in Ps* 118.11.3; CC 40: 1697,25/27

*141. *De Gen. Contra Manich.* 2.8.11; PL 34: 202

*142. *Ep.* 147.4.11; CC 44: 284,19–285,3. Nothing seems to be known about Paulina, to whom this letter is addressed.

of this? *We have not received the spirit of this world, but the Spirit that is from God, so that we may be aware of what God has bestowed on us.* Whatever is good has been bestowed by him. Therefore, because this too is good, our awareness of who bestows every good thing is surely given by him, so that in every way, for every good thing, 'the one who glories may glory in the Lord.'†

†1 Co 1:31 (Jr 9:24)

—from homily eighty-two on the Gospel of John, where the Lord says that 'the servant does not know what the master is doing'†*

†Jn 15:15

144. 'To those who have, more will be given.' What is 'having' in the full sense? Knowing the source of what you have. 'From those who have not'—that is, who are ignorant of the source of what they have—'even what they have will be taken away.'† Moreover, as the same author says, 'This too was a mark of wisdom, to know whose gift it was as well.'† So too the apostle Paul, when commending to us God's grace in the Holy Spirit, said, *We have not received the spirit of this world, but the Spirit that is from God.* And as if he were asked, 'How do you tell the difference?' he went on, *so that we may be aware of what God has bestowed on us.*† The Spirit of God is a Spirit of love, and the spirit of this world is a spirit of self-esteem. Those who have the spirit of this world are proud, they are ungrateful to God. They have many of his gifts, but do not worship him from whom they have them. Hence, they are unhappy.

†Mt 13:12; Mk 4:25

†Ws 8:21. Augustine had just been referring to the author of this book.

†**1 Co 2:12**

—from a sermon on the birthday of the holy martyrs of Massyla*

145. *Natural persons*† *do not perceive the gifts of God's Spirit.*†

†*animalis homo*

†**1 Co 2:14**

The apostle Jude openly declares that those separated from the Church do not have the Spirit when he says, 'who separate themselves, natural persons, not having the Spirit.'† Hence the apostle Paul reproves those, even within the Church itself, who

†Jude 19

*143. *Tract. in Ioh.* 85.3; CC 36: 540,34/42

*144. *Serm.* 283.2.2–3.3; PL 38: 1287. Massyla is presumably the North African town mentioned by Pliny, *Nat. Hist.* 5.4.32, and Vergil, *Aen.* 4.483.

were creating schisms in the names of individuals, even though they were included within the Church's unity. He says, among other things, *Natural persons do not perceive the gifts of God's Spirit, for they are foolishness to them, and they are unable to know them since they are spiritually discerned.* He is explaining what he means by *do not perceive*—they do not grasp knowledge.

He calls those within the Church infants, not yet spiritual but still carnal, needing to be nourished with milk, not solid food. He says, *As infants in Christ I gave you milk to drink, not solid food, for you were not able as yet; you are still not able.*† When he says *not yet* **†1 Co 3:1–4**
or *still not* you have no reason to despair if you are tending toward the point where what is *not yet* will someday be. *You are still carnal,* he says, and, showing what makes them carnal, *Since among you are jealousy and quarreling, are you not carnal,* he asks, *and behaving in a purely human way?* And making his point more precisely he asks, *When someone says, 'I am of Paul,' and another, 'I am of Apollos,' are you not merely human?*

They—that is, Paul and Apollos—were united in the unity of 'the Spirit and the bond of peace.'† And yet, because [their partisans] †Eph 4:3
had begun to divide them among themselves, and to be puffed up for one against the other, [Paul] describes them as *merely human, carnal* and *natural,* not strong enough to perceive the gifts of God's Spirit. And yet because they have not been separated from the Church he calls them *infants in Christ.* Of course he wanted those he was reproving for being merely human to be either angels or gods—that is, in these quarrels they were not concerned with the things of God but rather with what was purely human.† †Mt 16:23; Mk 8:33; Rm 8:5

He does not describe those separated from the Church as 'not perceiving the gifts of the Spirit' as though referring to the perception of knowledge. [Jude] describes them as 'not having the Spirit.' It does not follow, however, that those who have [the Spirit] also consciously perceive that they have it. *Infants in Christ* within the Church, still *natural* and *carnal* because not strong enough to perceive that they have him—that is, to understand and recognize him—have the Spirit. How could they be *infants in Christ* unless they had been reborn of the Holy Spirit?† We should not be surprised that †Jn 3:5
people have something and are ignorant of what they have. If I may

pass in silence over the divinity of the almighty and unchangeable Trinity, who easily perceives by knowledge what the soul is? And who does not have a soul?

Finally, that we may be perfectly sure that *infants in Christ* who do not yet perceive *the gifts of God's Spirit* still have the Spirit of God, let us observe, a little farther along, how he rebukes these same people, when he asks, 'Do you not know that you are God's temple, and that God's Spirit dwells in you?'† He would not by any means say this to people separated from the Church—[Jude] describes them as 'not having the Spirit.'

†1 Co 3:16

—from a sermon on blasphemy against the Holy Spirit†*

†Mt 12:31; Mk 3:29; Lk 12:10

146. *Those who are spiritual judge all things, but are themselves judged by no one.*†

†1 Co 2:15

So is humanity 'renewed in knowledge of God according to the image of the one who created it; and having become spiritual they *judge all things* which are there to be judged, *but are themselves judged by no one.* As to their judging all things, this means that they have dominion over the fish of the sea, the birds of heaven, the cattle and wild animals, the whole earth, and every creeping thing that crawls on the earth. This they do through the grasp of their minds, by which they *perceive the gifts of God's Spirit.* On the other hand, 'humans in a position of honor did not understand; they are like foolish beasts, and have become like them.'†

†Col 3:10; Gn 1:26; **1 Co 2:14**; Ps 49:12, 20

And a little further on: *Those who are spiritual* also *judge* by approving what they find right and reproving what they find wrong in the actions and morals of believers—in chastity, in fastings, in holy thoughts about what they perceive by the bodily senses. They are said now to judge in these matters in which they have the authority to correct.

—from *Confessions* 13, speaking of the beginning of Genesis, when humanity received dominion over all living creatures*

---

*145. *Serm.* 71.18.30–31; PL 38: 461–62. For a fuller explanation of Saint Paul's use of *animalis* see Bede's *Commentary on the Seven Catholic Epistles* (CS 82.44 and note [6] 66).

*146. *Confess.* 13.22 (32)-24 (34); CC 27: 260,24–261,7; 262,49/51,52/54

147. *Brothers and sisters, I could not speak to you as to spiritual people, but rather as people of the flesh. As infants in Christ I gave you milk to drink, not solid food.*† †1 Co 3:1–2

The crucified Christ preached by the apostles was both a stumbling block to Jews and foolishness to Gentiles, and 'to those who are called, both Jews and Greeks, the power of God and the wisdom of God.'† Carnal infants held this only by faith, while spiritual people †1 Co 1:23–24 of greater ability perceived it by their understanding as well.

Being aware at the outset that the very things *spiritual people* and *people of the flesh* hear simultaneously each group grasps in its own way—the latter as infants, the former as adults; the latter as the nourishment of milk, the former as the solid substance of food—there appears to be no need to veil any secret teachings in silence, and to conceal them from infant believers as things to be spoken of apart to adults, that is, to those of greater understanding. We may suppose that this is to be done because the Apostle said, *I could not speak to you as to spiritual people, but rather as people of the flesh.* The fact that he decided to know nothing among them 'except Jesus Christ, and him crucified,'† [indicates] that he *could not speak* †1 Co 2:2 to them *as to spiritual people* since they were incapable of grasping it as spiritual people. Those among them who were *spiritual* grasped by their spiritual understanding the same thing that others heard as people *of the flesh.* Thus we shall take his words, *I could not speak to you as to spiritual people, but rather as people of the flesh,* to mean, 'You have not been able to grasp what I was saying as spiritual people, but as people of the flesh.'

—from homily ninety-five on the Gospel of John*

148. *Since among you are jealousy and quarreling, are you not carnal and behaving in a purely human way?*† †1 Co 3:3

What does *behaving in a purely human way* mean? It means to be 'people of the flesh,' because we take 'flesh,' a part of a human being, to mean the whole human being. [Paul] earlier called 'natural' the same people he later describes as 'of the flesh,' saying, 'Natural

*147. *Tract. in Ioh.* 98.2–3; CC 36: 577,8/12; 1–578,17

persons do not perceive the gifts of God's Spirit, for they are foolishness to them.' To such as these—that is, natural persons—he says further on, 'Brothers and sisters, I could not speak to you as to spiritual people, but rather as people of the flesh.'† Both employ the same figure of speech, that is, a part is taken for the whole. Soul† and flesh, which are parts of a human being, can signify a whole, which is a human being. And so the 'natural' person and the person 'of the flesh' are not different, but both are one and the same thing, that is, a human person living *in a human way*.

†1 Co 2:14, 3:1

†*Anima*, from which is derived *animalis*, translated 'natural' in 1 Co 2:14 and elsewhere. See note for section145.

In the same way nothing else than 'human being' is meant, whether we read, 'No flesh will be justified by the works of the law,' or the statement that seventy-five 'souls' went down with Jacob into Egypt.† This is more evident in what [Paul] has added: *When someone says, 'I am of Paul,' and another, 'I am of Apollos,' are you not merely human?* What he expressed by 'you are natural' and 'you are of the flesh' he now says with more precision, 'you are merely human.' This means, 'You are living *in a human way*, not as God lives. If you lived as God lives, you would be gods.'

†Rm 3:20; Gn 46:27 LXX and Ac 7:14

—from *On the City of God* 14*

149. *I planted, Apollos watered, but God gave the growth.*†

†**1 Co 3:6**

What did Simon [Magus] want except to be praised for miracles and to be uplifted by pride? [Pride] impelled him to suppose that the gift of the Holy Spirit could be purchased with money. The Apostle set himself against this sort of pride by remaining humble. Aglow with the Spirit as the midday sun, shining with practical wisdom, he says, *Neither the one who plants nor the one who waters amounts to anything, but God who gives the growth*—since he had just said, *I planted, Apollos watered, but God gave the growth*, and again, 'Was Paul crucified for you? Were you baptized in the name of Paul?'† [Notice] how he refused to be worshipped in place of Christ, and chose not to display himself to an unchaste soul in the bridegroom's place. Do planting and watering not seem important? But *neither*

†Ac 8:18–19; **1 Co 3:7**; 1:13

*148. *De Civ. Dei* 14.4; CC 48: 418,31–419,36, 43/54, 60/65 *the one who plants nor the one who waters amounts to anything.* How anxious he was! He says he amounts to nothing with respect to the salvation of those whom he was yearning to upbuild in Christ.

—from a sermon against the pagans, on January first*

150. *The one who plants and the one who waters are one.*† †1 Co 3:8

I do not know whether we find *they are one* said of things different in nature anywhere in the Scriptures. If more than one should be of the same nature and different convictions, they are not one insofar as their convictions are different. If they were already one in that they were human beings, [Jesus] would not have asked, when committing his disciples to the Father, 'that they may be one even as we are one.'† Because Paul and Apollos were both human †Jn 17:22 beings, and had the same convictions, [Paul] said, *The one who plants and the one who waters are one.* When we say *one* without adding what they are one of, and several things are called *one*, we are indicating that they are of the same nature and essence, without difference or disagreement. When we add the respect in which they are one we can be indicating that one thing has been made out of many, even though they are different in nature. Thus soul and body are certainly not one (what things are as different?) unless we add or understand what they are one of—that is, one person or one living being. Hence the Apostle says that 'anyone who is united to a prostitute is one body [with her].'† †1 Co 6:16

—from *On the Trinity* 6.2*

151. *No one can lay another foundation than the one that has been laid, which is Christ Jesus. If anyone builds on this foundation [with] gold, silver, precious stones, wood, hay, straw, the work of each one will be made visible.*† †1 Co 3:11–13

Nothing in a building is more important than the foundation. All those, then, who have Christ in their hearts, so that nothing

*149. *Serm.* 197.3; PL 38: 1023
*150. *De Trin.* 6.3.4; CC 50: 231,1–232,16

earthly and temporal—not even what is lawful and permitted—is more important, have Christ as a foundation. If they put something else first, even though they may appear to have faith in Christ, in their case Christ is not the foundation since they put such things ahead of him. If in contempt of the salutary commandments they do what is unlawful, much more are they convicted of putting Christ not first but last.

Any Christian who loves a prostitute and, being united to her,
†1 Co 6:16 becomes one body,† does not now have Christ as a foundation. If
anyone loves a spouse, and does this in the way of Christ, who can
doubt that Christ is the foundation? If, however, this is done in the
way of the world, if done carnally, with the disease of lust, 'like the
Gentiles who do not know God,' even this the Apostle—or rather
†1 Th 4:5; Christ, through the Apostle—allows 'by way of concession.'† Even
1 Co 7:6 such persons, therefore, can have Christ as a foundation. If they do
not place any such affection or pleasure ahead of him, even though
they build with wood, hay or straw, Christ is the foundation, and
†1 Co 3:15 for this reason *they will be saved through fire*.† Certainly the fire of
tribulation consumes the delights of this world and earthly love,
which because of the marriage bond are not to be condemned.
This fire includes both bereavements and all the calamities that take
these [delights] from us. On this account will the buildings be a loss
for those who have built them, since they will possess nothing of
what they have built. They will be tormented by the loss of those
things whose enjoyment brought them pleasure. But *they will be
saved through* this *fire* by virtue of the foundation, since even if a
persecutor should put before them the choice of these things or
Christ, they would not put them before Christ.

See in the Apostle's words those *building on the foundation with
gold, silver or precious stones*: 'One who is without a spouse,' he says,
'thinks about the things of God, how to please God.' See others
building with wood, hay or straw: 'One joined in marriage,' he says,
†1 Co 7:32, 33 'thinks about things of this world, how to please a spouse.'† *The
work of each one will be made visible; for the day*—surely 'a day of
†Zp 1:15 tribulation'†—*will disclose it, because it will be revealed with fire*. He
calls tribulation *fire*, as we read elsewhere, 'The kiln tests the potter's
†Si 27:5 vessels, and the trial of tribulation [tests] the righteous.'† *The fire*

will test what kind of work each has done. If the work someone has built survives—for the work of one who 'thinks about the things of God, how to please God' lasts—*[the builder] will receive a reward*—that is, will receive it from the object of the thoughts. *If the work is burned up, [the builder] will suffer loss* since deprived of what was loved; *[the builder] will be saved*, because separated from the firm foundation by no tribulation, *but only as through fire*, for what is possessed with the allurement of love is not lost without burning pain.

—from *On the City of God* 21.27*

152. That something of this sort happens even after this life is not beyond belief. We can ask whether it is so—and either find out, or leave unresolved, that some believers are saved slower or faster by a kind of cleansing fire† in proportion as they loved perishing goods more or less. These are not, however, like those of whom it is said that 'they will not possess the kingdom of God'†—unless after appropriate repentance their faults are pardoned.

†*ignem purgatorium*

†1 Co 6:9, 10

—from *Enchiridion* 69*

153. *No one can lay another foundation than the one that has been laid, which is Christ Jesus. . . .* †

†**1 Co 3:11–15**

Those who live a good life, who honor and praise God, who are patient in tribulations, who long for their homeland—these build *with gold, silver or precious stones*. Those who still love worldly things, who are involved in earthly affairs, and are given over to certain bonds and passions of the flesh, to their homes, to marriages, to possessions—and yet are Christians, so that their hearts do not draw back from Christ and they put nothing before Christ (just as in building they put nothing before the foundation)—these build *with wood, hay or straw*.

---

*151. *De Civ. Dei* 21.21.26; CC 48: 786,5/9; 796,19/27; 797,29/67
*152. *Enchir.* 18.69; CC 46: 87,74/80

But what follows? *The fire will test what kind of work each has done*—the fire of tribulation and temptation. This fire has tested many martyrs here and now; it is going to test the whole human race at the end. Martyrs have been found who possessed those worldly goods. How many wealthy persons and senators have suffered! Some of them were building *with wood, hay, or straw* because of their disposition toward carnal and worldly concerns. Still, because they had a foundation on which they were building, the hay was burned up and they remained upon the foundation. As the Apostle says, *If someone's work survives, [the builder] will receive a reward*; they are going to lose nothing, because they will find what they have loved. What then has the fire done for them? It has tested them. *If someone's work survives, [the builder] will receive a reward. If someone's [work] is burned up, [the builder] will suffer loss*, and so on.

Being unharmed by fire is one thing, being saved by fire is another. Why does this come about? On account of the foundation. Do not let the foundation recede from your heart! Do not lay your foundation on hay—that is, do not lay down hay before [you lay] the foundation, with the result that hay has first place in your heart, and Christ second place. However, if you can have only hay there now, at least let Christ have the first place, and hay the second.

—from the treatise on Psalm 29*

†**1 Co 3:16** 154. *Do you not know that you are God's temple?*†

Scripture cries out in the Apostle's writings that the Holy Spirit is God. [Paul] says, *Do you not know that you are God's temple*, and at once he adds, *and that God's Spirit dwells in you?* God dwells in his
†Ps 11:4; Hab 2:20 temple.† God's Spirit does not dwell in God's temple as an attendant, since in another place [Paul] says more plainly, 'Do you not know that the temple of the Holy Spirit within you is your bodies? You have him from God, and you are not your own, for you were bought
†1 Co 6:19–20 with a great price. Therefore, glorify God in your body.'†

—from *On the Trinity* 7.3*

---

*153. *En. in Ps* 29.2.9; CC 38: 180,7–181,39
*154. *De Trin.* 7.3.6; CC 50: 254,91/99

155. *And again, 'The Lord knows the thoughts of humans, that they are vain.'*† †1 Co 3:20 (Ps 94:11)

The Lord knows the thoughts of humans, that they are vain. You do not know the thoughts of God, that they are righteous; he knows your thoughts, *that they are vain.* Even humans have known the thoughts of God, but he makes his intention known to those whose friend he has already become.† Therefore, brothers and sisters, abandon the thoughts of humans that are vain, that you may take hold of the thoughts of God that are wise. †Ex 33:11; Si 45:1–5; Jn 15:15

—from the treatise on Psalm 93*

156. . . . *until the Lord comes, who will both bring to light what is hidden in darkness, . . .* † †1 Co 4:5

As mortals, we do not know the hearts of mortals. Then will the Lord *bring to light what is hidden in darkness and disclose the thoughts of the heart; and then each one will have praise from God*, because neighbor will praise and love in neighbor what God himself will bring to light, that it may not remain concealed.

—from *Enchiridion* 124*

157. *Who confers distinction upon you? Who makes you different from another?*† †1 Co 4:7

The Apostle lays down a prohibition when he says, 'Let no one glory in a human,' and in another place he says, 'Let the one who glories glory in the Lord.'† Those heretics who suppose that they become righteous on their own—as if God has not granted them this, but they themselves—surely are not glorying in the Lord but in themselves. The Apostle asks such persons, *Who makes you different from another?* He asks this because only God makes people different from the lump of perdition that came into being from Adam, to make of them 'vessels for honor' and not 'for shame.'† †1 Co 3:21, 1:31 †Rm 9:21; 2 Tm 2:20

---

*155. *En. in Ps* 93:14; CC 39: 1314,1/5; 1315,11/13

*156. *Enchir.* 32.121; CC 46: 114,18/23

But because persons carnal and vainly puffed up, on hearing *Who makes you different from another?* may be able to answer in word or thought and say, 'My faith makes me different, my prayer makes me different, my righteousness makes me different,' the Apostle immediately challenges such thoughts and asks, *What do you have that you have not received? And if you received it, why do you glory as if you did not receive it?* Those who suppose they have become righteous on their own glory as if they did not receive it, and as a result they glory in themselves and not in the Lord.

—from a letter to the monk Valentine*

158. *When any of you has a case against another, do you dare to have it*
†**1 Co 6:1** *judged by the unjust and not before the saints?* and so on.†

Here we may suppose that the sin did not consist in having a lawsuit against another but only in wanting it judged outside the Church, had [Paul] not gone on to add, *It is in any case already*
†**1 Co 6:7** *a failure on your part that you have lawsuits with one another.*† To prevent them from excusing themselves by saying that they have a just case, and that they suffer an injustice they want to have taken from them by an opinion of the judges, [Paul] immediately challenges such thoughts and excuses, and asks, *Why not rather suffer the injustice? Why not rather be defrauded?* He wants them to recall the Lord's words, 'If anyone wants to take away your tunic and go to law with you, give up your cloak as well'; and in another place [Jesus] said, 'If anyone takes away your goods, do not ask
†Mt 5:40; Lk 6:30 for them again.'† Thus he forbade his followers to have lawsuits with others over worldly things, and on the basis of this teaching the Apostle calls this a *failure*. Still, although such lawsuits to be decided among the members, with members giving the decisions, exist in the Church, [Paul] forbids this outside the Church in

*157. *Ep.* 214.3; CSEL 57: 382,10–383,8. Valentine was abbot of a monastery at Hadrumetum, today called Sousse, in Tunisia.

terrible words, and clearly some concession is being granted to the weak here.

—from *Enchiridion* 80*

159. *Do you not know that we will judge angels? How much more worldly matters!*† †1 Co 6:3

'You will sit,' [Jesus] said, 'on twelve thrones, judging the twelve tribes of Israel.'† If twelve seats are there, the thirteenth apostle, Paul, †Mt 19:28 will have no place to sit, and no position from which to judge. Yet he himself said that he was going to judge not only humans but even angels. Which angels [did he mean] if not the apostate ones? *Do you not know that we will judge angels?* he asked. Many people may respond, 'Why do you boast that you are going judge? Where will you sit? Our Lord mentioned twelve seats—one of the apostles fell away, Saint Matthias was elected in his place,† and the twelve †Ac 1:25–26 thrones have been filled. First, find [yourself] a place to sit, and then boast that you are going to judge.'

—from the treatise on Psalm 86*

And a little further on:

160. As the five brothers of the man being tormented in hell [signify] thousands of Jews, and the one hundred and fifty-three fish [signify] thousands upon thousands of saints, so the twelve thrones [signify] not twelve individuals but the huge number of the perfect.†* †Lk 16:28; Jn 21:11; Mt 19:28

161. *All things are lawful for me, but not all things are advisable.*† †1 Co 6:12

*158. *Enchir.* 21.78; CC 46: 92,17–93,40 passim
*159. *En. in Ps* 86.4; CC 39: 1201,11/21
*160. *En. in Ps* 49:9; CC 38: 584,85/89

Something can be lawful but inadvisable, but what is unlawful cannot be advisable. Therefore not everything lawful is advisable. Everything unlawful, however, is inadvisable.

—from *To Pollentius* 1*

162. What is lawful is inadvisable in a case when it is, indeed, allowed, but the use of that privilege brings with it a hindrance to the salvation of others.

—again, the same book*

163. Those things appear to me lawful but inadvisable which are allowed by justice before God, but which must be avoided in the sight of human beings if they produce a hindrance to salvation. But things not lawful are so forbidden that they must not be done.

—again, the same book*

164. *Food for the stomach and the stomach for food—and God will do*
†**1 Co 6:13** *away with both one and the other.*†

We repair the daily deterioration of the body by eating and drinking, until you do away with food and the stomach, when you kill this emptiness with a wonderful fullness, and clothe this
†1 Co 15:54 corruptible [body] with incorruption.†

—from *Confessions* 10*

165. *Do you not know that anyone who is united to a prostitute is one*
†**1 Co 6:16** *body [with her]?*†

*161. *De Adulter. Coniug.* 1.15.16; CSEL 41: 365,2/4. Nothing is known about Pollentius to whom this treatise *On Adulterous Marriages* is addressed.
*162. *Ibid.* 1.18.22; CSEL 41: 369,14/16
*163. *Ibid.* 1.17.18; CSEL 41: 366,6/11
*164. *Confess.* 10.31 (43); CC 27: 177,2/5

When we say *one* without adding what they are one of, and several things are called *one*, we are indicating that they are of the same nature and essence, without difference or disagreement. When we add the respect in which they are one we can be indicating that one thing has been made out of many, even though they are different in nature. Thus soul and body are certainly not one (what things are as different?) unless we add or understand what they are one of—that is, one person or one living being.

Hence the Apostle says that *anyone who is united to a prostitute is one body [with her]*. He did not say just 'are one' or 'is one,' but he added *body*—just as *one body* is formed by the joining together of two different elements, masculine and feminine. And he says that *anyone who is united to the Lord is one spirit [with him]*.† He did not say that anyone who is united to the Lord 'is one' or 'are one,' but he added *spirit*. The spirit of a human and the spirit of God differ by nature, but by being united one spirit is made from the two different ones—in this way, that God's spirit is happy and perfect without the human spirit, but the spirit of a human is only happy with God.

†**1 Co 6:17**

—from *On the Trinity* 6.2*

166. For this reason whether we say 'God from God,'† so that this name is appropriated to each [namely, Father and Son]—yet not so that both together are two gods, but one God—the two are united with one another in a way that the Apostle testifies occurs even in separate and different substances. The Lord by himself is spirit, and a human by itself is of course a spirit—yet if *united to the Lord* it *is one spirit [with him]*.† How much more [is this true] where an absolutely inseparable and eternal connection exists!

†Nicaean-Constantinopolitan Creed.

†Jn 4:24; **1 Co 6:16–17**

—again, from [*On the Trinity* 6.] 4*

*165. *De Trin*. 6.3.4; CC 50: 232,8/25. The first paragraph repeats the second half of section 150.
*166. *Ibid*. 6.4.6; CC 50: 234,19/26

167. The [human] mind is so placed in the order of natures, not of places, that only God is superior to it. Moreover, when it is wholly united to him, [the two] will be *one spirit*. The Apostle bears witness to this when he says, *Anyone who is united to the Lord is one spirit [with him]*. [This comes about] by the mind's approaching participation in [the Lord's] nature, truth and happiness, yet not with [the Lord's] increasing in nature, truth and happiness. [The mind] will see as unchangeable everything it sees in that nature to which it has blissfully been united. Then, as divine Scripture promises it, its desire will be satisfied with good things—unchangeable good things—the Trinity itself—its God, whose image it is. And that it may henceforth suffer no harm it will be in the shelter of his presence, and so filled with his abundance† that it will never again take delight in sin.

†**1 Co 6:17**; Ps 103:5, 31:20, 36:8

—from *On the Trinity* 14.14*

168. *Every sin that a person commits is outside the body; those who commit fornication sin against their own bodies.*†

†**1 Co 6:18**

Do you not know, [Paul] writes, *that anyone who is united to a prostitute is one body [with her]? 'They will be,' it says, 'two in one flesh.*† We cannot say this of any other human misdeeds, can we? In other forms of wrongdoing the human spirit is free to commit one of them and be at the same time engaged elsewhere in thought. During the act and moment of fornication the human mind cannot be free to think of something else. The whole person is so engrossed by the body and in the body that the mind cannot be said to be the person's own—even though at the same time we can say of a whole person that it is flesh and a breath that passes and does not return.†

†**1 Co 6:16** (Gn 2:24)

†Ps 78:39

So we can thus understand that *every sin that a person commits is outside the body, but those who commit fornication sin against their own bodies.* The Apostle seems to have wanted to magnify the evil of fornication as much as he could. He says that in comparison with it we should consider other sins of whatever kind as occurring outside

*167. *Ibid.* 14.14.20; CC 50A: 448,84–449,96

the body, and he says that only by this great evil of fornication does one sin against one's own body. By the great fierceness of the passion—none is more intense—the body's own pleasure holds a person enslaved and takes a person captive.

—from a sermon on the same subject*

169. *You are not your own, for you were bought with a great price.*† †**1 Co 6:19–20**

There are two commandments,† and two kinds of sins. A person sins either against God or against another person. You also sin against God by defiling his temple in yourself; God has redeemed you by the blood of his Son. Although whose were you even before you were redeemed, if not his who made all things? He wished to possess you in a particular way as redeemed by the blood of his Son. *You are not your own*, [Paul] says, *for you were bought with a great price; glorify and bear God in your body*. And so the one by whom you were redeemed made you his home. Do you want your home overthrown? Neither does God [want this of] his—this is you yourself! If you do not spare yourself for your own sake, then spare yourself for the sake of God, who has made you his temple. 'God's temple is holy, which you are'; and, 'God will destroy anyone who profanes God's temple.'† †1 Co 3:17

†Mt 22:37–39; Mk 12:29–31; Lk 10:27

—from a sermon on the two kinds of sin*

170. Which sins are trivial and which sins are serious is for divine, not human, judgment to decide. We see that clemency has been granted in certain matters even by the apostles themselves—for example, what the venerable Paul says to married persons: *Do not deprive one another [of your conjugal right] except by agreement for a set time, to be free for prayer; and return to it again, so that Satan may not tempt you because of your lack of self-control.*† We may suppose that being united †**1 Co 7:5** in the marriage act not for the sake of begetting children—which is the blessing of marriage—but for the sake of carnal pleasure, so

*168. *Serm.* 162.2; PL 38: 887
*169. *Serm.* 278.7.7; PL 38: 1271

that the incontinent in their weakness may escape the deadly evil of unchastity—whether adultery, or some other impurity which it is unseemly even to mention, into which lust can draw them when Satan tempts them—is not a sin. We may, as I said, suppose that this is not a sin if [Paul] had not added, *I say this by way of concession, not of*
†1 Co 7:6 *command.*† Who can deny that this is a sin when apostolic authority grants it as a concession to those who do it?

—from *Enchiridion* 80*

171. *If they are not practicing self-control, let them marry; it is better to*
†1 Co 7:9 *marry than to be consumed with passion.*†
†Mt 19:12 'Let anyone accept this who can.'† 'But I cannot,' someone says. 'You cannot?' 'I cannot.' An instructive statement from the Apostle supports you: *If they are not practicing self-control, let them marry.* Something granted as a concession can be done. It belongs to a concession not to rush headlong to eternal punishment. What is licit can be done where what is not licit can be forgiven.

What follows shows this: *I would prefer them to marry than to be consumed with passion.* [Paul] said that he yielded something to incontinence because he feared something greater. He feared eternal punishment and he feared what awaits and befalls adulterers, even what [awaits] married persons who are overcome by their desires and use each other beyond what is necessary for producing children—which is the punishment of those things for which we say daily,
†Mt 6:12 'Forgive us our debts, as we also forgive our debtors.'†

—from a sermon on the benefit of marriage*

172. *To married women I give this command—not I but the Lord—that a*
†1 Co 7:10 *woman should not leave her husband.*†
The Lord accepts only unchastity as a reason [for divorce] in
†Mt 5:32, 19:9 order to confirm that a wife should not be divorced easily.† He

---

*170. *Enchir.* 21.78; CC 46: 92,1/16
*171. *Serm.* See PL 39: 1732

orders that every other difficulty, if any should be present, must be borne steadfastly for the sake of married fidelity and chastity. He also calls the man who marries a woman separated from her husband an adulterer. The Apostle reveals the limit of this situation when he says that it is to be observed as long as her husband is alive; when he has died, [Paul] allows her to marry.† †Rm 7:2–3

He himself held to this rule, and in this matter he is not revealing his own advice, as he did in some cases, but a commandment of the Lord who enjoined it. *To married women I give this command—not I but the Lord—that a woman should not leave her husband; if she does leave him, [she must] remain unmarried or be reconciled to her husband; and a husband should not divorce his wife.*† I believe that in a similar manner if he divorces [her] he should not marry another woman but be reconciled to his wife. It can happen that he may divorce his wife on account of unchastity, which the Lord intended to be an exception. Of course, if she is not allowed to marry while the husband she has left is alive, and he is not allowed to marry another while the wife he has divorced is alive, much less is it right [for either of them] to commit illicit acts of passion with any other person. †1 Co 7:10–11

To the rest I say—not the Lord.† First we must see to what *rest* [he is speaking]. Earlier he was speaking on behalf of the Lord to those who are married. Now he is speaking on his own behalf *to the rest.* Perhaps, then, [he is speaking] to those who are not married. But this does not follow, for he adds, *If any brother has an unbelieving wife, and she consents to live with him, he should not divorce her.* So even now he is speaking to those who are married. What then does he mean when he says *to the rest* if not that earlier he was talking to those who were so united in marriage as to be equally in the Christian faith, whereas now he is speaking *to the rest*, that is, to those so united in marriage that one is an unbeliever? †1 Co 7:12

What is he saying to them? *If any brother has an unbelieving wife, and she consents to live with him, he should not divorce her. And if any woman has an unbelieving husband, and he consents to live with her, she should not divorce her husband.*† †1 Co 7:12–13

A commandment is one thing, advice another, indulgence still another. A wife is commanded not to leave her husband; *if she does*

leave him, [she must] remain unmarried or be reconciled to her husband. She is not allowed to do otherwise. A man who is a believer is advised that if he has an unbelieving wife who consents to live with him, he is not to divorce her. He is, then, allowed to divorce her, because not to divorce her is not the Lord's commandment but the Apostle's advice. So too, a virgin is advised not to marry. If she marries, she will not be following his advice, but she will not be acting
†1 Co 7:25–28 contrary to a commandment.† He grants indulgence when he says,
†1 Co 7:6 'I say this by way of concession, not of command.'† Therefore if an unbelieving spouse can be divorced—although not to divorce is better—and yet according to the Lord's commandment a spouse is not to be divorced except for unchastity, then even unbelief itself is unchastity.

Apostle, what are you saying? Surely that a man who is a believer should not divorce an unbelieving wife who consents to live with him. 'So I do,' he answers. Since, then, the Lord too commands that a man is not to divorce his wife except for unchastity, why do you say here, *I say—not the Lord*? Undoubtedly because the idolatry that unbelievers follow, and harmful superstition of any kind, is unchastity. The Lord permitted a wife to be divorced because of unchastity, and because he permitted it without commanding it he provided an opportunity for the Apostle to advise that one who chose should not divorce an unbelieving wife, since in this way she could perhaps become a believer.

[Paul] says, *An unbelieving man is made holy in his wife, and an*
†1 Co 7:14 *unbelieving wife is made holy in her brother.*† I imagine that it had already happened that some women came to faith through husbands who were believers, and men through wives who were believers. Although he did not give names, yet he encouraged them, using examples to support his advice.

Then he continues, *Otherwise your children would be unclean, but as it is, they are holy.* Already there were Christian children who had become holy, influenced by one of their parents, or by the agreement of both. This would not have happened if the marriage had been dissolved when one came to believe, and a spouse's unbelief was not borne with until an occasion came for believing.

—from *On the Lord's Sermon on the Mount* 1*

173. *From now on, let those who have wives be as though they had none.*† †1 Co 7:29

We should judge those marriages happier in which [the partners] have been able by mutual consent to observe continence, whether after begetting children, or even because they choose not to have earthly offspring. This is not contrary to that commandment by which the Lord forbids a spouse's being divorced. [A husband] who does not live with [his wife] carnally but spiritually is not divorcing her, but is observing the Apostle's words, *From now on, let those who have wives be as though they had none.*

—from *On the Lord's Sermon on the Mount* 1*

174. *For the form of this world is passing away.*† †1 Co 7:31–32

With the judgment over, this heaven and this earth will cease to exist when a new heaven and a new earth begin to exist.† This †Rv 21:1
world will pass away through a change in things, not through a wholesale destruction. Hence the Apostle says, *For the form of this world is passing away. I want you to be without anxiety.* The *form*, not the nature, is passing away.

And a little farther on: When those who have not been written in 'the book of life' have been judged and thrown into eternal fire, then will *the form of this world* pass away by a conflagration of terrestrial fires, just as the flood was brought about by an inundation of terrestrial waters.† Accordingly, the properties of the corruptible †Rv 20:15; Gn 7:17–18
elements appropriate to our corruptible bodies will utterly perish by being burned by the terrestrial conflagration, as I have said, and

*172. *De Serm. Dom. in Monte* 1.14.39, 16.44–45; CC 35: 42,908–43,927; 49,1051–50,1064; 1071–52,1104

*173. *Ibid.* 1.14.39; CC 35: 43,927/34

our substance itself will have those properties which by a wonderful change are appropriate to immortal bodies. As a result, a world renewed for the better will be suitably adapted to human beings renewed for the better, even in the flesh.

—from *On the City of God* 20.14*

†1 Co 8:1

175. *Knowledge puffs up, but love builds up.*†

We misunderstand this unless knowledge only does us good if it includes love. Without love [knowledge] puffs up—that is, it expands into a pride empty as wind.

—from *On the City of God* 9.20*

†1 Co 9:13–17

176. *Do you not know that those who are employed in the temple get their food from the temple? . . .* †

[Paul] says that it is lawful for him, and has been granted by the Lord, that *those who proclaim the gospel should get their living by the gospel*—that is, they should get what they need for this life *by the gospel*—and that he has not taken advantage of this privilege. Many people were longing to have an opportunity for acquiring and selling the gospel. The Apostle, wanting to cut off the opportunity, supported himself with his own hands. He says of these people in another place, 'That I may cut off the opportunity for those who seek an opportunity.'†

†Ac 20:34; 2 Co 11:12

†Mt 10:10; Lk 10:7

Even though he, like the rest of the good apostles, may with the Lord's permission† have lived *by the gospel*, he would not have been making his own support his reason for preaching the gospel; instead he would have been making the gospel the reason for his support. In other words, he would not be preaching the gospel in order to get food and whatever else he needed, but would be accepting these things in order to fulfill his purpose. Otherwise he would have been preaching the gospel from necessity, not willingly.

---

*174. *De Civ. Dei* 20.14 &16; CC 48: 724,19/24; 726,9/21 passim
*175. *Ibid.* 9.20; CC 47: 267,5/8

This [Paul] rejects when he says, *Do you not know that those who are employed in the temple get their food from the temple, and those who serve at the altar partake with the altar? In the same way the Lord ordained that those who preach the gospel should get their living by the gospel. But I have used none of these things.* He is showing that this was permitted, not commanded; otherwise we will hold that he acted against the Lord's commandment.

Then he goes on and says, *I have not written these things so that they may be applied to me. It is good for me to die rather than that anyone should make my glory of no account.* He said this because he had already decided to make his living with his own hands on account of certain persons who were seeking an opportunity. *If I preach the gospel,* he says, *this brings me no glory*—that is, if I preach the gospel in order *that they may be applied to me*—that is, if I preach the gospel for the purpose of obtaining these things, and make my reason for proclaiming the gospel food and drink and clothing. Why does this bring him no glory? *An obligation is laid on me,* he says—that is, I do not preach the gospel because I have no other way of making my living, nor do I do it to get a temporal return from preaching what is eternal. So will there then be obligation in the gospel, not volition.

Woe to me, he says, *if I do not preach the gospel!* But how ought he to preach it? He should place his reward in the gospel itself, and in the kingdom of God. In this way he can preach the gospel not from compulsion but willingly.

If I do this willingly, he says, *I have a reward; but if not of my own will, I am entrusted with a stewardship*—in other words, if I preach the gospel compelled by a lack of what is necessary for temporal existence, others, who love the gospel I preach, will have the reward of the gospel on my account, while I will have nothing, because I do not love the gospel itself but its price as set in those temporal things. What a monstrous thing comes about, that any should serve the gospel, not as children, but as servants to whom a stewardship has been entrusted! In that case they would be handing out what belongs to someone else, and themselves getting nothing from it beyond their allowance of food, which is outwardly given them not by way of sharing in the kingdom, but only as a support for their wretched condition of servitude.

†1 Co 4:1 In another place, however, [Paul] does call himself a steward.† Even a servant who has been adopted into the status of children can act faithfully as steward for those with whom he shares that in which, as a joint heir, he has deserved a portion. But when he now says, *if not of my own will, I am entrusted with a stewardship*, he means the kind of steward who is steward of what belongs to someone else, from which the steward himself receives nothing.

—from *On the Lord's Sermon on the Mount* 2*

†1 Co 9:20–22 177. *To the Jews I became like a Jew, in order to win Jews, . . .* †

As to my saying that [Paul] became like a Jew to the Jews, and like a Gentile to the nations, not with a liar's cunning but with the sensitivity of a fellow-sufferer, you seemed to me to have paid too little attention to how I meant this—or perhaps I was not able to explain it satisfactorily. I did not say this because he was feigning these things out of pity, but [I meant] that he was not feigning when he acted like the Jews, just as he was not feigning when he acted like the nations. You also reminded me of this, and in doing so helped me, for which I admit that I am not ungrateful. When I sought from you in my letter† how you supposed that he became like a Jew to the Jews, since [you said that] he accepted the religious rites of the Jews deceitfully, while he became like a Gentile to the nations without accepting their religious rites, [you said that] he became like a Gentile to the nations by receiving the circumcised and allowing indiscriminate eating of foods the Jews condemned. And a little farther on:

†Letter 40.4.4

He owed to both [Jews and Gentiles] 'love from a pure heart, a good conscience, and sincere faith,'† and in this way he *became all things to all people* that he *may gain all*, not with a liar's cunning but with the sensitivity of a fellow-sufferer—that is, not by deceitfully committing all the evil things that people were doing, but by carefully administering the medicine of mercy to everyone else for all their evils just as though they were his own.

†1 Tm 1:5

*176. *De Serm. Dom. in Monte* 2.16.54; CC 35: 144,1154–147,1207

Accordingly, when he did not refuse even to carry out for himself the religious rites of the old covenant he was not being deceitful out of pity, but he was acting altogether without deceit. In this way he was showing his respect for things enjoined by the Lord God as the procedure for a certain period of time, and distinguishing them from the sacrilegious religious rites of the nations. He became like a Jew to the Jews, not with a liar's cunning but with the sensitivity of a fellow-sufferer, when he yearned to set them free from the error of being unwilling to believe in Christ, and imagining that they could be cleansed of their sins and saved by their own ancient sacrifices and ceremonial observances, as if he himself was being gripped by the error. Surely he was loving his neighbor as himself, and doing to others what he wanted them to do to him if he had need of it. When our Lord gave this counsel he went on to say, 'For this is the law and the prophets.'†

†Mt 22:39, 7:12; Lk 10:27, 6:31; Mk 12:31

[Paul] enjoined this sensitivity of a fellow-sufferer in the same letter to the Galatians when he wrote, 'If anyone is detected in some transgression, you who are spiritual, instruct such a one in a spirit of gentleness, taking note of yourself lest you too be tempted.'† See if he did not tell them to become like such persons in order to gain them—they were certainly not meant to commit the same transgression deceitfully, or to feign that they had it, but they were to consider in the case of someone else's trespass what may also happen to themselves, and so mercifully come to another's assistance in the way that they would want to be helped by another. This is 'not with a liar's cunning but with the sensitivity of a fellow-sufferer.' In this way Paul *became all things to all people in order to gain them all*—not by feigning what he was not, but by having compassion because, on the grounds that he thought of himself as a human being, he could be [compassionate] toward the Jew, toward the Gentile, toward every person enmeshed in error or in some sin.

†Ga 6:1. On 'the same letter' see note below.

—from a letter to Saint Jerome on the same question*

*177. *Ep*. 82.3.26–29; CC 34: 378,1/16; 379,14–381,2 (*Ep*. 40.4.4; CC 34: 73,7–74,9). Augustine and Jerome were engaged in a celebrated dispute over Jerome's interpretation of Galatians 2:11–14.

178. Therefore let us display toward those whose weakness we wish to bear what we would want them to display toward ourselves, if perhaps we were subject to weakness and the others not. The Apostle's words, *I became all things to all people in order to gain them all*,† are related to this. Of course he was reflecting that he may also be subject to the very vice from which he desired to free someone else. He was bringing about what he said by having compassion, not by lying, as some persons surmise—especially those who seek the cover of some notable example for defending their own lies, which they cannot deny.

†**1 Co 9:22**

—from *On Eighty-Four Questions**

179. To let you know that the faith is one, listen to [Paul] saying, 'Having the same spirit of faith, we also believe,' and likewise in another place, *I do not want you to be unaware, brothers and sisters, that our ancestors were all under the cloud, and all passed through the sea, and all were baptized into Moses in the cloud and in the sea, and all ate the same spiritual food, and all drank the same spiritual drink.*† The Red Sea signifies baptism; Moses, their leader through the Red Sea, signifies Christ; the people who passed through signify the faithful; and the death of the Egyptians signifies the obliteration of sins.

†2 Co 4:13; **1 Co 10:1–4**

Did not those through whom these signs were shown, through whom these events that we believe were foretold in prophesy, believe the same things? Of course they believed—but they believed what was to come, while we believe that they have already come. That is why [Paul] said, *They drank the same spiritual drink*—the same spiritually, not the same materially. What did they drink? *For they drank from the spiritual rock that followed them, and the rock was Christ.* See how the signs were different, while the faith remained [the same]. There *the rock was Christ.* For us what is placed on God's altar is Christ. They drank water flowing out of the rock as a great sacramental sign of the same Christ. We, the faithful,

*178. *De Div. Quaest. LXXXIII* 71.4; CC 44A: 203,79–204,87

know what we drink. If you regard the visible form, it is different; if [you regard] the intelligible meaning, *they drank the same spiritual drink.*

—from homily forty-two on the Gospel of John*

180. But what will [Manichaeans] say in opposition to the Apostle who writes, *All these things happened to them as a figure, and they were written down for our sake?*† See how [Paul] himself revealed †**1 Co 10:11**
why we should accept these writings, and why we no longer have to observe these signs of the realities. When he says, *they were written down for our sake,* he is surely indicating the great care with which we should read and understand them, and the great authority we should accord them, because *they were written down for our sake.* When, however, he calls them figures for us, and says they *happened to them as a figure,* he is showing that since we are carrying out the very realities that have been revealed we no longer need to keep the remembrance of figures that were merely foreshadowings.

—from *Against Faustus* 6*

181. *We must not put Christ to the test, as some of them did, and were destroyed by serpents.*† †**1 Co 10:9** (Nb 21:6)

The one who commanded us to tread spiritually on every kind of serpent† is also the God of the prophets who sent visible serpents †Lk 10:19
to an unfaithful people to admonish them. [These visible serpents] were to represent their sins, from whose poison they were invisibly dying. This corrective affliction symbolized by the death of bodies the death of souls.

—from *Against the Opponent of the Law and the Prophets* 2*

*179. *Tract. in Ioh.* 45.9; CC 36: 392,22/31; 36–393,48
*180. *Contra Faust. Manich.* 6.2; CSEL 25: 285,23–286,6
*181. *Contra Adv. Leg. et Prophet.* 2.11.37; CC 49: 125,1147/52

†1 Co 10:13 182. *Let no temptation take hold of you but what is human.*†

Human temptations also exist, I believe, when someone with a good intention, yet in accord with human frailty, fails in some resolve, or is irritated against another person out of eagerness for setting things right, but with a trifle more zeal than Christian composure calls for. Of these the Apostle says, *Let no temptation take hold of you but what is human.*

—from *On the Lord's Sermon on the Mount* 2*

183. *Therefore, my beloved, flee from the worship of idols . . . I do not*
†1 Co 10:14–20 *want you to become partners with demons.*†

He brings out the Apostle as a witness to what he says: 'Look at Israel carnally. Are not those who eat the victims participants in the altar? What then am I saying? That an idol is anything? But those who sacrifice sacrifice to demons.' This [passage] is not written that way, but like this: *Look at Israel according to the flesh. Are not those who partake of the sacrifices partners in the altar? What then am I saying? That what is immolated to idols is anything, or that the idol is anything? But what they immolate they immolate to demons and not to God. I do not want you to become partners with demons.*

It could happen that in accord with differences of interpretation, not in the realities but in the words, where I said *according to the flesh* other manuscripts have 'carnally'; where I said *those who partake of the sacrifices* some have 'eat the victims'; where he and I have both set down *are partners in the altar* some may have 'are participants in the altar'; and where I put down *What then am I saying? That what is offered in sacrifice to idols is anything?* he may have put down less—or his manuscript may have less—and therefore he only put down 'That an idol is anything?'

What follows is more to the point, because he has put it down differently. The Apostle says, *But what they immolate they immolate to demons and not to God, whereas* he said, 'But those who sacrifice sacrifice to demons'—as if all those who offer sacrifice sacrifice only

*182. *De Serm. Dom. in Monte* 2.9.34; CC 35: 124,746/51

to demons. The Apostle does not say 'those who sacrifice' but *what they sacrifice,* or, as I put it down, *what they immolate*—that is, what those who worship idols sacrifice *they* sacrifice or *immolate to demons and not to God.*

This is the reason [Paul] added *I do not want you to become partners with demons*—he was of course keeping them from idolatry. Therefore he wanted to show them that they *become partners with demons* if they partake of the sacrifices offered to an idol, in the same way that Israel after the flesh, which partook of the sacrifices, was a partner of the altar in the temple. He says, then, 'carnally,' or *according to the flesh,* because it is Israel spiritually, or according to the spirit, which no longer follows the ancient adumbrations, but the truth coming after that was signified by those preceding adumbrations.

This is why [Paul] begins by saying, *Therefore, my beloved, flee from the worship of idols.* Then as he continues he shows with what sacrifice they ought now to be associated, saying, *I speak as to sensible people—you judge what I say. The cup of blessing that we bless, is it not a sharing of the blood of Christ? The bread that we break, is it not a sharing of the body of the Lord? Because there is one bread, we who are many are one body, for we all partake of the one bread.* And this is why he added, *Look at Israel according to the flesh. Are not those who partake of the sacrifices partners in the altar?*—that they may understand that they are now partners in the body of Christ, just as [the Jews] were partners in the altar. As he said this he was keeping them from idolatry.

Hence, this section of his discourse takes its inception, as I have recalled, to keep them from supposing that because 'an idol is nothing'† their eating from the sacrifices belonging to idols makes †1 Co 8:4
no difference, on the supposition that these things, as being superfluous, do them no harm. [Paul] too confirms that an idol is nothing. He does not prohibit these things because they were immolated to senseless idols, but because *what they*— that is, worshippers of idols—*immolate they immolate to demons and not to God. I do not want you to become partners with demons.*

—from *Against the Opponent of the Law and the Prophets* 1*

*183. *Contra Adv. Leg. et Prophet.* 1.19.38; CC 49: 68,986–69,1037

†1 Co 10:17 184. *Because there is one bread, we who are many are one body, and we all partake of the one bread and the one cup.*†

Because he suffered for us, [Jesus] commended his body and blood to us in this sacrament—which he even made us into as well! We too have become his body, and through his mercy we are what we have received. Recall both that you did not exist, and that you were created. You were brought to the Lord's threshing floor. You were treaded out by the labor of oxen—that is, by those who proclaim the gospel. When you were held back as catechumens you were being stored up in the barn. You handed in your names; you began to be ground into flour by fasts and exorcisms. Afterwards you came to the water, you were sprinkled and became one. When the heat of the Holy Spirit came upon you, you were baked, and became the Lord's bread. Look what you receive! As you see that what has been made is one, so become one by loving one another, by holding to one faith, one hope and indivisible love. When heretics receive this [sacrament] they receive a testimony against themselves, because they seek division while it is a sign of unity.

So too the wine existed in many clusters of grapes and is now in one—one in the sweetness of the cup after the pressure of the wine press. You too, after the fasts, after the labors, after being brought low and crushed, have now come in Christ's name into the Lord's cup, so to speak. You are there on the table, and you are there in the cup—you are with me. We take it together, we drink together, because we live together.

—from a sermon on the sacraments of the faithful, Easter Monday*

†1 Co 10:32–33 185. *Give no offense to Jews and Greeks and the Church of God, as I too please everyone in everything.*†

†Ga 1:10 The Apostle says, 'If I were still pleasing people, I would not be a servant of Christ,'† while in another place he says, *as I too please everyone in everything*. Those who do not understand it reckon

*184. *Serm.* 229 (Fragm.); PL 38: 1103

this a contradiction. He said he did not please people because he was not doing good in order to please people, but to please God, toward whose love he wanted to turn people's hearts by pleasing them. Accordingly, he rightly said that he was not pleasing people because in this very thing he was looking to please God, and he rightly commanded us to please people—not that we were to seek this as a reward for doing right, but because those who do not offer themselves for imitation by the ones whom they want saved cannot please God.

People can by no means imitate a person who is not pleasing to them. Therefore just as a person who says, 'By my efforts to find a ship, I am not seeking a ship but my native land,' would not be speaking foolishly, so the Apostle may say consistently, 'By my efforts to please people, I am not pleasing people but God. That is not what I want—I attend to it so that those whom I want saved may imitate me.'

—from *On the Lord's Sermon on the Mount* 2*

186. *The head of Christ is God.*† **†1 Co 11:3**

If God exists only as all three [persons] together, how is God the head of Christ—that is, [how is] the Trinity the head of Christ, since Christ is in the Trinity in order that it may be a trinity? Or is what the Father and the Son are together the head of what the Son is alone? The Father and the Son together are God, but the Son alone is Christ—especially since the Word already [made] flesh is speaking in accord with his lowliness. The Father is greater than this—as he says, 'The Father is greater than I.' Thus this very God that consists of himself as one with his Father may be the head of the human mediator,† which he alone is. †Jn 1:14; 14:28; 1 Tm 2:5

If we rightly call the mind the principal part of a human being—that is, the head of the human substance, so to speak, since the mind makes a human human—why is it not more appropriate and more truly the case that the Word, which is God together with the Father,

*185. *De Serm. Dom. in Monte* 2.1.3; CC 35: 93,58–94,75

is the head of Christ—although we cannot understand the human Christ except together with the Word which became flesh?

—from *On the Trinity* 6.9*

187. *A man ought not to cover his head, since he is the image and glory of*
†**1 Co 11:7** *God; woman, however, is the glory of man.*†

'As many of you as were baptized into Christ have put on Christ, there is neither Jew nor Greek, slave nor free, male nor female; for
†Ga 3:27–28 you are all one in Christ Jesus.'† Have female believers, then, lost their bodily sex? But as they are being renewed in the image of God there where there is no sex—'human beings were made in the image of God' there where there is no sex, that is, in the spirit of their
†Col 3:10; Gn 9:6; Eph 4:23 minds†—what is the reason *a man ought not to cover his head, since he is the image and glory of God*, whereas a woman ought to, because she is *the glory of man*—as though the woman is not being renewed in the spirit of her mind, 'which is being renewed in knowledge of
†Eph 4:23; Col 3:10 God according to the image of the one who created it'?†

Because a woman differs from a man by her sex, her bodily cover can well represent that part of [human] reason directed to the management of temporal matters. The image of God remains, then, only in that part of the human mind that holds fast to eternal reason, contemplating and reflecting upon it. This, it is evident, females as well as males possess. Therefore, we recognize their common nature in their minds; the division in the one mind is represented in their bodies.

—from *On the Trinity* 12.7*

188. *For just as woman came from man, so also man comes through woman;*
†**1 Co 11:12** (Gn 2:21–22) *but all things come from God.*†

For just as woman came from man, so also man comes through woman. Woman was made *from man* so that *man* may also afterward be born

*186. *De Trin.* 6.9.10; CC 50: 240,32/46
*187. *De Trin.* 12.7.12–13; CC 50: 367,91/109. Paul appears to deny that woman is made in the image of God. Augustine will not allow this, and in *De Trinitate* 12 he proposes an allegorical treatment of 1 Corinthians 11:7.

through woman. If Victor makes a division, so as to say that *woman comes from man* as far as her body is concerned, while her soul and spirit come from God, how can the Apostle's words, *but all things come from God,* be true, if a woman's body *came from man* in such a way as not to be from God? Therefore, allowing that the Apostle is more likely to be speaking the truth than that we ought to prefer [Victor] to the Apostle, *woman came from man,* whether we think of her body, or of the whole of which human nature consists—I am claiming neither of these views as certain, but am still asking which of them is true—and *man comes through woman,* whether his whole human nature, which is born through a woman, is derived from his father, or only his flesh—which is still in question. Yet *all things come from God*—concerning this there is no question—that is, body, soul and spirit,† of both man and woman. Even if these were not born †1 Th 5:23
or derived from God, or did not emanate from him so as to be of his nature, yet they are *from God.* What was created, formed, and made by [God] has from [God] its existence.

—from *To Renatus on the Origin of the Soul,* for Victor, who denied that souls have their origin in procreation*

189. *For there must also be heresies, so that those who have been approved may become evident among you.*† **†1 Co 11:19**

Those touched with ill will through sin are compelled to misunderstand, so that this itself may be a punishment for sin. Yet by their [spiritual] death the children of the Catholic church are aroused from slumber as by a kind of thorn, and they make progress toward an understanding of the divine Scriptures. *For there must also be heresies,* [Paul] says, *so that those who have been approved may become evident among you*—that is, among human beings, since they are [already] evident to God.

—from the explanation of Psalm 7*

*188. *De Nat. et Orig. Animae* 1.17.27; CSEL 60: 327,3/5; 27–328,11. Renatus was a monk in North Africa; Augustine addressed the first book of this work to him. Victor, also called Vincent Victor, had written against Augustine's explanation of the origin of the human soul. See Augustine's *Letter* 93, and *Retractations* 2.82 (CSEL: 36,2.56; PL 32).

*189. *En. in Ps* 7.15; CC 38: 46,8/14

†1 Co 11:27 190. *Whoever, therefore, eats the bread,* and so on.†

Why are you surprised if Christ's bread, by which Judas was to be made over to the devil, was given to him, when you see that conversely an angel of the devil, by which Paul was to be made perfect in Christ, was given to him?† Thus good was prejudicial to an evil man, and evil beneficial to a good one. Recall why *Whoever eats the bread and drinks the Lord's cup unworthily will be answerable for the Lord's body and blood* was written. When the Apostle said this, he was speaking of people who were taking the Lord's body in an indifferent and careless manner, as they would any other food. Therefore, if a person is being rebuked for not discerning—that is, for not distinguishing the Lord's body from other foods—how is an enemy who approaches his table pretending to be a friend condemned!

†Jn 13:26–27; 2 Co 12:7

—from homily fifty-nine on the Gospel of John*

191. *Therefore I make known to you that no one speaking in the Spirit of God says 'Jesus be accursed.'*†

†1 Co 12:3

'Not everyone who says to me, "Lord, Lord," will enter into the kingdom of heaven, but the one who does the will of my Father who is in heaven, that one will enter into the kingdom of heaven.'† We can ask with good reason how the Apostle's statement, *No one speaking in the Spirit of God says 'Jesus be cursed,' and no one can say 'Jesus is Lord' except in the Holy Spirit,* agrees with this. We cannot say that those who possess the Holy Spirit will fail to enter the kingdom of heaven if they persevere to the end,† nor can we say that those who say, 'Lord, Lord,' and yet fail to enter the kingdom of heaven possess the Holy Spirit.

†Mt 7:21

†Mt 10:22

How, then, does *no one say, 'Jesus is Lord,' except in the Holy Spirit* unless the Apostle used the word *say* to signify precisely the intention and understanding of the one speaking. On the other hand, the Lord used the word in a general sense when he said, 'Not everyone who says to me, "Lord, Lord," will enter into the kingdom

*190. *Tract in Ioh.* 62.1; CC 36: 483,21/32

of heaven.' Even those who neither intend nor understand what they are saying appear to be saying it; strictly speaking, however, only those who use vocal sounds to express their intention and mind actually *say* it.

—from *On the Lord's Sermon on the Mount* 2*

192. Finally we have the apostolic phrase, *No one says 'Jesus is Lord' except in the Holy Spirit.*† And who says *Jesus is Lord* except those who love him, if they say it in the way the Apostle intended this to be understood? Many say it with their lips but deny it in their hearts and deeds—as [Paul] says of such people, 'They profess to know God, but they deny him by their deeds.'† If he is denied by deeds, beyond any doubt he is also spoken by deeds. Accordingly, *no one says 'Jesus is Lord'* with mind, word, deed, heart or work—*no one says 'Jesus is Lord' except in the Holy Spirit.* And no one speaks thus except one who loves.

†**1 Co 12:3**

†Tt 1:16

—from homily seventy-one on the Gospel of John*

193. *One and the same Spirit accomplishes all these things.*† **†1 Co 12:11**

What the Apostle says of the Holy Spirit, *One and the same Spirit accomplishes all these things*, does not mean that the Father and the Son do not work with him, but that one Spirit and not many are present in what he accomplishes, and also that in his various operations [the Spirit] is not at variance with himself. But when [Paul] goes on and says, *allotting to each one individually just as he chooses*, is he not also pointing to the Spirit's authority, [authority] completely inseparable from the Father and the Son?

—from a sermon on blasphemy against the Holy Spirit*

*191. *De Serm. Dom. in Monte* 2.25.82–83; CC 35: 182,1897/1900; 1905–183,1920

*192. *Tract. in Ioh.* 74.1; CC 36: 513,37/45

*193. *Serm.* 71.16.26; PL 38: 459–60 passim

194. *For just as the body is one and has many members, and all the members of the body, although they are many, are one body, so also is*
†1 Co 12:12 *Christ.*† Speaking of the members of Christ—that is, of the faithful—[Paul] does not say, 'So also are the members of Christ,' but he calls the whole of which he is speaking *Christ. For just as the body is one and has many members, and all the members of the body, although they are many, are one body, so also is Christ.* Many members, one body: Christ.

Therefore all of us together with our head are Christ; apart from our head we are good for nothing. Why? Because with our head we are a vine; apart from our head—do not even think of it!—we are branches that have been cut off, intended not for any work of the vinegrowers but only for the fire. This is why [Christ] himself [said] in the gospel, 'I am the vine, you are the branches. My Father is the vinegrower. Apart from me you can
†Jn 15:1–6 do nothing.'†

—from the treatise on Psalm 30*

†1 Co 12:31 195. *And I show you a still more excellent way.*†

'Those who say they abide in Christ ought themselves to walk
†1 Jn 2:6 just as he walked.'† What is the way Christ walked? What other way is there but love, concerning which the Apostle says, *I show you a*
†*adhuc superemi-nentiorem*, where the Vulgate has *adhuc excellentiorem*. *still more supereminent*† *way.* If then we want to imitate Christ we ought to run in the way which Christ deigned to walk even while he was hanging on the cross. He had been nailed to the cross, and as he ran in the way of love he prayed for his persecutors. [Jesus] said, 'Father, forgive them, for they do not know what they are
†Lk 23:34 doing.'† Let us also, then, pray this continually for all our enemies, that the Lord may grant them amendment of life and forgiveness of sins.

—from a sermon on the text, 'Our struggle is not
†Eph 6:12 against flesh and blood'†*

---

*194. *En. in Ps* 30.2.4; CC 38: 193,24–194,37
*195. *Serm.* See PL 39: 1734

196. *Love is great-souled, it is generous, it is not arrogant, it is not envious, it does not act perversely.*† What is as *great-souled* as to die for the ungodly? What is as *generous* as to love even one's enemies? Love alone is not oppressed by the good fortune of others because *it is not envious*. Love alone is not conceited over its own good fortune because *it is not arrogant*. Love alone does not feel remorse because *it does not act perversely*. †1 Co 13:4

[Love] bears all things, believes all things, hopes all things, endures all things.† It *bears all things* in this present life because it *believes all things* concerning the future life, and it *endures all things* inflicted on it here because it *hopes all things* that are promised there. †1 Co 13:7

—from a sermon in praise of love*

197. *[Love] does not seek what is its own.*† †1 Co 13:5

People would not be lovers of money unless they supposed that their excellence would increase with their wealth. *Love*, being the opposite of this disorder, *does not seek what is its own*—that is, it does not derive its happiness from its individual excellence. Rightly, then, *it is not arrogant.*† †1 Co 13:4

—from the *Literal Commentary on Genesis* 11*

198. Love *believes all things*†—among those, surely, whom it binds to itself and makes one. †1 Co 13:7

—from *Confessions* 10*

199. *Now we see through a mirror, in a riddle, but then face to face.*† †1 Co 13:12

'Your knowledge is too wonderful for me; it has grown strong and I cannot attain it.'† I understand from myself how wonderful and †Ps 139:6

*196. *Serm.* 350.3; PL 39: 1534–35 passim
*197. *De Gen. ad Litt.* 11.15; CSEL 28,1: 347,23/26
*198. *Confess.* 10.3; CC 27: 156,11/12

incomprehensible is the knowledge by which you made me, seeing that I am not capable of comprehending myself whom you have made. And yet 'in my meditation a fire will flame out' so that I will seek your face continually.† I know that wisdom is an incorporeal substance and the light by which we see things not seen by eyes of flesh. And yet so great and spiritual a man [as Paul] says, *Now we see through a mirror, in a riddle, but then face to face.*

†Ps 39:3, 105:4=1Ch 16:11

If we ask what sort of *mirror* this is, and what it is, we realize that nothing but an image is perceived in a mirror. What we have been trying to do is to see somehow, as *through a mirror*, the one by whom we were made, by means of this image which we ourselves are.

But Paul added, *in a riddle.* Many people unacquainted with the writings that teach us about the figures of speech the Greeks call 'tropes' do not understand this. Expressing the name of each mode or trope in Latin is very difficult and uncommon. Hence some of our translators, being unwilling to use a Greek word when the Apostle says, 'This is an allegory,'† translate it by a circumlocution, saying, 'These things signify one thing by another.'

†Ga 4:24

This trope—that is, allegory—is of several kinds, including the one called *riddle.* What is an allegory, then, but a trope where one thing is understood by another? This to the Thessalonians is one: 'So then let us not fall asleep as others do, but let us keep awake and be sober; for those who sleep sleep at night, and those who get drunk are drunk at night; but let us, who belong to the day, be sober.'† Nevertheless, this allegory is not a riddle, as its meaning is obvious except to the very dimwitted. A *riddle*—to explain it briefly—is an obscure allegory, like 'The leech had three daughters,'† and others like it. When the Apostle wrote 'allegory' he found it not in words but in a fact—he pointed out that by the two sons of Abraham, one from a slave woman, the other from a free woman, we are to understand the two covenants.† This was not just said, but it actually took place. Before he explained it this was obscure. Such an allegory—which is the general name—could be specifically called a *riddle.*

†1 Th 5:6–8

†Pr 30:15. One manuscript, M, reads 'two daughters' like the Vulgate.

†Ga 4:22–24

It seems to me, therefore, that as by the word *mirror* he wanted us to understand an image, so by the word *riddle,* although it is a likeness, it is obscure and difficult to see through. By the words *mirror* and *riddle*, then, the Apostle meant whatever likenesses are adapted to understanding God, as far as this can be done. Yet nothing is better adapted [to this] than what [i.e., the soul] we do not call his image for nothing. Accordingly, no one should be surprised that, even in the mode of seeing that is granted us in this life, namely *through a mirror, in a riddle*, we labor to see anything at all. [Paul] would not have used the word *riddle* here if the act of seeing was easy.

—from *On the Trinity* 15.7*

200. *Now we see through a mirror, in a riddle.* 'I tell you, their angels in heaven continually see the face of my Father, who is in heaven.' Just as they see, so we too are going to see; but we do not yet see in their way. For this reason the Apostle says, *Now we see through a mirror, in a riddle, but then face to face.* That sight is reserved for us as a reward for our faith. John also spoke of it: 'We know that when he appears we will be like him, for we will see him as he is.'† We must take God's face as being his appearance, not a part of the body, such as we have and call by that name.

†**1 Co 13:12**; Mt 18:10; 1 Jn 3:2

The saints are going to see God in the body, but whether by means of it—as we now see the sun, the moon, the stars, sea and land and what is in them by means of the body—is no trifling question. To say that the saints will then have bodies of such a kind that they cannot close and open their eyes when they choose is harsh, but that those who close their eyes there will not see God is harsher. If the prophet Elisha, when physically elsewhere, saw his servant Gehazi accepting the gifts that Naaman the Syrian gave him,† how much more will the saints in the spiritual body see everything, not only if they close their eyes, but even when they are physically elsewhere! And a little farther on:

†2 K 5:26

The Apostle's words, *face to face*, do not compel us to believe that we are going to see God by means of this physical face, where our physical eyes are, since we will be seeing him uninterruptedly in spirit. If the interior self had no face the same Apostle would not

*199. *De Trin.* 15.7.13–9.16; CC 50A: 479,117/9; 480,2–481,5; 481,7/15; 19–482,33; 41/52

have said, 'But we, seeing with unveiled face the glory of the Lord, are being transformed into the same image from glory to glory, as
†2 Co 3:18 by the Spirit of the Lord.'†

—from *On the City of God* 22.29*

†1 Co 13:12 201. *Now I know only in part; then I will know even as I am known.*†

†1 Jn 2:16 Let us not try to carry over 'the desire of the eyes'† from this world to that vision of God promised us at the resurrection, but let us strive with holy zeal to cleanse our hearts. Let us not think of a physical face when the Apostle says, *Now we see through a mirror, in*
†1 Co 13:12 *a riddle, but then face to face,*† especially as he said more clearly, *Now I know only in part; then I will know even as I am known.* If we will know God then by a physical face, we are known now by a physical face—*then I will know,* [Paul] says, *even as I am known.*

Who does not understand that in this passage he means our face as well, the face of which he says in another passage, 'But we, seeing with unveiled face the glory of the Lord, are being transformed into
†2 Co 3:18 the same image from glory to glory, as by the Spirit of the Lord'†—he means from the glory of faith to the glory of eternal contemplation? The transformation by which 'our inner self is being renewed from
†2 Co 4:16 day to day'† brings this about.

—from *To Paulina, On Seeing God**

202. *Now faith, hope, and love abide, these three; and the greatest of these*
†1 Co 13:13 *is love.*†

These three exist, *faith, hope, and love*; all knowledge and prophecy are at their service. The sight we will see displaces faith, and the happiness we will attain displaces hope; but love, even as these others pass away, will only increase. If we love by believing what we do not yet see, how much more when we begin to see! And if we love by

*200. *De Civ. Dei* 22.29; CC 48: 857,25/26; 36/45; 49–858,62; 860,143/49 passim
*201. *Ep.* 147.22.51; CC 44: 327,4/21.

hoping for what we have not yet attained, how much more when we do attain it! *Now faith, hope, and love abide,* [Paul] says, *these three; and the greatest of these is love.* Even when everyone reaches what is eternal, and the first two pass away, love, enlarged and more certain, will remain.

—from *On Christian Doctrine* 1*

203. *For those who speak in a tongue speak not to human beings but to God . . .* † †1 Co 14:2, 6, 14, 16

Spirit is distinguished from mind by the most obvious testimony. *If I pray in a tongue,* [Paul] says, *my spirit prays but my mind is unproductive.* If we take the *tongue* in this passage to be expressing obscure and mystical meanings, and if we remove from them the mind's understanding, no one derives profit from hearing what is not understood. Hence [Paul] also says, *For those who speak in a tongue speak not to human beings but to God, for no one hears; yet the Spirit is speaking mysteries.* Here he is indicating well enough that in this passage he is using the word *tongue* where there are meanings like images and likenesses of things—to understand them one needs to apply the mind. When they are not understood, however, he says that they are in the spirit, not in the mind. Hence he states more clearly, *If you say a blessing with the spirit, how can those who hold the place of the uninstructed say 'Amen' to your blessing when they do not know what you are saying?*

Since the tongue—that is, the member of the body that we move in the mouth when we speak—presents signs of things and does not produce the things themselves, by a transference of the word [Paul] has called any production of signs before they are understood a *tongue.* When understanding, which is proper to the mind, is added, revelation, or knowledge, or prophecy, or teaching occurs Therefore [Paul] says, *If I come to you speaking in tongues, what profit shall I provide for you unless I speak to you in revelation or knowledge*

---

*202. *De Doct. Christ.* 1.37.41–39,43; CC 32: 30,14–31,6; 11/14

or prophecy or teaching—that is, with signs? This is understanding added to tongues, so that what is accomplished is accomplished not only by the spirit but also by the mind.

Consequently, prophecy did not yet exist for those to whom signs were manifested in the spirit by means of certain likenesses of bodily things, without the mental function being added so that these things may be understood as well: the one who interpreted what another saw was more a prophet than the one who saw. Hence, it is evident that prophecy is related more to the mind than to the spirit. The 'spirit' is called this in a special sense—it is a power of soul inferior to the mind, where likenesses of bodily things are represented.

Accordingly, Joseph, who understood what the seven ears of grain and the seven cows signified, was more a prophet than
†Gn 41:1–31 Pharaoh, who saw them in his dreams.† Pharaoh's spirit provided the form that enabled him to see them; Joseph's mind was enlightened so that he could understand [what they represented]. Pharaoh had the *tongue*, and Joseph the *prophecy*, since the mental image of the things was in the former, and the interpretation of the mental image in the latter. Therefore, one who sees in the spirit only the signs of the things represented by means of bodily images is less a prophet, and one endowed only with the understanding of these is more a prophet; the one, however, who excels in both—so as to see in the spirit significant likenesses of bodily things, and to understand them by natural vigor of mind—is most of all a prophet. Such was the pre-eminence of Daniel, which was tried and proven. He told the
†Dn 2:26–45 king the dream he saw, and revealed what it represented.† Physical images were represented in his spirit and the understanding of them revealed in his mind.

—from the *Literal Commentary on Genesis* 12.14*

204. *And that he rose on the third day, in accordance with the Scriptures,*
†1 Co 15:4–8 *and that he appeared to Cephas.*†

---

*203. *De Gen. ad Litt.* 12.8–9; CSEL 28,1: 390,5–392,1

[Paul] did not say, 'He appeared first to Cephas,' for that would be inconsistent with what we read in the gospel, that he appeared first to the women.† Later, [Paul] says, he appeared to the Twelve—although to which, and at what time [is not stated]—but [he appeared] on the actual day of the resurrection. *Then he appeared to more than five hundred of the brothers at one time.* Whether when they were assembled with the eleven behind closed doors 'out of fear of the Jews'—when, Thomas having left them, Jesus came to them—or a week later,† at a time he chose, we have no incompatibility here. *Later,* [Paul] says, *he appeared to James.* We should not take this as his first appearance to James, but that [he appeared to him] individually, in a special manifestation. *Then to all the apostles.* This was not his first appearance to them, but he would now converse more familiarly with them right up to the day of his ascension. *Last of all,* [Paul] says, *he appeared also to me, as one born out of due time.* This was now [an appearance] from heaven, some considerable time after his ascension.†

†Mt 28:9; Mk 16:9; Jn 20:14

†Jn 20:19, 26

†Ac 9:3–4

—from *On the Harmony of the Gospels* 3.25*

205. *Not I, but the grace of God that is with me*†—not because [Paul] was doing nothing good, but because he would have done nothing had [God] not helped him.

†**1 Co 15:10**

—to Paulinus [of Nola]*

206. *For as death came through a human being, so the resurrection from the dead has also come through a human being.*†

†**1 Co 15:21–22**

[Paul] calls Christ *a human being* here, although he is also God. This is to prevent anyone from thinking that the righteous of old could have been set free by Christ as God only—that is, by the Word that was in the beginning†—and not also by faith in his incarnation, by which Christ is called *a human being* as well. *Death came through*

†Jn 1:1

*204. *De Cons. Ev.* 3.25.85; CSEL 43: 390,23–391,16
*205. *Ep.* 186.10.36; CSEL 57: 76,5/7

one *human being*, [Paul] says, and *the resurrection from the dead has also come through* one *human being; for as in Adam all die, so also in Christ all will be made alive.* He is surely speaking of the resurrection of the righteous, where there is eternal life, not of the resurrection of the wicked, where there will be eternal death. That is why he says *they will be made alive*, since the others will be condemned.

—from a book in response to the queries of Hilary*

†1 Co 15:22 207. *As in Adam all die, so also in Christ all will be made alive.*†

As no one is in the realm of death except through Adam, so no one is in the realm of life except through Christ. As all human beings exist through Adam, so all righteous human beings exist through Christ. As through Adam all have become mortal children of this age in punishment, so also through Christ all are becoming immortal children of God in grace.

—from a letter to Bishop Optatus on the origin of the soul*

†1 Co 15:22 208. *As in Adam all die, so also in Christ all will be made alive*†—then, surely, that will be in a spiritual body in a life-giving spirit. Not that *all* who *die in Adam* will be members of Christ, for the great majority of them will be punished for ever by a second death. He says *all* in both clauses because, just as no one dies as a natural body except in Adam, so no one is brought to life as a spiritual body except in Christ.

—again, *On the City of God* 30*

209. *Then [comes] the end, when he hands over the realm to God and*
†1 Co 15:24 *the Father.*†

*206. *Ep.* 157.3.14; CSEL 44: 461,13–462,1 passim

*207. *Ep.* 190.2.8; CSEL 57: 143,20–144,5. Optatus was bishop of Mauretania Tingitana, modern Tangin.

*208. *De Civ.Dei* 13.23; CC 48: 408,113/20. The reference to book 30 is an error in the MSS.

Our Lord Jesus Christ will hand over *the realm to God and the Father*—not that he has been divided from the Father and the Holy Spirit—seeing that he will lead believers to the contemplation of God, which is the final purpose of all good deeds. It is also everlasting rest, and the joy that will not be taken from us. The Lord indicates this in his words, 'I will see you again, and your hearts will rejoice, and no one will take your joy from you.'† His faithful, of course, whom he has redeemed by his blood, are called his *realm*.† †Jn 16:22 †Rv 1:5–6; 5:9–10

—from *On the Trinity* 1.10*

210. *When he brings to nothing all sovereignty, and all authority and power*†—that is, so that the dispensation of appearances by means of angelic sovereignties and authorities and powers will not be needed. We may appropriately take these personages as saying what is said to the bride in the Song of Songs, 'We will make for you appearances of gold with differences of silver, as long as the king is on his couch'†—that is, as long as Christ is in his secret place, since 'our life is hidden with Christ in God. When Christ, your life, appears,' [Paul] says, 'then you too will appear with him in glory.'† †**1 Co 15:24** †Sg 1:11–12. Augustine's text differs considerably from the Vulgate (Sg 1:10–11). †Col 3:3–4

We should not suppose that Christ will hand over *the realm to God and the Father* in such a way as to deprive himself of it. Certain idle talkers have even believed this. When he is said to hand over *the realm to God and the Father*, he himself is not excluded, because he together with the Father is one God.

A word used here, however, misleads those who are indifferent about the holy scriptures and eager for controversy—*until*. The passage continues, *For he must reign until he puts all his enemies beneath his feet*†—as if he is not to reign when he has put them there. They fail to understand that the word is used as in the text, 'His heart has been strengthened; he will not be moved until he looks over his enemies.'† [This does not mean that] when he looks he will be moved. †**1 Co 15:25** (Ps 8:6; Eph 1:22) †Ps 112:8

When people hear the Apostle's words, *When it says that everything has been made subject to him, clearly this does not include the one*

*209. *De Trin.* 1.10.20–21; CC 50: 56,1/7; 59,66/67

†1 Co 15:27 *who made everything subject to him*,† they should not suppose that they are to understand of the Father that he has made everything subject to the Son in such a way that the Son has not also made everything subject to himself. The work of the Father and Son cannot be separated. Otherwise the Father has not made everything subject to himself, but the Son, who hands over the realm to him, and who brings to nothing *all sovereignty, and all authority and power*, has made everything subject to him. These words, *When he hands over the realm to God and the Father, when he brings to nothing all sovereignty, and all authority and power*, were spoken of the Son. The one who 'brings to nothing' is the one who 'makes subject'

The passage in which [Paul] says, *When everything is made subject to him, then he himself will be made subject to the one who made everything*
†1 Co 15:28 *subject to him,*† was said to prevent anyone from supposing that Christ's condition, which he received as a human creature, was later to be changed to divinity itself, or—to speak more precisely—to deity, which is not a creature but the incorporeal and unchangeable unity of the Trinity, a nature consubstantial and coeternal with itself.

—from the same, chapter 8*

†1 Co 15:28 211. *So that God may be all in all.*†

What else did [God] mean when he said through the prophet, 'I
†Jr 24:7, 30:22, 31:1, 32:38; Ezk 11:20 will be their God, and they will be my people,'† than that 'I will be the source of their satisfaction, I will be whatever people honorably desire—life and health and food and abundance and glory and honor and peace and all that is good?' This, when properly understood, is what the Apostle states: *That God may be all in all.* He himself will be the end of our desires, he who will be seen without end, loved without satiety, and praised without weariness. This gift, this emotion, this activity will surely be common to all, like eternal life itself.

—from *On the City of God* 22.30*

---

*210. *Ibid.* 1.8.15–16; CC 50: 49,68–50,77; 49,48/58; 48,32/36; 41–49,47; 46,1–47,8

*211. *De Civ. Dei* 22.30; CC 48: 863,27/36

212. *I die every day, brothers and sisters, by your glory.*† †1 Co 15:31

To keep us from supposing that this means, 'Your glory makes me die every day'—as we say, 'Through that one's teaching he became learned,' or, in other words, 'By that one's teaching it comes about that he is fully taught'—the Greek manuscripts in which *ne ten humeteran kauchesin* is written determine [the meaning]. Only someone making an oath says this. We should understand that our Lord commanded us not to swear† so that no one would look †Mt 5:34 upon an oath as something good, and by persistent swearing slip by habitual use into false swearing.

The Lord teaches that nothing among God's creatures is of so little value that anyone may decide to swear falsely by it. Divine Providence governs created things from the highest to the lowest, beginning from God's throne, right down to white or black hair.† †Mt 5:34, 36

In this we should also understand other [forms of oath], not all of which I can mention, like the passage I just recalled from the Apostle: *I die every day by your glory*. To show that he was bound [to carry out] this oath to the Lord, [Paul] added, *which I have in Christ Jesus our Lord.*

—From *On the Lord's Sermon on the Mount* 1*

213. *But someone will ask, 'How do the dead rise? With what kind of body do they come?'*† †1 Co 15:35

When [Paul] wanted to convince those who said that there is no resurrection from the dead that there is a resurrection from the dead, he first put forward Christ's resurrection as a model. Among the other things that he discussed then, he put a question to himself and said, *But someone will ask, 'How do the dead rise? With what body do they come?'*—that is, with *what kind* of *body*? Then, using seeds as an example, he said, *Fool! What you sow does not come to life unless first it dies. And as for what you sow, you do not sow the body that is to be, but a bare seed, usually of wheat or of one of the rest. God gives it a body, as he wishes, and to each of the seeds its own body.*† By *you do not* †1 Co 15:36–38

*212. *De Serm. Dom. in Monte* 1.17.51–52; CC 35: 58,1242/51; 59,1278–60,1282, 1296/1300

sow the body that is to be he did not mean that wheat will not come from wheat, but that no one sows the green stalk or the blade, and the many coverings of the grains in the chaff with which the seeds come up. And so he says *but a bare seed*, wanting to show that if God can add what was not in the bare seed, much more can he restore what was in the body of a human being.

What [Paul] now adds refers to the diversity of those who rise, owing to the various [degrees of] glory of believers and saints. *Not all flesh is the same flesh*, he says; *one kind is of human beings, another of animals, another of birds, another of fish. Both heavenly bodies and earthly bodies exist, but the glory of the heavenly is of one kind, and that of the earthly is another. The glory of the sun is of one kind, the glory of the moon is another, and the glory of the stars is another; for star differs from star in*
†**1 Co 15:39–42** *glory. So also is the resurrection of the dead.*†

All of this means that, if the kinds of flesh, though all are mortal, differ among themselves by virtue of the varieties of living things; and if bodies, though all are visible, differ among themselves by virtue of the varieties of places—hence the *glory of the heavenly is of one kind, and that of the earthly is another*; and if in the highest places, though all [the bodies] are heavenly, they differ in the brightness of their lights, we should not be surprised that in the resurrection of the dead the glory of the deserving will be distinctive.

[Paul] comes now to what *all flesh* that rises to eternal life has in common. *It is sown in corruption*, he says; *it will rise in incorruption; it is sown in dishonor, it will rise in glory; it is sown in weakness, it will*
†**1 Co 15:42–44** *rise in power; it is sown a natural body, it will rise a spiritual body.*†
Given these words of the Apostle, are we allowed to suppose that our bodies are going to rise better than Christ's, since it is put before us as the model which we ought confidently to look to, and through his grace to hope for? Christ's body could not possibly have risen in a state of corruption if we are promised that ours *will rise in incorruption*. Accordingly, it is certain and beyond all doubt that Christ's body, although it did not see the corruption of decay in the sepulcher—hence Scripture says, 'You will not give your holy
†Ps 16:10 one to see corruption'†—but could be pierced by nails and lance, now exists in a state of perfect incorruption. What was sown *in the dishonor* of his passion and death now exists *in the glory* of eternal life.

What could be crucified because of *weakness* now reigns in *power*. What was a *natural body*, since it was derived from Adam, is now *spiritual*, since it is now joined inseparably to spirit.

When the Apostle wanted to produce the testimony of Scripture concerning the *natural body*, he set down what we read in Genesis, and said, *If there is a natural body, there is also a spiritual one, as it is also written, 'The first Adam became a living being,'* or *'a live being.'*† Of course you remember how Scripture says, 'And God breathed into his face the breath of life, and the man became a live being,' while it says of the animals, 'Let the earth bring forth a live being.'† We understand, then, that the *natural body* is said to be similar to other living things on account of the disintegration and corruption of death; it is renewed every day with food, and afterwards, when the bond of life gives out, it disintegrates. The *spiritual body*, however, because now with the spirit, is immortal.

†**1 Co 15:44–45** (Gn 2:7)

†Gn 2:7, 1:24

Although some people are of the opinion that a body becomes *spiritual* when the body itself is changed into spirit, and what was a human being composed of body and spirit will become wholly spirit—as if the Apostle had said, 'It is sown a body, it will rise a spirit.' The Apostle said, *It is sown a natural body, it will rise a spiritual body.*

Consequently, as the *natural body* is not a soul but a body, so we have to reckon the *spiritual body* not a spirit but a body. Moreover, who would dare hold the opinion either that Christ's body did not rise a *spiritual* one, or, that if it did rise a spiritual one, it was no longer body but spirit? He rejected this idea of his disciples when, on seeing him, 'they thought they were seeing a spirit'; he said, 'Touch me and see; a spirit does not have bones and flesh, as you see that I have.'† The flesh, then, was now a spiritual body. Yet it was not a spirit, but a body, never again to be unbound and separated from the soul by any further death, as is a *natural body* such as that given life by God's breath when 'the man became a live being.' Even this would have passed from *natural* to *spiritual* without the intervention of death, if the transgression of a commandment had not inflicted a punishment for sin committed before God could bestow a crown for righteousness preserved.

†Lk 24:37, 39

Hence the Lord Christ came to us, through us, when the righteous one found sinners through the covering, so to speak, of our lowly condition. He appeared to us through a *natural*, that is, a mortal *body*, when surely, if he had chosen, he could have come to us with an immortal body from the first. Because it was fitting that we be healed by the humility of the Son of God, he came all the way down to the level of our weakness, and revealed the merit and reward of our faith by the power of his resurrection.

Therefore the Apostle goes on to say, *The last Adam became a life-*
†**1 Co 15:45** *giving spirit.*† Whether we should take the first Adam to be the one who was formed out of dust in the beginning, and the last Adam to be the one born of the Virgin, or whether both are complete in each human being—so that the first Adam would be a human being in a mortal body and the last Adam the same one in an immortal body—in either case [Paul] wanted this distinction [to be made] between a living being and a life-giving spirit, that the former is a *natural body*, the latter a *spiritual* one. Certainly life resides in a *natural body*, but it does not give life to the point of taking away corruption. In a *spiritual body*, since a person perfectly 'united to the Lord is
†1 Co 6:17 one spirit [with him],'† it gives life in such a way as to produce a *spiritual body*, destroying all corruption and being apprehensive of no separation.

Hence there follows, *But the spiritual is not first, but the natural; afterwards the spiritual. The first human being was from the earth, earthly; the second human being was from heaven, heavenly. As was the earthly one, so also are the earthly, and as was the heavenly one, so also are the heavenly. As we have borne the image of the earthly one, let us also bear the image of*
†**1 Co 15:46–49** *the one who is from heaven.*†

What does *as was the earthly one, so also are the earthly* mean if not that they are mortals sprung from a mortal? And what does *as was the heavenly one, so also are the heavenly* mean if not that they are immortal because of one who is immortal—the former through Adam, the latter through Christ? The Lord, although he was heavenly, became earthly for a purpose, to make those who were earthly heavenly. In other words, from being immortal he became mortal by taking on
†Ph 2:7 'the form of a servant,'† not by changing his nature as Lord. This was

to make those who were mortal immortal by imparting his grace as Lord, not by retaining their damaged form as servants.

—from a letter to Consentius on the Lord's body after the resurrection*

214. [Paul] evidently wanted us to take Christ as the heavenly being and Adam as the earthly one—not on account of his earthly body, but on account of sin. To Adam [God] said, 'You are earth, and into earth you shall go† since you are guilty and destined for the punishment of death.' Our Lord, not falling down on his own account, but descending on ours, took on flesh without sin. In his taking on of flesh he could demonstrate the resurrection of all flesh, and for the present we may bear by faith the heavenly human being—for the present [we may bear] by faith an image of the heavenly human—for the present in the heart, but afterward, in the resurrection of the dead, in the body as well. *As was the earthly one, so also are the earthly*—that is, all will die—*and as was the heavenly one, so also are the heavenly*†—that is, all will rise, for the heavenly one has already risen and ascended into heaven.

†Gn 3:19

†**1 Co 15:48**

—from a sermon on the resurrection of the dead*

215. When the Apostle was discussing the resurrection of the body he taught that from being corruptible our bodies would become incorruptible, from being mean they would become glorious, from being weak, strong, from being natural, spiritual—in other words, from being mortal they would become immortal. He then added, *This I say, brothers and sisters, that flesh and blood cannot possess the kingdom of God.*† And to keep people from supposing that the Apostle had decided this with regard to the material substance of flesh, he

†**1 Co 15:50**. Here Augustine says *cannot possess*; in a few lines he will say *will not possess*.

*213. *Ep*. 205.2.6–12; CC 57: 328,1–329,23; 330,10–333,23. Little is known about this Consentius.

*214. *Serm*. 362, *Serm*. 362.14.15; PL 39: 1621

clarified what he was saying by adding, *nor will corruption possess incorruption*, as if he was saying, 'What I have said about flesh and blood not possessing the kingdom of God I said because corruption will not possess incorruption.' In this passage, then, he wanted us to understand by the words *flesh and blood* the corruption of mortality.

Then, as if someone asked him, 'How will it be flesh and not be flesh?'—it will indeed be flesh, since the Lord said after the resurrection, 'Touch me and see; a spirit does not have flesh and
†Lk 24:37, 39 bones, as you see that I have,'† while it will not be flesh, since *flesh and blood will not possess the kingdom of God*—he explains what he says by adding, *Behold, I tell you a mystery! We will all rise* (or, as the Greek manuscripts have it, *We will all fall asleep*) *but we will not all*
†1 Co 15:51 *be changed*.† Whether he wanted us to take this change as being for worse or for better what comes next demonstrates.

In a moment, he says—that is, in an indivisible point of time—*in the twinkling of an eye*—that is, with the greatest swiftness—*at the last trumpet*—that is, at the last signal that will be given for the completion of these things—*the trumpet will sound, and the dead will*
†1 Co 15:52 *rise incorrupt, and we will be changed*.† We must undoubtedly take this change as being for the better, since all, both righteous and unrighteous, are going to rise—as the Lord says in the gospel, 'Those who have done good to the resurrection of life, those who have done evil to the resurrection of judgment.' He calls everlasting punishment 'judgment,' as elsewhere, 'those who do not believe,' he says, 'have already been judged.' Consequently, those who are to rise to judgment will not be changed into that incorruption that cannot suffer the corruption of pain. That belongs to the faithful and to saints. The others will be tormented by everlasting corruption, 'for their fire will not be quenched, and their worm
†Jn 5:29, 3:18; Is 66:24 will not die.'†

What does the distinction mean, *the dead will rise incorrupt, and we will be changed*, except that all will rise incorrupt, but from among these the righteous will be changed into the state of incorruption that no corruption can harm in any way? Those who will not be changed into this state will indeed rise incorrupt with regard to their bodily integrity, yet they are to be corrupted by the pain of their punishments when they hear, 'Go into the eternal fire prepared for the devil and his angels.' 'The righteous will not fear the evil news.'† †Mt 25:41; Ps 112:7, probably from memory.

But when he has said of this change in the righteous that *we will be changed*, as if we were asking how this is to come about, and what this change will be like, [Paul] adds, *For this corruptible [body] must put on incorruption, and this mortal [body] must put on immortality*.† I think that we cannot doubt that this is consistent with the words *flesh and blood will not possess the kingdom of God* because the corruption and mortality of flesh and blood will not exist there. In this passage he uses the words *flesh and blood* in reference to these qualities. †**1 Co 15:53**

—from the letter to Consentius*

216. *We will all rise*—or, as other manuscripts have it, *We will all fall asleep*.† Since no resurrection can take place without a preceding death, and since we cannot take sleep in this passage as meaning anything but death, how will *all* either *fall asleep* or *rise* if so many whom Christ will find in the body will neither fall asleep nor rise? If we believe that the saints who will be discovered alive when Christ comes, and who will be caught up to meet him,† are going to leave their mortal bodies in that 'catching up' and immediately return to the same bodies, now immortal, we will experience no difficulties in the words of the Apostle, either where he says, 'What you sow does not come to life unless first it dies,'† or where he says, We *will all rise*—or, *We will all fall asleep*. Not even the saints will come to life through immortality without previously dying, however briefly. For this reason they will not be excluded from a resurrection preceded by a sleep; although brief, it will occur. †**1 Co 15:51** †1 Th 4:17 †1 Co 15:36

—from *On the City of God* 20.20*

217. [Paul] did not intend to build them up into thinking that they were going to do in the kingdom of heaven such things as they

*215. *Ep.* 205.2.13–15; CC 57: 334,1–336,15
*216. *De Civ. Dei* 20.20; CC 48: 734,50–735,65

were doing in this life—the mortal actions of eating and drinking, marrying and giving in marriage, producing children. These pertain to the mortal nature of flesh, not to its form. The Jews believed in resurrection, but thought that it would take place carnally, so that life after resurrection would consist in continuing to do what they were doing at the time. Thinking this carnally, they could not answer the Sadducees when they propounded a question concerning the resurrection,† and so forth.

†Mt 22:23–32

We will all rise, but we will not all be changed. In a moment,† in the twinkling of an eye, at the last trumpet.† Many of you do not know what an *atom* [that is, a *moment*] is. *Atom* [is derived from the word] *tome*, [meaning] a cutting, a division; in Greek an *atom* is what cannot be cut or divided. An *atom* in a body is a very small body with no capacity for being cut. An *atom* in time is a brief moment with no capacity for being divided. Take, for example, a stone—divide it into parts, divide these parts into pebbles, divide the pebbles into grains of sand, divide the grains of sand into dust—you come to some small thing which you cannot divide further. This is a material *atom*. As for time, a year, for example, is divided into months, months are divided into days, days can still be divided into hours, hours into groups of moments that still allow divisions of some length, until you come to a very small point of time, and to a kind of drop [of time] that cannot have any length since it has no center. This is an *atom* [that is, a *moment*] of time.

†Augustine's text read *in atomo*, hence the following explanation.
†**1 Co 15:51–52**

After [Paul] had said *in a moment*, he added how much of an action or movement can take place in that moment of time. *In the twinkling of the eye*, he said. The *twinkling of the eye* is not the length of time in which we close and open the eye by moving the eyelid. He calls the sending out of rays to see something *the twinkling of the eye*. As soon as you open your eye your ray is sent out toward—I do not say to a nearby wall, but to a far distant mountain—nor do I say a mountain seen close to earth, but one that is neighbor to the stars, the moon and the sun. As great as is the distance these are from the earth, as soon as you send out the ray it is there, so swiftly does it fly over [the intervening] space. *In a moment, in the twinkling of an eye, at the last trumpet*—the sign given from heaven on the day of judgment.

—from a sermon on the resurrection of the dead*

218. *Then the saying that is written will come about: 'Death has been swallowed up in victory. Where, O death, is your strife? Where is your sting? The sting of death is sin.'*† †**1 Co 15:54–56** (Is 25:7; Ho 13:14). Augustine's text of verse 55 began *Vbi est, mors, contentio tua?*

I think that in this passage *death* represents a carnal habit that resists a good intention by the pleasure to be enjoyed in temporal things. [Paul] would not have asked, *Where is your strife?* if it did not offer resistance and opposition. Its *strife* is also described in this passage: 'The cravings of the flesh are against the spirit, and the cravings of the spirit are against the flesh, so that you do not do what you want.'† Perfect sanctification brings about the subjection of all our carnal longings to good intention by our spirit that has been enlightened and given life. †Ga 5:17

We earned this death by sin, since sin resulted entirely from our freedom of choice. In paradise no pain from pleasure denied stood in the way of the human's good intention. *The sting of death is,* then, *sin,* because by sin came the pleasure that can now stand in the way of our intention and only be restrained with pain. We rightly call this pleasure *death* because it is a failing, the result of a weakened soul. *And the power of sin is the law,* because what the law prohibits is committed with much more wickedness and shame than if no law prohibited it. And so death will be *swallowed up in victory* when through sanctification fleshly pleasure will be consigned to oblivion in every part of a human being by the perfect pleasure of things spiritual.

—from *On Eighty-Four Questions**

219. *The sting of death is sin.*† †**1 Co 15:56**

By sin's pricking us death occurs. Sin is a kind of scorpion. It pricked us and we died. When will we say, *Where, O death, is your*

*217. *Serm.* 362.15.18–17.20; PL 39: 1623–25 passim

*218. *De Div. Quaest. LXXXIII* 70; CC 44A: 197,5/17; 198,25/28; 34–199,43

†1 Co 15:55. Here Augustine's text agrees with the Vulgate. The Greek MSS reveal the same discrepancy (between *neikos* and *nikos*).

victory?† We are not promised this in this life, but at the resurrection. Then the saints will be granted to have neither the slightest desire nor the ability to sin.

—from a sermon to the people on this reading*

†**1 Co 15:44–48** conflated

220. *The first man, [who was] from the earth, earthly, became a living being,* not *a life-giving spirit,*† something reserved for him until he earned it by obedience. His body required food and drink not to be affected by hunger and thirst. It was not preserved from the necessity of death and kept in the bloom of youth by unconditional and indestructible immortality, but by the tree of life. Beyond all doubt [his body] was *natural* and not *spiritual*, yet it would not have died if he had not fallen by transgressing under the sentence of God, who pronounced it and made it the subject of a threat.† Nourished, even outside paradise, he was delivered up to time and old age to be brought to an end, at least with respect to the life he could have had perpetually in paradise—although in a natural body, until it would become spiritual as a reward for obedience, had he not sinned. And a little farther on:

†Gn 2:17

To show what a natural body is [Paul] said, *As it is also written, 'The first man became a living being.'* In this way he intended to show what a *natural body* is, even though Scripture does not say of the first man, who was called Adam, when his being was created by God's breath, 'And the man became a natural body,' but, 'The man became a living being.'† By the words, *The man became a living being*, the Apostle intended us to understand a *natural* human *body*. He showed how we are to understand a *spiritual [body]* by adding, *The last Adam became a life-giving spirit.* Surely he means Christ, who has now so risen from the dead that henceforth he cannot die at all.†

†Gn 2:7

†Rm 6:9

Furthermore, he goes on to say, *But the spiritual is not first, but the natural; afterwards the spiritual.* Here he has declared much more clearly that he meant the natural body when he wrote that *the first man became a living being*, and the spiritual [body] when he said that

*219. *Serm.* 151.7.7; PL 38: 818

the last Adam became a life-giving spirit. First was the *natural body* such as the first Adam had—although it would not have died had he not sinned—and such as we now also have, but with its nature changed and marred to the degree brought about in [Adam] after he sinned. From this it would now have the necessity of dying. Such [a body] Christ condescended to have for our sake at first, not out of necessity but by his power. *Afterward [came] the spiritual [body].* Such [a body] came first in Christ as in our head. It will follow in his members at the final resurrection of the dead.

Then the Apostle added the most obvious difference between these two people, saying, *The first human being was from the earth, earthly; the second human being was from heaven, heavenly. . . .* This the Apostle set down so that what he says elsewhere, 'As many as have been baptized in Christ have put on Christ,' may now take place in us in accord with the sacrament of rebirth. In reality this will be accomplished fully when what is *natural* to us by birth will have become *spiritual* by resurrection. To make use of his words in the same way, 'By hope we have been saved.'† We have put on the image of the earthly one by the transmission of transgression and death. Birth produces this in us. But we have put on the image of the heavenly one by the gift of forgiveness and of everlasting life. Rebirth bestows this on us—but only through 'the mediator between God and humanity, Jesus Christ, himself human.'† [Paul] intends us to take him as being the heavenly one, because he came from heaven to be clothed with a body of earthly mortality, which he would clothe with heavenly immortality.

†Ga 3:27; Rm 8:24

†1 Tm 2:5

[Paul] also describes other people as *heavenly*, since through grace they become Christ's members in order that he may be one with them as head and body.† We must not take the words, *As was the earthly one, so also are the earthly*, as saying that they became [earthly] by the admission of sin. We should not suppose that [the first human being] had a *spiritual body* before he sinned, and that this was changed by sin into a *natural* one. To think this we would have to pay too little attention to the words of the great teacher who said, *If there is a natural body, there is also a spiritual one, as it is written, 'The first man, Adam, became a living being.'* This cannot have occurred after sin, since it was the original condition of human

†1 Co 12:12, 27; Eph 5:23

beings. Blessed Paul adopted the testimony of the law concerning this in order to reveal a *natural body* to us.

—from *On the City of God* 13*

221. Even the apostle Paul may appear to have thought about the
†Mt 6:34 morrow† when he said, *Concerning the collection for the saints: you also should do as I ordered the churches of Galatia. On the first day of the*
†**1 Co 16:1–2** *week, each of you should put aside something, saving it up*.† From these and other such passages of Scripture we see clearly that our Lord does not condemn this if we amass possessions in an ordinary way, but only if we serve God for their sake. In their endeavors, then, they would have not the kingdom of God but the acquisition of possessions in view.

—from *On the Lord's Sermon on the Mount* 2*

*220. *De Civ. Dei* 13.23; CC 48: 405,10–406,23; 407,65–408,111; 122–32
*221. *De Serm. Dom. in Monte* 2.17.57; CC 35: 150,1277–151,1280; 152,1315–153,1318

Saint Augustine's Commentary

the Second Letter of Paul to the Church at Corinth

PAUL, AN APOSTLE OF CHRIST JESUS by the will of God.† †2 Co 1:1

Paul appreciates having us speak of his sins so that the one who healed such a disease may be glorified. The Physician's hand cut and healed the greatness of the wound. The voice from heaven brought down a persecutor and raised up a preacher; it slew Saul and brought Paul to life. Saul was the persecutor of a holy man [David], and hence [Paul] had his name when he was persecuting the Christians. Later, from Saul he became Paul.† †Ac 9:1–6; 1 S 19; Ac 13:9

What does 'Paul' mean? 'Little.' When he was Saul he was proud and exalted; when he was Paul he was humble and little. That is why we say, 'I will see you *paulo post*'—that is, 'after a little while.' Hear that he became little: 'for I am the latest of the apostles'; and, 'to me, the very least of the saints,' as he says in another place.† He was among the apostles like the fringe on a garment—but the church of the Gentiles, like [the woman] suffering from a hemorrhage, touched him and was healed.† †1 Co 15:9 (Augustine's text read *novissimus* rather than *minimus*); Eph 3:8 †Mt 9:20–22

—from homily eight on the Letter of Saint John*

223. How is the door of the Word opened except when the mind of a listener is opened to belief? Hence the Apostle said, *When I came to Troas for the gospel of Christ, and a door was opened to me in the Lord, I had no rest for my spirit because I did not find Titus, my brother. But, making my farewell to them, I left for Macedonia.*† To whom did he make his farewell if not to those who believed, in whose hearts a door was opened for his preaching of the gospel? †2 Co 2:12–13

But notice what he adds: *Thanks be to God*, he says, *who always makes us triumph in Christ, and manifests through us the aroma of the knowledge of him in every place. We are the good aroma of Christ for God, in those who are being saved and in those who are perishing; to some the aroma of death to death, for others the aroma of life to life.*† †2 Co 2:14–16

See why this most ardent soldier and invincible defender of grace gives thanks; see why he gives thanks—because the apostles

*222. *In Ioh. Ep.* 8.2; PL 35: 2037

are *the good aroma of Christ for God, in those who are being saved* by his grace as well as *in those who are perishing* by his judgment. But so that those with too little understanding of these things may be less provoked to anger, he adds to his admonishment and asks, *And who is sufficient for these things?*

—from *To Prosper and Hilary**

224. 'The house,' [John] said, 'was filled with the aroma of the perfume.' The world was filled with a good report. Now a good report is a good aroma. Listen to the Apostle: *We are the good aroma*
†Jn 12:3; **2 Co 2:15, 14** *of Christ*, he says, *in every place.*† And a little farther on:

Fortunate are those who live by a good aroma. What is more unfortunate than those who die by a good aroma? 'And who,' someone asks, 'does the good aroma slay?' This is what the Apostle
†**2 Co 2:16** says: *And who is sufficient for these things?*† In what wonderful ways does God bring it about that the good live and the wicked die by a good aroma? Some loved the apostle Paul, who did good, who lived uprightly, who preached righteousness by his words and demonstrated it by his deeds, who was an admirable teacher and a
†1 Co 4:1–2 trustworthy steward,† whose reputation spread everywhere; others envied him. Have you loved some who do good? You have lived by their good aroma. Have you envied some who do good? You have died by their good aroma.

–in homily forty-seven on the Gospel of John*

†**2 Co 3:6** 225. *For the letter kills, but the Spirit gives life.*†

The law that is read only, and not understood and not fulfilled, surely *kills*. Then do we call it *the letter. But the Spirit gives life* because 'the fulfilling of the law is the love which has been poured out in
†Rm 13:10, 5:5 our hearts through the Holy Spirit who has been given to us.'†

—from *To Simplician, Bishop**

*223. *De Praedest. Sanc.* 20.40–41; PL 44: 989–90 passim
*224. *Tract. in Ioh.* 50.7–8; CC 36: 435,1–436,19 passim
*225. *De Div. Quaest. ad Simpl.* 1.1.17; CC 44: 23,367/72; 21,316/32

226. *Now if the ministry of death, chiseled in letters on stones, was glorious.*† †**2 Co 3:7**

Why does he speak of a *ministry of death* if the law is good? Because 'sin, that it may appear as sin, worked death in me through what is good.'† This should not surprise you since it is said of the very preaching of the gospel, *We are the good aroma of Christ, in those who are being saved and in those who are perishing; to some the aroma of life to life, for others the aroma of death to death.*† The law is said to be a *ministry of death* for the Jews, for whom it was written on stone to symbolize their rigidity, [but] not for those who fulfill the law through love. 'The fulfilling of the law is love.' 'The one who loves another has fulfilled the law,' for, 'you shall not commit adultery, you shall not murder, you shall not steal, and if there is any other commandment it is summed up in this word, You shall love your neighbor as yourself.' This too is written in the same law.†*

†1 Tm 1:8; Rm 7:12–13

†**2 Co 2:15–16**

†Rm 13:10, 8–9; Lv 19:18

227. We must be wary of taking a figurative expression literally. The Apostle's words apply here: *The letter kills, but the Spirit gives life.*† When we take what is figuratively said as being said literally we have our minds set on the flesh. No death is more aptly called a death of the soul than when that in [the soul] that makes it superior to the beasts is subjected to the flesh by adherence to the letter. A follower of the letter who hears 'sabbath,' for example, understands nothing but one day out of the seven that are repeated in a continuous sequence. And when such people hear 'sacrifice' they do not go beyond the thought of what ordinarily happens to animal victims and the fruits of the earth.

†**2 Co 3:6**

—from *On Christian Doctrine* 3*

228. *Now if the ministry of death, chiseled in letters on stones, was so glorious that the children of Israel could not gaze on Moses' face because of*

*226. The MSS give no title to this excerpt. The reference is the same as for section 225.
*227. *De Doct. Christ.* 3.5.9; CC 32: 82,3–83,16 passim

the glory of his countenance, [a glory] that fades, how much more glorious †**2 Co 3:7–8** *will be the ministry of the Spirit?*†

†Rm 7:12 The law, though just and holy and good,† brought death to the transgressors whom God's grace did not help to fulfill the righteousness of the law. Under the old covenant the law had to be imposed on the proud and on those who trusted in the strength of their own wills. [This law] did not bestow righteousness, but only commanded it. Thus those embraced by the death brought on by transgression were to have recourse to the grace revealed under the new covenant. [Grace] not only commands, but offers help. What wonder, then, if the former—where the letter kills by forbidding the evil that is done and enjoining the good that is not done—is called a *ministry of death*, and the latter is called a *ministry of the Spirit*! This one is undoubtedly life-giving, so that we rise from the death brought on by transgression; we do not, as guilty persons, read about righteousness on tablets of stone, but as free persons we possess it in our hearts and in our lives. The new covenant differs from the old in that there the old self was confined by the narrowness of fear, while here the new self spreads out across the broad expanse of love.

[Paul] said of the minister of the old covenant, Moses, that *the children of Israel could not gaze on* his *face because of the glory of his countenance*. This was a sign that they were not going to perceive Christ in the law. A veil was put over Moses' face for their sake, *to* †**2 Co 3:13** *keep the children of Israel from gazing to the end*, as it is written.†

What is the end of the law? Let me not answer this, but the Apostle. He said, 'Christ is the end of the law for the justification of †Rm 10:4 everyone who believes.'† The end fulfills, not kills. The purpose for which we perform our duties we call an 'end.' A duty and an end differ in this way: a duty consists of what we ought to do, and an end is why we do it. Surely all these things came about on account of Christ, whom the children of Israel did not perceive in the events that came about. The veil signified this—it did not allow them to *gaze to the end*, that is, to Moses' face, which signified Christ.

This glory is said to fade because all semblances that signify something fade when the reality signified appears. Our present knowledge will fade, as the same apostle says, when the [knowledge] he describes as 'face to face' comes,† and so too that handed down to the Jews in semblances under the old covenant had necessarily to fade before the revelation of the new covenant. Not everyone, of course, among [the Jewish] people failed to perceive Christ prefigured by the semblances of the old covenant, for Moses himself, and the rest of the prophets—who foretold him to the rest—did not fail to perceive [him]. †1 Co 13:10, 12

—from *Against the Opponent of the Law and the Prophets* 2*

229. *But we, seeing with unveiled face the glory of the Lord as in a mirror, are being transformed into the same image.*† **†2 Co 3:18**

'Now,' [Paul says, 'we see through a mirror, in a riddle, but then face to face.'† If we ask what sort of mirror this is, and what it is, we realize that nothing but an image is perceived in a mirror. What we have been trying to do is to somehow see as 'through a mirror' the one by whom we were made, by means of this image, which we ourselves are. †1 Co 13:12

The same apostle indicates this in another text. *But we, seeing with unveiled face the glory of the Lord as in a mirror, are being transformed into the same image from glory to glory, as by the Spirit of the Lord.* [Paul] used the word *speculantes*, 'seeing as in a mirror'—he means *per speculum videntes*, 'seeing through a mirror,' not *de specula prospicientes*, 'looking out from a watch-tower.' This is not ambiguous in the Greek language from which the apostolic letters have been translated into Latin. There *speculum*, where the images of things appear, differs even by sound from *specula*, from whose height we look at something far away. That the Apostle described [us] as *seeing the glory of the Lord* by means of a mirror, not by means of a watch-tower, is entirely and sufficiently clear, then.

When he says that *we are being transformed into the same image* he surely intends us to understand the image of God. When he says

---

*228. *Contra Adv. Leg. et Prophet.* 2.7.24–27; CC 49: 109,697/701; 110,712/19; 737–111,771

the same he means 'the very one''—that is, the one we see as in a mirror. *The same image* is also the glory of God, as he says elsewhere, 'A man ought not to cover his head, since he is the image and glory
†1 Co 11:7 of God.'†

Therefore he says that *we are being transformed*—we are being changed from form to form, and passing from a dark form into one filled with light. The dark form is the image of God, and if it is the image, then it is also the glory in which we human beings were created, surpassing other living beings. Of our human nature Scripture says, 'A man ought not to cover his head, since he is the image and glory of God.' When its Creator makes this nature, which is preeminent among created things, righteous from being wicked, it is transformed from deformed to finely formed. In its ungodly state, as its fault is more damnable, its nature is more certainly laudable.

On this account [Paul] added *from glory to glory*, from the glory of creation to the glory of righteousness—although his words, *from glory to glory*, can be understood in other ways: from the glory of faith to the glory of sight, and from the glory by which we are God's children to the glory by which 'we will be like him, for we will see
†1 Jn 3:2 him as he is.'† The words he adds, *as by the Spirit of the Lord*, show that the good of so desirable a transformation is conferred upon us by the grace of God.

—from *On the Trinity* 15.8*

230. This perfection of the image will be achieved at some time in the future. Our good master instructs us in the way to acquire it—by Christian faith and holy doctrine. Then *with unveiled face*—without the veil of the law, which is the semblance of things to come—*seeing the glory of the Lord as in a mirror,* we may be transformed *into the same*
†2 Co 3:18 *image from glory to glory, as by the Spirit of the Lord.*†

—again, from the same book, chapter 11*

*229. *De Trin.* 15.8.14; CC 50A: 479,3–480,41. Two sentences of section 199 are repeated at the beginning of this excerpt.

*230. *De Trin.* 15.11.20; CC 50A: 489,78/83

231. The Jews keep a veil over the face by not passing over to Christ, since when anyone passes over to Christ the veil will be lifted. *We, with* the same *face unveiled, are being transformed into the same image.* [Paul] says with perfect clarity, *A veil lies over their hearts.* There [in the heart], then, is the face with which, unveiled, we see now in faith—although 'through a mirror' and 'in a riddle'—'but then face to face.'† †**2 Co 3:18, 15**; 1 Co 13:12

—from *To Paulina, On Seeing God**

232. *In the case [of those who are perishing] the god of this world has blinded the minds of unbelievers.*† †**2 Co 4:4**

Quite a few people of our time interpret this statement as saying that the true God has blinded the minds of unbelievers. They read *In the case [of those who are perishing] God . . .* and pause, and then attach the phrase *of this world* to *the unbelievers* rather than to *the god*, so that they read, 'In the case [of those who are perishing] God has blinded the minds of the unbelievers of this world.'

Such an act, by which the minds of unbelievers are blinded, can in a sense be attributed to the true God. He does not do it from malice, but from justice. As Paul says elsewhere, 'Is God unjust, who brings forth anger?' Some hidden decision precedes these hidden things, when God exercises the most righteous scrutiny of his judgment, by which the minds of some are blinded [while] those of others are enlightened, and [God] is told with perfect truth, 'Your judgments are a great deep.'† †Rm 3:5; Ps 36:6

—from *Against Faustus* 21*

233. *For God, who told light to shine out of darkness, has shone in our hearts.*† †**2 Co 4:6** (Gn 1:3)

---

*231. *Ep.* 147.22.51; CSEL 44: 328,4/10

*232. *Contra Faust. Manich.* 21.2; CSEL 25: 569,22–570,7; 571,7/11. The first paragraph is a paraphrase. Augustine's text of 2 Corinthians 4:4 read *In quibus deus saeculi huius excaecavit mentes infidelium*, where *saeculi huius* can modify either *deus/Deus* or *mentes infidelium*.

[The opponent] attributes to the writer's folly his saying that darkness always existed without a beginning, while light took its beginning from darkness—as if he read of perpetual darkness in that book which he scorns. Yet there it is written, 'In the beginning God made heaven and earth; the earth was invisible and disordered, and darkness was over the great deep.'† Darkness began from him, then, from whom the confused mass of heaven and earth began to exist, before the light which would illumine what had been dark, without light, came into being.

†Gn 1:1–2. Augustine's Latin is a literal translation of the Septuagint.

What then would be inappropriate if the dark primordial things [heaven and earth] were the material out of which the earth was made, so that when light came upon it what had been made would be improved, and in this way would yield the allegorical meaning of the disposition, as it were, of a person making progress, which would come later? On the other hand, if he is displeased that light took its beginning from darkness, let the Apostle who wrote to believers, 'Once you were darkness, but now in the Lord you are light,' tell it to him. Who did this if not the one who, when darkness was over the great deep, said, 'Let there be light, and light was made.'† The same apostle Paul expressed this more clearly in another place when he said, *For God, who told light to shine out of darkness, has shone in our hearts.*

†Eph 5:8; Gn 1:3

—from *Against the Opponent of the Law and the Prophets* 1*

234. *Having the same spirit of faith, in accord with what is written, 'I believed, therefore I spoke,' we too believe, therefore we too speak.*†

†**2 Co 4:13** (Ps 116:10)

[Paul] would not have said *the same spirit of faith* if he was not advising us that even the righteous of old had this spirit—that is, [of faith] in the incarnation of Christ. But because what is told us as having taken place already was foretold to them as something to come in the future, and what is revealed during the period of the new covenant was veiled during the time of the old covenant, its

*233. *Contra Adv. Leg. et Prophet.* 1.8.11–11.15; CC 49: 43,259–44,271; 46,335/42. See *Confessions* 12.11; 13.8 and 14.

sacred signs were different. They were of one kind under the old covenant, another under the new, while the faith itself does not vary.

—from a letter in reply to the queries of Hilary*

235. The blessed apostle Paul presented testimony from Scripture by which he commended to us the glory of the martyrs. He said, *In accord with what is written, 'I believed, therefore I spoke,' we too believe, therefore we too speak.*† If they had only believed, and not spoken, they would not have suffered. By believing they laid hold of life, and by speaking they incurred death, but a death in which they would sow a corruptible body and reap incorruption. The same apostle expounded the meaning of this—that what *we believe, therefore we too speak*—in another passage as follows: 'One believes with the heart for righteousness, and one confesses with the mouth for salvation.'†

—from a sermon on the birthday of Saint Quadratus*

†**2 Co 4:13** (Ps 116:10)

†1 Co 15:42; Rm 10:10

236. The same faith in the Mediator saved the people of old, the small along with the great—not the old covenant, 'which bore children for slavery.'†

—to Count Valerius*

†Rv 11:18, 19:5; Ga 4:24

237. *Even if our outer nature is wasting away, out inner nature is being renewed day by day.*†

†**2 Co 4:16**

This renewal does not happen in one moment of conversion, like the renewal that happens in baptism in one moment by the forgiveness of all sins—not even one, however small, remains

*234. *Ep*. 157.3.14; CSEL 44: 462,6/16

*235. *Serm*. See PL 39: 1731. This is undoubtedly part of the sermon preached in honor of the third century North African martyr-bishop of Utica, Quadratus, mentioned by Possidius in his list of Augustine's works (PL 46: 19).

*236. *De Nupt. et Concup*. 2.11.24; CSEL 42: 277,8/10. For Valerius see section 33.

unforgiven. But as getting rid of a fever is one thing and recovering from the weakness brought on by the fever is another; and again, pulling a spear out of a body it has pierced is one thing and healing the wound it made by a complete cure is another. Thus, the first stage of healing is to remove the cause of the infirmity, which is done by the remission of every sin, and the second is to heal the infirmity itself, which is done gradually by advancing in the renewal of this image.

†Ps 103:3

These two [stages] are demonstrated in the psalm.† We read there, 'Who forgives all your iniquities'—this is done in baptism; and then, 'who heals all your infirmities'—this is done by daily movements forward as this image is being renewed. Thus those being renewed by advancing day by day in the knowledge of God, and in righteousness and holiness of truth,† transfer their love from things temporal to things eternal, from things visible to things intelligible, from things of the flesh to those of the spirit, and they diligently endeavor to restrain and lessen their desire for the former and to bind themselves by love to the latter. And a little farther on:

†Col 3:10; Eph 4:24

The image which is being renewed day by day 'in the spirit of the mind' in the knowledge of God—not outwardly, but inwardly—will be brought to perfection by the vision we will then have 'face to face' after the judgment, but which now advances 'through a mirror, in a riddle.'†

†Eph 4:23; Col 3:10; 2 Co 4:16; 1 Co 13:12

—from *On the Trinity* 14.17*

238. *We know that if our earthly house of this habitation is dissolved, we have a building from God, a house not made with hands, eternal in the heavens.*†

†2 Co 5:1

Although we yearn to cling to Christ, we are yet unwilling to die. We endure [death] willingly—or rather, patiently—because we are given no other means of passing to union with Christ. If we

*237. *De Trin.* 14.17.23–19.25; CC 50A: 454,1/15; 20–455,24; 457,14/17

could reach Christ by some other way, who would be willing to die? Explaining our human nature—that is, a kind of association of soul and body—a sort of intimate state of doubleness and union in these two—in a certain place, the Apostle says that *we have a house not made with hands, eternal in the heavens*—that is, a state of immortality prepared for us. We are to be clothed with this in the end, when we rise from the dead.

—from the treatise on Psalm 68*

239. *Truly we who are in this habitation groan under our burden, because we wish not to be stripped but to be further clothed, so that what is mortal may be swallowed up by life.*† †2 Co 5:4

We are then burdened by a corruptible body, and knowing that the cause of this burden is not the body's nature and substance, but its corruption, *we wish not to be stripped* of the body, but to be clothed with its immortality. It will then be a body, but because it will not be corruptible it will not be a burden.

—from *On the City of God* 14*

240. 'You have saved my soul from its constraints.'† What shall I †Ps 31:7
now say of the constraint of mortality? We are constrained, and no one wants what constrains us. A harsh constraint, not to want what we cannot escape! If it were possible, we would be unwilling to die, and would will to become what angels are—but by some kind of change, not by death. As the Apostle says, *Truly we who are in this habitation groan under our burden, because we wish not to be stripped but to be further clothed.*† We want to reach God's kingdom, but we do †2 Co 5:4
not want death.

—from the treatise on Psalm 30*

*238. *En. in Ps* 68.1.3; CC 39: 903,21/31 passim
*239. *De Civ. Dei* 14.3; CC 48: 416,11–417,18
*240. *En. in Ps* 30.2.13; CC 38: 200,3/25 passim

241. *We groan under our burden*. This agrees with what is written in another place: 'The body that is perishing burdens the soul, and the earthly habitation presses down the mind that muses on many things.'† So [Paul] says, *We groan under our burden*, under the load of a perishable body. *We groan under our burden*. If you are groaning, lay down this load willingly! [Paul] said that he was groaning under this weight, he said that he was burdened under the load of a perishable body. See whether he wants to be stripped of this weight with which he is burdened, under which he groans.

†**2 Co 5:4**; Ws 9:15

It does not follow. What does he say? *In which we wish not to be stripped*. O voice of nature, admission of pain! The body is burdensome, the body is weighty, the body is perishable. People groan under it—and do not willingly abandon it. *We wish not to be stripped*, he says. Are you going to go on groaning? And if you are groaning under your burden, why do you not want to be stripped?

'No,' he says. See what follows. *We wish not to be stripped but to be further clothed*. I groan under an earthly garment, I hasten toward heavenly clothing. I want to receive the latter; I don't want to take off the former. *In which we wish not to be stripped but to be further clothed*.

Paul, may I understand you? What you are saying? For so great a heavenly garment to come to you over these rags of mortality and corruption, so that it is underneath and the other on top, the rags inside, the heavenly garment outside, would be an outrage. 'God forbid!' he says. 'This is not what I am saying. I *wish not to be stripped but to be further clothed*—not so that corruption may be concealed beneath incorruption, but *so that what is mortal may be swallowed up by life*.

You who know the Scriptures did well to shout out. But that no one ignorant of the Scriptures may suppose that the following words are mine—they are Paul's words, all of them are apostolic words: *We groan under our burden, in which we wish not to be stripped but to be further clothed, so that what is mortal may be swallowed up by life*. [Paul,] you are maintaining well what you say elsewhere, speaking of the resurrection of the body: 'For this corruptible [body] must put on incorruption, and this mortal [body] must put on immortality. When this corruptible [body] puts on incorruption, and this mortal [body] puts on immortality, then the saying that is written will come about: Death has been swallowed up in victory.' What he says here, *that what is mortal may be swallowed up by life*, is there, 'Death has been swallowed up in victory.' Death is nowhere—not below, not above, not inside, not outside. 'Death has been swallowed up in victory. Where, O death, is your strife?'† †1 Co 15:53–54

—from a sermon on the birthday of the apostles Peter and Paul*

242. *The one who perfects us in this very thing is God, who has given us the Spirit as a pledge.*† **†2 Co 5:5**

I have already given an answer when I spoke of the difference between present and future ages. Here we receive the strength both to contend and to be victorious through the Spirit as a pledge; there, lacking enemies outside and inside, we will enjoy an indescribable and everlasting peace. Those who want to possess here all that is to be had there give evidence that they have no faith

—from the second book against Julian*

243. *For all will stand before the judgment seat of Christ . . .* † **†2 Co 5:10**

Those [rites] the Church celebrates in committing the departed are not contrary to the Apostle's statement where he says, *For all will stand before the judgment seat of Christ, that each one may answer for what has been done through the body, whether good or evil.* Even the merit that makes these [rites] capable of benefiting them each one earned when alive in the body. They do not benefit everyone. Why do they not benefit everyone, unless on account of the different kinds of life which each led in the body?

—from *Enchiridion 113**

*241. *Serm.* 299.9; PL 38: 1374–75
*242. *Contra Sec. Iul. Resp.* 2.140; CSEL 85,1: 264,16/21
*243. *Enchir.* 29.110; CC 46: 108,16/24

244. We must do the judgment and righteousness that will benefit us later on, when each one will receive recompense *for what has been*
†Ibid. *done through the body, whether good or evil.*† By *through the body* the Apostle meant during the time each lived in the body. If somebody blasphemes with evil purpose and godless intent, but does not do it with any member of the body, that person will be guilty even though it was done without a movement of the body, since it was done during the bodily existence of that person.

—from *On the City of God* 17.4*

245. We may aptly reflect on the Apostle's words. He did not say that the one being judged must receive recompense *for what has been*
†Ibid. *done*† 'before the body.' Obviously souls do not exist before bodies. If they did exist before [bodies] the Apostle would surely have said, 'Just as *through the body*, so also before the body.'

—to Vitalis*

246. *If we are transported in mind, it is for God; if we are sober, it is*
†2 Co 5:13 *for you.*†

'You will see heaven opened, and angels ascending and descending upon the Son of Man.' Listen to the Apostle himself ascending and descending in a single passage, in a single sentence: *If we have been transported in mind, it is for God; if we are sober-minded, it is for you*. What does *we have been transported in mind* mean? That we see things 'of which no one is permitted to speak.' What does *we are sober-minded for you* mean? 'Have I decided to know anything
†Jn 1:51; 2 Co 12:4; 1 Co 2:2 among you except Jesus Christ, and him crucified?'† If the Lord himself ascended and descended, clearly his preachers too ascend by illumination and descend by preaching.

—from sermon seven on the Gospel of John*

*244. *De Civ. Dei* 17.4; CC 48: 560,223/30

*245. *Ep.* 217.6.22. This excerpt is not included in the MSS of the letters now extant. Vitalis was a layman of the church at Carthage.

*246. *Tract. in Ioh.* 7.22–23; CC 36: 80,9; 81,40/48

247. The word *exstasis* is Greek. In Latin, as I have been given to understand, we can explain it by one word if we say *excessus* or 'transport.' We understand two things by 'transport of mind,' either alarm,† or a direction toward things above, so that in some way things below slip from memory. All the saints who have had God's hidden mysteries that surpass this world revealed to them have experienced this 'ecstasy.' †Ps 31:22

Of this transport of mind—that is, ecstasy—Paul, when he spoke, implying [that he was speaking of] himself, said, *If we have been transported in mind, it is for God; if we are sober-minded, it is for you, for the love of Christ constrains us.*† He means, if we wanted to do and to contemplate only such things as we see in a transport of mind, we would not be with you, but would be engaged above—as if despising you. And when you follow us with faltering steps to higher and more interior matters, unless, again, we were constrained by the love of Christ, 'who, though he was in the form of God, did not regard equality with God as something to be grasped, but emptied himself, taking the form of a servant,'† and considered ourselves to be servants, not ungrateful to the one from whom we received such august things for the sake of those who are weak, we would not despise lower things, and would be indulgent toward those who cannot see the lofty things along with us. †**2 Co 5:13–14** †Ph 2:6–7

Therefore [Paul] said, *If we have been transported in mind, it is for God.* He saw what we see in a transport of mind, but he alone revealed his secrets. He says this, who says that he was caught up and borne off 'to the third heaven,' and heard unutterable 'words, which humans are not allowed to speak.' So great was his transport of mind that he could say, 'Whether in the body or out of the body I do not know; God knows.'† †2 Co 12:2–4

—from the treatise on Psalm 30*

248. *For the love of Christ constrains us; we are convinced of this: because one has died for all, therefore all have died.*† †**2 Co 5:14–15**

*247. *En. in Ps* 30.2.2; CC 38: 191,1/26 passim

†Jn 5:25 It is good for all to hear 'the voice of the Son of God,'† and to live by passing over to the life of godliness from the death of ungodliness. The apostle Paul says of this death, *Therefore all have died; and [Christ] died for all, so that they too who live may live no longer for themselves, but for him who died and rose on their behalf.*

All, without one exception, *have died* in sins, whether original sins or those added by [our] choice, either from ignorance, or by knowing and not doing what is right. And for all the dead one living person—that is, one having no sin at all†—died, *so that they who live* through forgiveness of their sins *may live no longer for themselves, but for him who* on behalf of all *died* for our sins *and rose* for our justification.†

†2 Co 5:21; 1 P 2:22; 1 Jn 3:5

†Rm 4:25

—from *On the City of God* 20.6*

249. *From now on, therefore, we know no one according to the flesh; and if we knew Christ according to the flesh, now we no longer know [him that way].*†

†2 Co 5:16

Of course it is clear to everyone now that the Apostle said this because of Christ's resurrection, since these words came immediately before: *so that they who live may live no longer for themselves, but for him who died and rose on their behalf.*† What does to live not for oneself but for him mean except to live, not according to the flesh, in the hope of earthly and perishable goods, but according to the spirit, in the hope of the resurrection, which has already taken place for them in Christ? And so the Apostle knew *according to the flesh* none of those for whom Christ *died and rose*, those who no longer lived for themselves, but for him, on account of their hope of future immortality, in the expectation of which they lived. In Christ this was no longer a hope but a reality. Even if he had known [Christ] according to the flesh while he was yet to die, [Paul] no longer knew him [that way], because he knew

†2 Co 5:15

*248. *De Civ. Dei* 20.6; CC 48: 707,17/28

that he had risen and that death would no longer have dominion over him.† †Rm 6:9

And because all of us are in this condition, in hope if not yet in reality, [Paul] goes on to say, *If there is a new creature in Christ, the old has passed away, and see, [everything] has become new! Everything is from God, who has reconciled us to himself through Christ.*† Everything, then, is a new creature—that is, a people renewed by faith, so that for the time being they may have in hope what will be brought to fruition later on in reality. They have now in Christ what they hope for in themselves. *The old has* now *passed away* with respect to hope, because this is no longer the period of the old covenant when people awaited a temporal and carnal kingdom from God, and *everything has become new* with respect to hope, so that we now possess the promised kingdom of heaven, where death and corruption will not exist. †**2 Co 5:17–18**

In the resurrection of the dead—with respect to hope no longer, but to reality—the old will pass away when 'the last enemy, death, will be destroyed,' and everything will become new when 'this corruptible [body] puts on incorruption and this mortal [body] puts on immortality.'† This has already taken place in Christ, whom Paul no longer knew *according to the flesh* with respect to the reality. Of those for whom [Christ] died and rose, with respect not to reality but to hope, [Paul] knew none *according to the flesh*, because it is by his grace, as same [apostle] says to the Ephesians, that we are saved.† †1 Co 15:26, 53 †Eph 2:5

—from *Against Faustus* 11*

250. *And if we knew Christ according to the flesh,* [Paul] said, *now we no longer know [him that way].* Surely those who know the Word become flesh spiritually do not know even Christ's flesh *according to the flesh.*† †**2 Co 5:16**; Jn 1:14

—from homily ninety-one on the Gospel of John*

*249. *Contra Faust. Manich.* 11.8; CSEL 25: 325,18–326,27
*250. *Tract. in Ioh.* 94.4; CC 36: 564,34/37

251. *We are ambassadors for Christ, as if God is exhorting you through us. We entreat you on Christ's behalf*—that is, as if Christ is entreating
†2 Co 5:20 you. For what? *To be reconciled to God.*†

If the Apostle exhorts and entreats us to be reconciled to God, we were enemies to God. No one is reconciled except from a state of enmity. Sins, not nature, made us enemies. How are we reconciled unless what separates us from him is removed? A medium separates us, but against this is a reconciling Mediator. The separating medium is sin; the reconciling Mediator is the Lord Christ. 'There is one God, and one mediator between God and
†1 Tm 2:5 humanity, Christ Jesus, himself human.'† To take away the barrier that separates us, which is sin, the Mediator came, and the priest himself became the sacrifice. Because he became a sacrifice for sin, offering himself as a whole burnt-offering on the cross of his passion, the Apostle, when he had said, *We entreat you on Christ's behalf to be reconciled to God*, as if we were asking, 'How can we be reconciled?' goes on to say, *Him who knew no sin [God] made sin*
†2 Co 5:21 *for us.*†

—from homily thirty-eight on the Gospel of John*

†Hos 4:8. Perhaps also Lv 6:24–26, 7:7; 1 S 2:12–17 in Augustine's text.

252. Under the old covenant the sacrifices for sins were called sins.† [Christ], whom these prefigured, truly became [sin]. Hence, after saying, *We entreat you on Christ's behalf to be reconciled to God,* the Apostle immediately added, *Him who knew no sin [God] made sin*
†2 Co 5:20–21 *for us, so that in him we may be the righteousness of God.*† He did not say, as we read in some faulty manuscripts, 'He who knew no sin made sin for us'—as if Christ himself sinned for us—but he said, *Him who knew no sin*—that is, Christ—God, to whom we need to be reconciled, *made sin for us*—that is, [made him] a sacrifice for sins capable of reconciling us.

[Christ], then, is made sin, as we are made righteousness—not ours but God's, and not in us but in him. In the same way [Christ] is made sin—not his but ours, not existing in him but

*251. *Ibid.* 41.5; CC 36: 360,9/14; 18/19; 23/33 passim

in us. By the likeness of sinful flesh† in which he was crucified he showed that, because sin was not in him, in a sense he would die to sin when he died in the flesh in which the likeness of sin was present. †Rm 8:3

—from *Enchiridion* chapter 41*

253. *Our mouth is open to you, O Corinthians.*† **†2 Co 6:11–12**

The breadth of the commandment is love, because where love is, nothing is restricted. The Apostle was in this breadth when he said, *Our mouth is open to you, O Corinthians, our heart is enlarged; you are not restricted in us.* In this, then, is 'your commandment exceedingly broad.' What is the 'broad commandment'? 'A new commandment I give you, that you love one another.'† Love, then, is not restricted. †Ps 119:96; Jn 13:34

Do you want to be unrestricted here on earth? Dwell in what is broad. Nothing anyone does to you restricts you, because you love what that person does not harm. You love God, you love the fellowship, you love the law, you love God's Church—they last for ever. You labor here on earth, but you will come to the promised recompense. Who takes from you what you love?

—from homily ten on the Letter of Saint John*

254. *The one who had much did not have more than enough, and the one who had less did not have too little.*† **†2 Co 8:15** (Ex 16:18)

What does *the one who had much did not have more than enough* mean? That what they had over they gave to those in need. And what does *the one who had less did not have too little* mean? That they received from one who had more than enough—*that there may be an equality*, as [Paul] says.† **†2 Co 8:14**

—in the explanation of Psalm 121*

---

*252. *Enchir.* 13.41; CC 46: 72,8–73,24
*253. *In Ioh. Ep.* 10.6; PL 35: 2058
*254. *En. in Ps* 121.9; CC 40: 1810,67–1811,71 passim

255. *For I have betrothed you to one husband, to present you as a chaste*
†2 Co 11:2 *virgin to Christ.*†

What [Matthew] said of the virgins coming to meet the bride-
†Mt 25:6 groom† we should understand, I think, in such a way that all those virgins taken together comprise the one who is called the bride—just as when all Christians come together in the Church we say that the children are coming together to their mother, although those same children comprise the one who is called their mother. The Church is now betrothed, and is a virgin to be brought to her wedding—that is, when she preserves herself from worldly corruption. She will be married at the time when, as all mortality passes away, she is made pregnant by an immortal conception. *I have betrothed you,* [Paul] says, *to one husband, to present you as a chaste virgin to Christ.* Moving from plural to singular, *you,* he says, *as a virgin.* [The Corinthians] can, then, be called both 'virgins' and *a virgin.*

—from *On Eighty-Four Questions* 61*

256. *And I am afraid that as the serpent deceived Eve by its cunning, so*
†2 Co 11:3 (Gn 3:1–6) *your minds too may be corrupted from the chastity that is in Christ.*†

A few women in the Church possess virginity of body, but all believers possess virginity of heart. In the matter of faith, the Apostle was afraid that virginity of heart may be corrupted by the devil—those who lose it are vainly virgins in body. A Catholic married woman takes precedence over a heretical virgin. The one is not a virgin in body; the other has become married in her heart—and not married to a husband, but to a serpent. And what of the Church? 'You will tread on the asp and on the basilisk.' The basilisk is king of serpents, as the devil is king of demons. 'And you will trample
†Ps 91:13 on the lion and the dragon.'†

—from the treatise on Psalm 90*

---

*255. *De Div. Quaest. LXXXIII* 59.4; CC 44A: 117,147–118,158
*256. *En. in Ps* 90.2.9; CC 39: 1276,18/30 passim

257. *If anyone gives you a slap in the face.*† †**2 Co 11:20–21**

The face is the feature by which people are recognized. We read in the Apostle's writings, *You put up with it if someone reduces you to slavery, or devours you, or takes [advantage of you], or puts on airs, or gives you a slap in the face.* Then he immediately added, *I say it to my shame,* in order to show what being slapped in the face means—it means being despised and disdained. The Apostle did not mean that they should not bear with such persons, but that they should bear with him. He loved them so much that he was willing to spend himself for them.† †2 Co 12:15

—from *On the Lord's Sermon on the Mount* 1*

258. *In Damascus, the governor of the nation of King Aretas guarded the city of the Damascenes in order to seize me, and I was let down in a basket through a window in the wall, and so escaped from his hands.*† †**2 Co 11:32–33** (Ac 9:25)

We recall, [Paul] says, the words of the one who said, 'When they persecute you in one town, flee to another.'† Who can believe that God intended that the flocks he purchased with his own blood should be deprived of the indispensable ministry without which they cannot live? Did he do this when the small child fled into Egypt, carried by his parents?† Can we say that he abandoned the churches he had not yet established? Was the Church which was there [at Damascus] deprived of an indispensable ministry when the apostle Paul was let down in a basket through a window, so that his enemy would not seize him, and so escaped from his [enemy's] hands? Was what had to be done not carried out by other brothers stationed in the same place? Surely the Apostle acted in accord with their wishes in keeping himself safe for the Church since he was the only one whom the persecutor was expressly seeking.

†Mt 10:23

†Ac 20:28; Mt 2:13–14

And so let Christ's servants, the ministers of his word and sacrament, do what he has prescribed or permitted. By all means let them flee from town to town when any one of them is being specially

*257. *De Serm. Dom. in Monte* 1.19.58; CC 35: 66,1432–67,1439

sought by persecutors, so long as the Church is not abandoned by others who are not being sought—let them provide nourishment for their fellow servants whom they know could not live otherwise. When the danger is common to all, however—that is, to bishops, clerics and laity—those who need the others must not be abandoned by those they need. Either all should move on to safe places, or those forced to remain should not be abandoned by those whose duty is to take care of their religious needs. Let them equally live, or equally suffer whatever the head of the household wishes them to endure.

—from a letter to Honoratus, bishop of the church of Thiara, when he asked whether bishops and clerics ought to withdraw from [their] churches at the onset of a barbarian attack*

†2 Co 12:7 259. *And lest the greatness of the revelations make me proud, I was given a sting of my flesh.*†

Here you recognize the Apostle enjoying *the greatness of the revelations* and fearing the onset of pride. That you may know that even the Apostle himself, who wanted to save others, still needed care—if you esteem his honor—hear what the physician prescribed to himself for his swelling: *And lest I grow proud over the greatness of the revelations.*

See, I can now ask the apostle Paul, 'Lest you grow proud, holy Apostle! Must you still be on guard against growing proud? Must you still be afraid of growing proud?' 'What are you saying to me?' he asks. 'Listen to what I am, and do not be high-minded, but be
†Rm 11:20 afraid.'† Listen to how a little lamb should go in where a ram is in such danger. *Lest I grow proud over the greatness of the revelations*, he says, *I was given a sting of my flesh, an angel of Satan to torment me.*

What sort of swelling is he afraid of, he who received such a stinging lotion? Say now that there was as much righteousness in him as there is in the holy angels. Or perhaps even a holy angel in heaven receives *a sting, an angel of Satan*, by whom to be tormented so as not to grow proud? God forbid that we suspect this of the

---

*258. *Ep.* 228.2; CSEL 57: 485,3–486,6

holy angels! We are human beings; we acknowledge that the holy apostles were human beings—chosen vessels, but still frail, still on a journey in the flesh, not yet triumphant in the heavenly homeland.

—from sermon two on the letter to the Romans, against the Pelagians who say that human beings can be sinless in this life*

260. *For this I appealed to the Lord three times, that it would leave me, and he said to me, 'My grace is sufficient for you, for power is made perfect in weakness.'*† †**2 Co 12:8–9**

We find that evil persons have asked and received, and good ones have asked and not received. What is worse than the demons? Yet they asked [to be sent into] swine and received [their request].† Do we find that God did not do what the apostles wanted, and fulfilled the desire of the demons? What shall we say, then, except that 'the Lord knows those who are his,' and that all of those who ask, receive.† But a doubt concerning the Apostle remains. Was the one who said, 'The Lord knows those who are his?' not among those who are his?

†Mt 8:31–32; Mk 5:12–13; Lk 8:32–33

†2 Tm 2:19 (Nb 16:5); Jn 16:24

Therefore, all who are his ask and receive. But we go on to inquire, in what respect [do they receive what they ask]? Those things we ask for on account of this temporal life sometimes help, sometimes harm. When God knows that they are harmful, he does not give them to those belonging to him who desire and ask for them. In the same way, a physician does not give whatever a sick person asks for, and refuses, as one who loves, what would be granted by one who does not love. [God], then, heeds all who are his with regard to their eternal salvation, but does not heed them all with regard to their temporal craving; he does not heed the latter in order to heed the former.

Finally, consider these words. When [Paul] did not receive what he *appealed to the Lord three times* for, [the Lord] said to him, '*My grace is sufficient for you, for power is made perfect in weakness.* Why do you want me to take from you *the sting of the flesh* which you have received

*259. *Serm.* 154.4.5–5.6; PL 38: 835–36 passim

to keep you from growing proud because of your revelations? Surely you are begging for this because you do not know the good it is doing you.'

Trust the physician. What he has laid on you is severe but useful. He causes grief, but brings forth health. *Power is made perfect in weakness.* Bear with weakness if you desire health; bear with weakness if you desire perfection, because *power is made perfect in weakness.*

—from a sermon on the Lord's words, 'Ask,
†Jn 16:24 and you will receive'†*

261. *If any do not love the Lord Jesus in incorruption, let them be anathema.*
†1 Co 16:22 *Maranatha.*†

[Paul] uses Greek and Syriac words together. He writes, *If any do not love the Lord, let them be anathema. Maranatha.* He wrote *anathema* in Greek—[it means] 'condemned'—and explained *Maranatha*—'until the Lord comes again.'

—in the dispute that [Augustine] had with Pascentius concerning faith, with Lawrence present as judge*

---

*260. *Serm.*; see PL 39: 1733

*261. *Appendix, Ep.* 20.15; PL 33: 1162–63. Pascentius was a layman, an Arian Count. This excerpt seems to be out of place.

Saint Augustine's Commentary

the Letter of Paul to the Church in Galatia

IF WE OR AN ANGEL FROM HEAVEN should preach a gospel to you different from what we preached, let that one be anathema!† †**Ga 1:8**

The Apostle did not want people to put their hope in him, but in the truth he was proclaiming. What he was saying was better than the person proclaiming it. *Even if we*, he says—that is not enough; listen to what follows—*or an angel from heaven*, he says, *should proclaim to you something different from what you have received, let that one be anathema!* He saw that a false mediator could transform himself into an angel of light and proclaim something false. Therefore, just as proud human beings want themselves worshipped in place of God,† to claim for themselves whatever they can, to make a name for themselves, and—if it were possible—to surpass Christ himself in glory, so too do the devil and his angels. The Donatists have Donatus in place of Christ; if they hear any pagan disparaging Christ, they bear it, perhaps, more patiently than if they hear someone disparaging Donatus. †2 Co 11:14; 2 Th 2:4

—from a sermon against the pagans, on January first*

263. *But even Titus, who was with me, was not compelled to be circumcised, though he was a Gentile.*† †**Ga 2:3**

[Paul] circumcised Timothy† for this reason, that they may not seem to the Jews, and especially to his relations on his mother's side—Gentiles who believed in Christ—to abhor circumcision as idolatry is to be abhorred, since the Lord enjoined the former and Satan prompted the latter. He did not circumcise Titus for this reason, that he may not give support to those who were saying that without that circumcision the Gentiles could not be saved, and who, to deceive the Gentiles, were boasting that Paul thought the same way. †Ac 16:3

He himself indicates this clearly enough when he says, *But even Titus, who was with me, was not compelled to be circumcised, though he was a Greek. Because of the false brothers brought in, who came in secretly to investigate our freedom, so that they may enslave us—to them we did*

---

*262. *Serm.* 197.4; PL 38: 1023

not submit even for a moment, so that the truth of the gospel may remain
†Ga 2:3–5 *with you.*† Clearly he understood that they had grasped his reasons for not doing what he had done to Timothy. In addition, because he could act with freedom he could show that these sacramental signs were neither to be sought as necessary nor condemned as sacrilegious.

—from a letter to Jerome on this text*

†Ga 2:9 264. *They gave to Barnabas and me the right hand of fellowship.*†

[Paul] says that he came to Jerusalem and discussed the gospel with the apostles. The right hand of fellowship was given him—that is, the sign of harmony, the sign of agreement—because in no way did he differ from what they had learned.

—from *On Eighty-Four Questions* 58*

265. *But when Cephas came to Antioch, I opposed him to his face, because clearly he was in the wrong. Until certain people came from James he used to eat with the Gentiles; but after they came he drew back and kept himself separate, fearing those of the circumcision party. The other Jews joined in his dissimulation, so that even Barnabas was led by them into this dissimulation. But when I saw that they were not walking consistently with the truth of*
†Ga 2:11–14 *the gospel, I said to Cephas before them all . . .* †

We must hold outright that in the teaching of religion no one is to lie in any respect. Hence the dissimulation on the part of Peter and Barnabas, by which they were compelling the Gentiles to behave like Jews, was rightly censured and reproved, lest it be harmful then, and prevail on later generations to imitate it. When the Apostle saw that they were not entering consistently

---

*263. *Ep.* 82.2.12; CSEL 34: 362,6–363,2

*264. *De Div. Quaest. LXXXIII*; Our printed editions lack this question; see the sermon of Caesarius of Arles (PL 38: 606) and *Clavis Patrum Latinorum*, nos. 368 and 1008.

into *the truth of the gospel* he said to Peter *before them all, 'If you, though a Jew, live like a Gentile and not like a Jew, how can you compel the Gentiles to live like Jews?'* But as to what he did himself by preserving and practicing certain legitimate observances according to Jewish custom to show that he was no enemy to the law and the prophets—God forbid that we believe that he acted dishonestly!

His opinion in this matter is certainly well known. It had been decided that the Jews who then believed in Christ were not to be kept from [observing] their ancestral traditions, nor were the Gentiles to be compelled [to observe them] when they became Christians. Thus those sacramental signs which had been established by divine command were not to be set aside as sacrilegious, nor yet accounted necessary now that the new covenant was revealed—as if without them no one who turned to God could be saved. There were some people who thought and preached this, even though Christ's gospel had already been received. These people Peter and Barnabas had joined in dissimulation, and therefore they were compelling the Gentiles to behave as Jews. It was a compelling—to proclaim that these things were so necessary—as if even after they had received the gospel, without them there would be no salvation in Christ. The mistaken opinion of some held this, Peter's fear dissimulated this, Paul's freedom refuted this.

—from *Against Lying*, to Consentius*

266. If Paul had done such a thing himself I would sooner believe that even he, after correction, could not neglect to reprove his fellow apostle, than that he could write dishonestly in his own or in any letter, much less in the one he prefaced with the words, 'In what I am writing to you, behold, before God, I do not lie.'† †Ga 1:20

—from a letter to Jerome on this question*

*265. *Contra Mend.* 11.25–12.26; CSEL 41: 504,12/13; 505,7–506,6. This Consentius seems to have been a Catholic layman living on one of the Balearic islands.
*266. *Ep.* 82.7; CSEL 34: 357,10/15

267. *And we believe in Christ Jesus, in order that we may be justified from the faith of Christ.*

†Ga 2:16 . . . *not from works*†—not because good works are in vain, since God repays according to each one's works, but because works come from grace, not grace from works. 'Faith that works through love' would accomplish nothing unless 'the love of God was poured out in our hearts through the Holy Spirit that has been given to us.' Faith itself would not exist in us if God did not 'distribute to everyone the measure of faith.'†

†Rm 2:6; Ga 5:6; Rm 5:5; 12:3

—from *To Paulinus, Bishop of Nola**

†Ga 2:16 268. [Paul] says that we are justified *from faith*,† because [faith] is the first thing out of which the rest are brought to pass.

—again, to Prosper and Hilary*

†Ga 2:20 269. *And I live, now not I, but Christ lives in me.*†

Listen to the Apostle Paul denying himself: 'The world has been crucified to me, and I to the world.'† Listen again to him denying himself: *I live*, he says, *not I*. The denial of himself is plain: *I live, not I*. But now follows a glorious confession of Christ: *but Christ lives in me*. What does 'deny yourself' mean? Do not choose to live for yourself. What does 'do not choose to live for yourself' mean? Do not do your own will, but the will of the one who dwells in you.

†Ga 6:14

—from a sermon on 'Those who love their life will lose it'†*

†Jn 12:25

†Ga 2:20 270. *Who loved me, and gave himself up for me.*†

The Apostle says, 'who did not spare his own Son, but gave him up for us all.'† Look, the Father 'gave up' Christ, and so did Judas.†

†Rm 8:32
†Mt 26:47–50; Mk 14:43–46; Lk 22:47–54; Jn 18:2–12

*267. *Ep.* 186.2.4; CSEL 57: 48,14/23 passim
*268. *De Praedest. Sanc.* 7.12; PL 44: 969
*269. *Serm.* 330.4; PL 38: 1459

Does it seem as if they did the same thing? Judas is a betrayer—is God the Father also a betrayer? 'Of course not!' you say. I do not say it, but the Apostle says 'who did not spare his own Son, but gave him up for us all.'

The Father gave him up, and he gave himself up. The same Apostle writes *who loved me, and gave himself up for me.* If the Father gave up the Son, and the Son gave himself up, what did Judas do? There was a giving up by the Father, a giving up by the Son, a giving up by Judas. One thing was done. What distinguishes the Father giving up the Son, the Son giving himself up, and Judas the disciple giving up his master?

Since the Father and the Son did this in love, while Judas did it in treachery, you see that you must consider not what people do, but the mind and purpose with which they do it. We find God the Father and Judas doing the same thing. We bless the Father, we abhor Judas; we bless love, we abhor wickedness. How much good has come to the human race from the giving up of Christ! Did Judas think of this, that he gave him up? God thought of our salvation, by which we were redeemed; Judas thought of the price for which he sold the Lord. The Son thought of the price he paid for us; Judas thought of the price he got for selling him. Different intentions bring about different results. One thing is done—if we measure it by the differing intentions, we find one thing to love, another to condemn, one to glorify, another to abhor.

—from homily seven on the Letter of Saint John*

271. *Abraham believed God . . .* † †**Ga 3:6**

Immediately he—that is, Abraham—was promised an heir, not the slave born in his house, but one who would come forth from Abraham himself. And again, [he was promised] countless offspring, not like the sand of the earth but like the stars of heaven.† Here it †Gn 18:10; 15:5,
seems to me the promise was of a posterity exalted in heavenly bliss. 22:17

*270. *In Ioh. Ep.* 7.7; PL 35: 2032–33 passim

The Apostle recalls this passage here in order to commend God's grace. *Abraham believed God, and it was reckoned to him as righteousness.* The circumcised were not to boast and be unwilling to admit the uncircumcised nations to the faith of Christ. When it came about that Abraham's faith was reckoned to him as righteousness, he had not yet been circumcised.

—from *On the City of God* 16.23*

272. *Christ redeemed us from the curse of the law, becoming a curse for us;*
†**Ga 3:13** (Dt 21:23) *for it is written, 'Cursed is everyone who hangs on a tree.'*†

Why is Faustus surprised that sin is a curse, that death is a curse, that the mortality of the flesh is a curse—found in Christ too, though he was without sin, from the fact of human sin? [Christ] took from Adam a body since the virgin Mary, who bore Christ, was from Adam. God had said in paradise, 'On the day you touch it you shall
†Gn 2:17, probably from memory; see Gn 3:3. die the death.'† This is the curse that hung on the tree. Let those who deny that Christ died deny that he was a curse; those, however, who admit that he died, cannot also deny that his death was from sin, and on this account is even called sin.

Let them hear the Apostle saying that 'our old self was crucified together with him,' and let him understand whom Moses called 'cursed.' For this reason the Apostle, following him, described Christ as *becoming a curse for us*, just as he was not afraid to say that 'he died
†Rm 6:6; 2 Co 5:15 for us all.'† 'He died' and 'he was cursed,' since death itself is the result of the curse, and all sin is cursed, whether it is the action that punishment follows, or the punishment itself—which in another way is called sin, because it results from sin.

Christ, however, took on our punishment without guilt in order to destroy our guilt, and also to bring our punishment to an end. 'God sent his own Son in the likeness of sinful flesh,' [Paul] said. By the fact of being mortal he possessed 'the likeness of sinful flesh.' [Paul] subsequently calls this 'sin,' saying 'so that from sin he may
†Rm 8:3 condemn sin in the flesh.'†

*271. *De Civ. Dei* 16.23; CC 48: 525,4/8; 19/25

But why would Moses shrink from calling *cursed* what Paul did not shrink from calling 'sin'? Moses added *everyone*—so as to say *Cursed is everyone who hangs on a tree*—not because he did not foresee that even righteous persons would be crucified, but because he clearly foresaw that heretics would deny that the Lord's death was real. They wished to separate Christ from this curse so that they may separate him from the reality of his death as well. If that death was not real, no curse hung on the tree when Christ was crucified because he was not really crucified. He added *everyone* so that no one would deny Christ's connection with real death if the foolish were to separate the honor shown him from the curse which is joined to death.

—from *Against Faustus* 14*

273. *The promises were made to Abraham and to his offspring. It does not say, 'and to offsprings,' as if to many, but as if to one, 'and to your offspring,' which is Christ.*† †**Ga 3:16** (Gn 13:15, 17:8)

Christ is one, head and body, as the Apostle teaches. He says of Abraham's offspring, 'If you belong to Christ, then you are Abraham's offspring,'† as he had said earlier, *It does not say, 'and to offsprings,' as if to many, but as if to one, 'and to your offspring,' which is Christ.* If Abraham's offspring is Christ, what else was said to those who were told 'then you are Abraham's offspring' except 'then you are Christ's'? †Ga 3:29

—from homily one hundred and five on the Gospel of John*

274. *Why then the law?*—as if to ask, 'What usefulness has the law?' *It was set down because of transgression.*† This is what [Paul] says elsewhere: 'The law came in so that trespass may increase.'† *It was set down because of transgression*—to bring low the neck of the proud, who attributed much to themselves, and who claimed sole credit for their wills, †**Ga 3:19** †Rm 5:20

*272. *Contra Faust. Manich.* 14.4–6; CSEL 25: 405,23–406,15; 18/19; 23/25; 28–407,1; 13/20; 408,5/8
*273. *Tract. in Ioh.* 108.5; CC 36: 617, 7/13

so that they supposed that their freedom of choice could achieve
righteousness on its own.

The law, then, *was set down because of transgression, until the
offspring would come to whom the promise was made, ordained by angels in*
†**Ga 3:19–20** *the hand of a mediator. Now a mediator is not of one. God, however, is one.*†
What does *a mediator is not of one* mean? It means that a mediator
is between two. We find what two things the mediator is between
when the same apostle says, 'There is one God, and one mediator
†1 Tm 2:5 between God and humanity, Christ Jesus, himself human.'† If you
were not lying there you would not need a mediator. Because you
are lying there and cannot get up, God has in a way extended to
you a mediator—his own arm. 'To whom has the arm of the Lord
†Is 53:1 been revealed?'†

If a law had been given that could give life, righteousness would come
†**Ga 3:21** *entirely from the law.*† If, then, no law *that could give life* was given, why
was [any law] given? [Paul] goes on to show why it was given—even
as it is, it was given as a help, so that you would not suppose yourself
healthy.

Scripture has included everything under sin, he says, *so that from the*
†**Ga 3:22** *faith of Jesus Christ the promise may be given to those who believe.*† When
you hear of one who makes a promise, look for the one who brings
it about. Human nature was capable of wounding itself through its
free choice, but, once wounded and injured, it is not capable of
healing itself through its free choice.

†1 Tm 1:8 'The law is good, if one uses it lawfully.'† What does using the law 'lawfully' mean? It means acknowledging one's illness
through the law, and seeking divine help for healing, since, as
I have said, *if a law had been given that could give life, righteousness would come* entirely *from the law*, and a Saviour would not
be needed, Christ would not come, and he would not seek the
lost sheep by his own blood. The same apostle says in another
place, 'For if righteousness comes through the law, then Christ died
†Lk 15:4; Ga 2:21 for nothing.'†

—from the fourth sermon on the letter to the Romans*

*274. *Serm.* 156.2.2–5.5; PL 38: 850–52 passim

275. *Therefore the law was our pedagogue in Christ, so that we may be justified by faith. But after faith has come, we are no longer under a pedagogue.*† †**Ga 3:24–25**

A follower of the letter treats allegorical words as if they were literal, and finds no other meaning beyond the literal word. One who hears 'sabbath,' for example, understands nothing but one day out of the seven that are repeated in a continuous sequence, and when such people hear 'sacrifice,' they do not go beyond the thought of what ordinarily happens to animal victims and the fruits of the earth.

Yet servitude [to the letter] among the Jewish people differed greatly from the practice of the other nations. They were indeed subject to temporal things, but in such a way that in them all one God was served. And although they were observing the signs of spiritual realities in place of the realities themselves, not knowing what they referred to, yet they considered it natural that by such servitude they were pleasing the one great God of all, whom they did not see. The Apostle writes that this observance was like that of small children *under a pedagogue*. For this reason those who clung stubbornly to such signs could not bear with the Lord's disparaging them when the time of their revelation had come, and hence they stirred up malicious accusations that he was performing cures on the sabbath.† †Mt 12:10; Mk 3:2; Lk 6:7

—from *On Christian Doctrine* 3*

276. *Whoever among you were baptized in Christ have put on Christ. There is neither Jew nor Greek, there is neither slave nor free, there is neither male nor female; for you are all one in Christ Jesus.*† †**Ga 3:27–28**

Have female believers, then, lost their bodily sex? But they are being renewed in the image of God there where there is no sex—'human beings were made in the image of God' there where there is no sex, that is, in the spirit of their minds.† †Col 3:10; Gn 9:6; Eph 4:23

—from *On the Trinity* 12.7*

*275. *De Doct. Christ.* 3.5.9–6.10; CC 32: 83, 9/12 passim. Some of section 227 is repeated here.

*276. *De Trin.* 12.7.12; CC 50: 367, 91/97. Some of section 187 is repeated here.

†Pr 31:21 277. 'All in her household have been clothed.'† Will her husband be concerned about the nakedness of their servants when he is living anywhere with such a wife? Who is this husband but Christ, and who is his wife but the Church? They 'have been clothed,' and with the best clothing! Do you want to know what the best is? *As many of you as were baptized in Christ* have been clothed, you *have put on*
†**Ga 3:27** *Christ.*† Absolutely 'all in her household' who *have put on Christ* 'have been clothed,' not only with regard to the procedures of the sacrament, but also in imitating his example, following in the steps
†1 P 2:21 of their Lord.†

—from a sermon on the valiant woman in the book of Proverbs*

†**Ga 3:27** 278. *As many of you as were baptized in Christ have put on Christ.*† Sometimes people put on Christ only to receive the sacrament, and sometimes to the point of sanctifying their lives. The first can be common to both good and bad, but this other belongs only to the good and devout.

—from *On the One Baptism* 5*

279. *When the fullness of time had come, God sent his Son, made of a*
†**Ga 4:4** *woman, made under the law.*†

The phrase *made of a woman* is offensive, since we profess that [Christ] was born of a virgin.

We profess only of the human that he was made—God is always making; he cannot be made in order to be. God cannot be made, but he is made to be something for someone, as we say, 'Lord, you have been made a refuge for us,' and, 'The Lord has been made
†Ps 90:1; 30:10 my helper.'† How many ways was he made, who never was made! Christ the Lord was made human in order to be—in order that the one who was always the creator may be a creature. While remaining

*277. *Serm.* 37.11.16; PL 38: 228–29 passim
*278. *De Bapt. Contra Donat.* 5.24.34; CSEL 51: 290,27–291,8 passim

God he was made a human, so that he may become what he was not, not that what he was may perish.

This is what he was *made of a* virgin. Why, [then], *of a woman*? Because among the Hebrews—this is the first language of Scripture—'woman' denotes the sex, not a loss of virginity. Read that when woman was formed, 'God,' it says, 'pulled out one of his'—that is, her husband's—'ribs, and built it into a woman.' Thus was Mary a woman. Thus was she told before she gave birth, before she conceived, 'Blessed are you among women.'† †Gn 2:22; Lk 1:28

—from a sermon on the prophetic words, that people should love righteousness and mercy and judgment, and should be prepared to walk with the Lord their God†* †Mi 6:8

280. When [Paul] said, *God sent his Son, made of a woman*,† he showed well enough that in being *made of a woman* the Son was sent. In that he was born of God he was in this world; in that he was born of Mary he was sent and came into this world. And a little farther on: †**Ga 4:4**

And so, since without any commencement of time 'in the beginning was the Word, and the Word was with God, and the Word was God,' without any time there was in the Word a time in which the Word may become flesh and dwell among us.† *When* that *fullness of time had come, God sent his Son, made of a woman*—that is, made in time—that people may see the Word incarnate. †Jn 1:1, 14

—from *On the Trinity* 2.5*

281. *To redeem those who were under the law*.† †**Ga 4:5**

See why Christ came, *to redeem those who were under the law*, that we may no longer be under the law but under grace. Who, then, gave the law? He gave the law who also gave grace—but the law he sent by a servant; he himself came down with grace. And how did people come to be under the law? By not fulfilling the law. One

*279. *Serm*. See PL 38: 316 b

*280. *De Trin*. 2.5.8; CC 50: 89,40/43; 91,87–92,93

who fulfills the law, then, is not under the law, but with the law. A person under the law is not raised but oppressed by the law.

The law makes everyone placed under the law guilty. This is the reason it is over their heads, to show sins, not to take them away. And because they could not fulfill the law by their own strength, and had become guilty under the law, they implored the help of a liberator. The law's guilt caused sickness to the proud; the sickness of the proud became the confession of the humble. Now the sick are confessing that they are sick—may a physician come and heal the sick! Who is the physician? Our Lord Jesus Christ.

—from sermon three on the Gospel of John*

282. *Because you are children, God has sent the Spirit of his Son into your*
†**Ga 4:6** *hearts, crying, 'Abba! Father!'*†

'You received a spirit of adoption of children in which we cry
†Rm 8:15 out, Abba! Father!'† See how [Paul] did not say here that the Spirit himself cries out in prayer, but [he said] 'in which we cry out, Abba! Father!' Yet he says in another place, *Because you are children, God has sent the Spirit of his Son into your hearts, crying, 'Abba! Father!'* Here he does not say, 'in which we cry out,' but he preferred to say that the Spirit himself cries out. The result is that we cry out, just as 'the Spirit himself intercedes with inexpressible groanings,' and 'it is the
†Rm 8:26; Mt 10:20 Spirit of your Father who speaks in you.'†

—from a letter to the priest Sixtus*

283. In accord with this will which God works in human beings, he too is said to will what he does not will himself, but what he causes those who belong to him to will—just as he is said to know what he has caused those who were ignorant of something to know. When the Apostle says, *coming to know God now, or rather to be known by God*, we are not allowed to believe that God is then coming to

*281. *Tract. in Ioh.* 3,2–3; CC 36: 20,15–21, 24; 28/1
*282. *Ep.*194.4.17; CSEL 57: 189,13/22

know those 'foreknown before the foundation of the world.'† He is said to know then what he then caused to be known. †**Ga 4:9**; 1 P 1:20

—from *On the City of God* 22.2*

284. Just as we rightly say that when God works in us he does whatever we do, so we rightly say that God rests when we rest by his favor. The Apostle admirably employed this way of speaking when he said, *coming to know God now, or rather to be known by God.* God was not then coming to know those 'foreknown before the foundation of the world,'† but because by his favor, not by their own merit or means, they were then coming to know him, [Paul] preferred to speak figuratively, in order to say that they were then known by him when he allowed them to know himself. He would rather correct the word, as if what he had said on his own was not rightly said, than to allow them to claim for themselves an ability [God] had granted to them. †**Ga 4:9**; 1 P 1:20

—from the *Literal Commentary on Genesis* 4.9*

285. *You observe days and seasons and months and years.*† †**Ga 4:10**

Certain things we may suppose to be trifling if the view of Scripture did not show them to be more serious. Who would think that the observation of days and months and years and seasons may be a grave sin—as those people observe them, who are willing or unwilling to begin anything on certain days or months or years because according to worthless human teachings they reckon such times lucky or unlucky—unless we weighed the seriousness of this evil from the anxiety of the Apostle, who tells such people, *I am anxious about you, that my work for you may have been wasted.*† †**Ga 4:11**

—from *Enchiridion* 81*

*283. *De Civ. Dei* 22.2; CC 48: 807,18–808,25
*284. *De Gen. ad Litt.* 4.9; CSEL 28, 1: 104,21/24; 106,4/13
*285. *Enchir.* 21.79; CC 46: 93, 46/47; 53/59

286. To be led into temptation is one thing, to be tempted is another. Without temptation people cannot be proved, whether to themselves—as is written, 'Those who have not been tempted, what kind of things do they know?'—or to others—as the Apostle says, *And your temptation in my flesh you did not scorn.*† This assured him that they were steadfast, because they were not turned away from love by those tribulations that had happened to the Apostle in his flesh. We are known to God, who knows all things before they occur, even before any temptations.

†Mt 6:13; Si 34:11; **Ga 4:14**

—from *On the Lord's Sermon on the Mount* 2*

287. *But you received me as an angel of God, as Christ Jesus.*†

†**Ga 4:14**

Because [Christ] himself speaks in his saints—as the Apostle says, 'Are you seeking a proof of him, of Christ, who is speaking in me?'—and although he may say, 'Neither the one who plants nor the one who waters amounts to anything, but God who gives the growth,'† because he did not want to be loved himself, but to have [God] in him loved—[Paul] bears witness to some people, saying that *you received me as an angel of God, as Christ Jesus.* In all his saints, then, [Christ] is the one to be loved, [Christ] who said, 'I was hungry and you gave me food.'† He did not say 'you gave them,' but 'you gave me.' So great is the love of the head for his body!

†2 Co 13:3; 1 Co 3:7

†Mt 25:35

—from a sermon against the pagans, on January first*

288. *Had it been possible, you would have plucked out your eyes and given them to me.*†

†**Ga 4:15**

Why was it impossible, except that in no way could it be done rightly? So too Job said, 'And would that I could slay myself'; so too the Lord said to Lot, 'I can do nothing until you arrive there.'† He said he could not, because without any doubt he could by might, but not by right.

†Jb 3:3, 10:18 (perhaps from memory); Gn 19:22

—from *Against the Letter of Gaudentius**

*286. *De Serm. Dom. in Monte* 2.9.30; CC 35: 119,646–120,654
*287. *Serm.* 197.5; PL 38: 1023–24
*288. *Contra Gaud.* 30.35; PL 43: 727 passim. Gaudentius was the Donatist bishop of Thamagudi in North Africa.

289. *It is written that Abraham had two sons, one from a slave woman and one from a free woman. The one from the slave woman was born according to the flesh, the one from the free woman through the promise. This is an allegory. These women are two covenants: one on Mount Sinai bearing children into slavery, which is Hagar. Sinai is a mountain in Arabia which corresponds to the present Jerusalem. It is in slavery with its children. The other is the Jerusalem above; it is free. . . .* † †**Ga 4:22–26**

This method of interpreting the passage, which comes down to us with apostolic authority, shows us how we ought to receive the scriptures of the two covenants, the old and the new. A portion of the earthly city became an image of the heavenly city, representing not itself but the other, and therefore being in bondage. It was not established for its own sake, but to represent the other, and since it was anticipated by another representation, the prefiguring image itself was prefigured. Sarah's slave Hagar and her son were a kind of image of this image. And since the shadows were to vanish with the coming of the light, [Paul] spoke of the free woman, Sarah, who represented the free city. Again, by another means of representation, she too served as a prefiguration. 'Cast out the slave woman and her son; the son of the slave woman will not inherit along with my son, Isaac'—or, as the Apostle says, *with the child of the free woman.*† †Gn 21:10; **Ga 4:30**

We find, then, in the earthly city two aspects. One reveals its own presence; the other serves to represent the heavenly city by its presence. Nature, flawed by sin, gives birth to the citizens of the earthly city, while grace, which frees nature from sin, gives birth to the citizens of the heavenly city. Hence the former are called 'vessels of wrath' and the latter 'vessels of mercy.'† †Rm 9:22–23

This also was represented in the two sons of Abraham. One, Ishmael, was born *according to the flesh* of the slave woman, who was called Hagar; the other, Isaac, was born according to the promise of the free woman, Sarah. Both were Abraham's offspring, but natural intercourse produced one, a promise representing grace bestowed the other. Ishmael, then, was born as humans are born, in nature's normal way of sexual intercourse. This explains *according to the flesh*—not that these blessings are not God's. But when God's gift, which God's grace would freely bestow on human beings to whom it was not owed, was to be represented, a son had to be given in a manner not indebted to the processes of nature.

—from *On the City of God* 15.2*

290. In the covenant properly called old, the one given on Mount Sinai, we find only earthly happiness explicitly promised. Hence that land to which the people was led through the wilderness is called the land of promise. There they were to find peace, a kingdom, spoils from victories over their enemies, an abundance of offspring and earthly produce, and other things of this kind. These are the promises of the old covenant. They also prefigure things of the spirit that belong to the new covenant—yet those who take on God's law for the sake of these earthly things are the heirs of the old covenant.

Those things craved in accord with the old self are promised and bestowed in accord with the old covenant, but those prefigured there as belonging to the new covenant require new people. The great Apostle knew what he was saying when he said that the two covenants were distinguished allegorically as the slave woman and the free woman. He attributed the children of the flesh to the old [covenant], and the children of the promise to the new, saying, 'It is not the children of the flesh who are the children of God, but the children of the promise are counted as descendants.' The children of the flesh, then, belong to the earthly Jerusalem, which *is in slavery with its children,* while the children of the promise belong to the
†Rm 9:8; **Ga 4:25–26** one that is *above*, our free and eternal mother in the heavens.† From this we clearly see who belongs to the earthly kingdom and who belongs to the kingdom of heaven. Those who by the grace of God understood this distinction even at that time became children of the promise; in God's hidden plan they were counted heirs of the new covenant, even though they appropriately administered the old covenant, which was divinely given in accord with the divisions of time, to the ancient people.

—from *On the Actions of Pelagius**

---

*289. *De Civ. Dei* 15.2–3; CC 48: 454,8–455,49; 457,7/13 passim
*290. *De Gest. Pelag.* 5.14; CSEL 42: 66,8–67,8

291. *These women are two covenants: one on Mount Sinai bearing children into slavery, which is Hagar. Sinai is a mountain in Arabia which corresponds to the present Jerusalem. It is in slavery with its children.*† †**Ga 4:24–25**

The old covenant properly belongs to the Jews. They were promised carnal blessings because they did not grasp spiritual ones. They were hoping from the Lord, in a wholly carnal way, for that earthly kingdom, and to be given an earthly life completely free from subjection to their enemies—and this is why they were serving [him]. Let us ask Christians if there are any such now? Such people belong to the old covenant. I am not asking their names, but their life. From such as these come heresies and schisms.

[Hagar] fled from Sarah's presence, and Sarah ill-treated her. Are you surprised? She ill-treated her physically. If the Donatist party has suffered some ill-treatment, on account of her pride the slave woman Hagar suffered from Sarah. Let Hagar hear the angel's voice: 'Return to your mistress!'† *But as at that time the one who was born according to the flesh persecuted the one who was born according to the Spirit, so now too.* We do not find Isaac physically persecuted by Ishmael, but only that the Apostle speaks of persecution. Note the passage where he says, *But as at that time the one who was born according to the flesh persecuted the one who was born according to the Spirit, so now too. But what does Scripture say? 'Drive out the slave and her child; for the child of the slave will not share the inheritance with the child of the free woman.'*† †Gn 16:6, 9 †**Ga 4:29–30** (Gn 21:10)

Let us look at the place where Scripture said this. What does it say in Genesis? It happened that while Ishmael and Isaac were playing, [Sarah] saw them playing.† Who did the persecuting? Who was persecuted? Sarah saw them playing and said, *Drive out the slave and her child.* Why? Because she saw them playing? Paul refers to the play as 'persecution' because that play was astray;† if astray, it is seduction and deception. All child's play is a semblance of more serious matters, and when an older boy plays with a younger one, he is, so to speak, leading him astray. He knows that he has other matters that he is intent on, and he feigns certain things to the boy—that is, to the weak one—when he plays with him. Ishmael was older, and steeped in wickedness. Playing with the boy, Isaac, he led Isaac astray, playing some tricks on the weak one. The mother perceived that the play was persecution. †Gn 21:9 †*quia lusio illa inlusio erat*

If Sarah, the mother, understands that play, the Church understands that play. Sarah said, 'Drive out the slave and her child; for the child of the slave will not share the inheritance with my son Isaac.' The Church says, 'Drive out the heresies and their children, for heretics will not share the inheritance with Catholics.' Why will they not share the inheritance? Were they not born of Abraham's seed? In what way have they the Church's baptism? They have baptism; Abraham's seed would make them heirs if pride did not cut them off from the inheritance. You were born by the same Word, by the same sacrament, but you do not come to the same inheritance of eternal life unless you return to the Catholic Church. You may be born of the seed of Abraham, but you will be outside, a child of the slave woman, on account of your pride.

—from a sermon on Hagar and Ishmael on the birthday of the martyrs*

292. *It is I, Paul, telling you that if you have yourselves circumcised, Christ*
†**Ga 5:2** *will be of no benefit to you.*†

Did he deceive Timothy, then, and make Christ of no benefit
†Ac 16:3 to him?† Or, if it was done deceitfully, was it then no hindrance? But [Paul] did not specify, and say either *if you have yourselves circumcised* truly, or deceitfully, but without limiting it he said, *if you have yourselves circumcised, Christ will be of no benefit to you.*

As you want to make room for your interpretation, so that you want us to supply the word 'deceitfully,' so I am not demanding unreasonably that you also allow me to interpret the words *if you have yourselves circumcised* as being addressed to people who wanted to have themselves circumcised because they supposed that they could not be saved by Christ otherwise. To those circumcised in this state of mind, with this desire and intention, Christ was of no benefit, as [Paul] clearly states elsewhere: 'If righteousness comes through the law, then Christ died for nothing.' He also makes this declaration, which you yourself have quoted: *You who are seeking to be justified by*

---

*291. *Serm.* 3; PL 38: 32–33

the law have been cut off from Christ; you have fallen from grace.† Surely he was rebuking those who were trusting in themselves, not those who were legitimately observing the [commandments] out of respect for the one who commanded them, not those who understood both why they were commanded—to foreshadow the truth—and how long they should endure. †**Ga** 2:21; **5:4**

—from a letter to Jerome on this question*

293. I say, then, that circumcision of the foreskin, and other things of this kind, were divinely given to the earlier people through the covenant that we call 'old,' to represent the future things that were to be fulfilled through Christ. When [the future things] had come, these were left for Christians to read solely for the purpose of understanding the prophecy that had gone before. They did not necessarily have to be carried out so that the revelation of faith, which was represented here as to come in the future, may come, as if it was still being awaited.

But although these things were not to be imposed on the Gentiles, they were not be withdrawn from Jewish practice as if abominable and reprehensible. Slowly and gradually, then, all this observance of prefigurations was to be ended by the passionate preaching of the grace of Christ, the only means believers have of knowing that they are justified and saved—not by those prefigurations of things once future, but then already coming and present, as at the calling of those Jews whom the Lord's physical presence and the period of the apostles found in this state. This was enough to suggest that [this observance] was not to be avoided as abominable and similar to idolatry, but that it had no further use, lest it be supposed necessary—as though salvation came from it and could not exist without it—as heretics supposed. [The heretics], while wishing to be both Jews and Christians, could be neither Jews nor Christians.

—again, from the same letter*

*292. *Ep.* 82.2.19; CSEL 34: 370,13–371,9
*293. *Ibid.* 2.15; CC 34: 364,21–365,16

†Ga 5:12 294. *Would that those who unsettle you would have themselves castrated!*†

Curses from prophecy do not come from the ill will of the one who calls them down, but from the prescient spirit of the one who declares them. Like a person vexed and displeased, the Apostle appears to have desired evil [when he said], *Would that those who unsettle you would even have themselves castrated!* Of course if you consider the character of the writer you will understand that by this choice and ambiguous expression he has wished them well. 'There are eunuchs who have had themselves castrated for the sake
†Mt 19:12 of the kingdom of heaven.'†

—from *Against Faustus* 16*

†Ga 5:13 295. *You were called to freedom, brothers and sisters.*†

This is our hope, brothers and sisters—that we may be set free by one who is free; and by setting us free he has made us servants. We were servants of overweening desire; now that we have been set free, we become servants of love. This the Apostle says: *You were called to freedom, brothers and sisters; only do not make freedom an occasion for the flesh, but serve one another through love.* No Christian should say, 'I'm free, I've been called to freedom. I was a slave, but I've been redeemed, and by my redemption I've been set free. I shall do what I want; if I'm free, no one can keep me from doing what I want.' However, if you commit sin because of what you want, you are the slave of sin. Then do not use your freedom to sin freely, but use it not to sin. Only if your will is holy will it be free. You will be free if you are a servant—free from sin, a servant to righteousness.

—from homily thirty-eight on the Gospel of John*

†Ga 5:13 296. *But serve one another through love.*†

---

*294. *Contra Faust. Manich.* 16.22; CSEL 25: 465,11/13; 18/23
*295. *Tract. in Ioh.* 41.8; CC 36: 362, 22/34

We cannot do this unless we all regard the weakness of others as our own, so that we bear it calmly, until those whose salvation concerns us are freed of it.

—from *On the Lord's Sermon on the Mount*★

297. *Walk in the Spirit, and do not carry out the cravings of the flesh.*† †**Ga 5:16**

[Paul] does not tell those who cannot avoid having them not to carry them, but not to carry them out—that is, not to fulfill them by consent of the will. His advice to the Galatians—*do not carry out the cravings of the flesh*—is the other side of what he says to the Romans, 'I do not find a way of carrying out the good.'† We do not carry out †Rm 7:18 [our cravings] in evil when we do not give the assent of our will to them, nor do we carry out our will in good as long as an impulse toward the things to which we refuse consent remains.

The cravings of the flesh are against the spirit, and the cravings of the spirit are against the flesh; for these are opposed to each other, so that you do not do what you want.† When *the cravings of the flesh are against the* †**Ga 5:17** *spirit, and the cravings of the spirit are against the flesh, so that* we *do not do what* we *want,* we do not carry out the cravings of the flesh, although they exist, nor do we carry through our good deeds, although they exist. As we carry out the craving of the flesh when our spirit also consents to evil deeds—with the result that its cravings are not against it but with it—so too do we carry out our good deeds when the flesh agrees with the spirit in such a way that it craves nothing contrary to it. This is what we intend when we crave the perfection of righteousness.

—from *Against Julian* 4★

298. It is most truly and accurately written that *the cravings of the flesh are against the spirit, and the cravings of the spirit are against the*

★296. *De Serm. Dom. in Monte* 2.19.65; CC 35: 162,1498/1501
★297. *Contra Iul.* 3.62; PL 44, 733–34 passim

†Ga 5:17 *flesh.*† Still, I suppose that the flesh can crave nothing apart from the soul. No one, learned or ignorant, can doubt this. The cause of this fleshly craving is not in the soul alone, much less in the flesh alone. It derives from both—from the soul, because no pleasure is felt apart from the soul, and from the flesh, because fleshly pleasure is not felt apart from the flesh. The Apostle describes the flesh that craves as *against the spirit*—no doubt the fleshly pleasure the spirit has from and with the flesh is *against* the pleasure it has by itself. Unless I am mistaken, it has this desire by itself, unmixed with the will of the flesh or the yearning for things of the flesh, when 'the soul longs and faints in the courts of the Lord.' [The soul] also has this by itself when it is told, 'You have craved wisdom; keep the commandment, and the Lord will give her to you.'†

†Ps 84:2; Si 1:26

Now when the spirit charges the members of the body with gratifying this desire which arouses only [the spirit]—as when we pick up a book, when we write, read, discuss or hear something, when we break bread for the hungry,† and offer other humane and merciful services—the flesh shows obedience, it does not produce a craving. When something that brings pleasure to the soul in accord with the flesh is *against* these and similar good desires, which the soul alone craves, then the flesh is said to have cravings *against the spirit*, and the spirit *against the flesh*.

†Is 58:7

—from the *Literal Commentary on Genesis* 10.16*

†Ga 5:18 299. *But if you are led by the Spirit, you are no longer under the law.*†

What being *under the law* in the way the Apostle finds faulty may be seems to me an important question. I do not believe that he said this on account of circumcision, or the sacrifices once made by our ancestors but not now made by Christians, or other things of this kind, but on account of this saying of the law, 'You shall not covet.'† This I grant Christians definitely must observe, and must preach with all the light the gospel sheds on it.

†Ex 20:17; Dt 5:21 (Rm 7:7)

*298. *De Gen. ad Litt.* 10.12; CSEL 28, 1: 309,8–310,8

[Paul] says that 'the law is holy, and the commandment is holy and righteous and good.' Then he adds, 'Did what is good, then, become death for me? By no means. Sin, that it may appear as sin, worked death in me through what is good, that the sinner, or the sin, may grow beyond measure through the commandment.' What he says here about sin growing beyond measure through the commandment he expresses elsewhere as, 'Law came in so that trespass may increase; but where trespass increased, grace abounded all the more.' Elsewhere again, when speaking earlier [in this letter] of the dispensation of grace which itself makes righteous, he says as if putting a question, 'Why then the law?' And he immediately responds to this question, 'It was set down because of transgression, until the offspring would come to whom the promise was made.'† He says that those whom the law makes guilty when they do not fulfill the law are *under the law* to their own condemnation when, by not understanding the blessing of grace, they proudly presume on their own strength, so to call it, for carrying out the commandments of God. 'Love is the fulfilling of the law'; 'God's love has been poured out in our hearts' not through ourselves but 'through the Holy Spirit that has been given to us.'†

†Rm 7:12–13 (see note to section 51), 5:20; Ga 3:19

†Rm 13:10, 5:5

The words of the law, 'You shall not covet,' bind a guilty person under it, and, if human weakness is not aided by God's grace, rather condemn a transgressor than set a sinner free. How much less, then, could those things commanded because of what they pointed to—circumcision and the rest, which had to be abolished while the revelation of grace was becoming more widely known—justify anyone? And yet they were not for this reason to be shunned, as if they were the diabolical sacrileges of the nations, even while the grace that such signs foreshadowed was beginning to be revealed. They were to be allowed for a while, especially to those who had come from that nation [of the Jews]. Later on, however, they were to be honorably buried, so to speak, by all Christians, and given up without blame.

—from a letter to Saint Jerome*

*299. *Ep.* 82.2.20; CSEL 34: 371,14–372,19; 21–373,9

300. *Now the works of the flesh are obvious. They are fornication, impurity, licentiousness, idolatry, sorcery, enmities, strife, jealousy, anger, quarrels,*
†Ga 5:19–21 *heresies, envy, drunkenness, orgies, and things like these.*†

An examination of the whole passage in this letter can answer the question of what it is to live according to the flesh. Among the works of the flesh that [Paul] called *obvious*, and listed and condemned, we find not only those connected with carnal pleasures, such as *fornication*, *impurity*, *licentiousness*, *drunkenness* and *orgies*, but also others not related to gratification of the flesh, which reveal vices of the soul. Do we not all understand that *idolatry*, *sorcery*, *enmities*, *strife*, *jealousy*, *anger*, *quarrels*, *heresies* and *envy* are vices of the soul rather than of the flesh?

It can happen that people abstain from sensual pleasure because of idolatry or the error of some heresy. Nevertheless, even then this apostolic authority convicts them of living according to the flesh, though they may seem to be restraining and repressing the appetites of the flesh. Their abstention from carnal pleasures proves that they are carrying out works of the flesh worthy of condemnation. Do those with *enmities* not have them in their minds? Do any speak in this way, to say to an enemy, or one they suppose is an enemy, 'Your flesh is set against me' rather than 'Your mind is set against me'? Why then does the teacher of the nations call all these, and others like them, in faith and truth, *works of the flesh*? His reason is that by the figure of speech by which a part signifies the whole he intends *flesh* to mean human nature itself.

If some people say that their flesh is the cause of whatever vices ruin their character, in that the soul lives this way because it is influenced by the flesh, they are not considering the whole nature of a human being carefully enough. The corruption of body that
†Ws 9:15 weighs down the soul† is not the cause but the punishment of the first sin. Corruptible flesh does not produce a sinful soul, but the sinful soul produces corruptible flesh.

Although certain inducements to the vices, and vicious desires themselves, may result from corruption of the flesh, we must not attribute all the vices of a wicked life to the flesh, lest we exonerate the devil, who has no flesh, from them all. Who is a greater enemy to the saints than he? Whom do we find more belligerent toward them, fiercer, a greater rival and more envious than he? And since he possesses all these [vices] but no flesh, how are they *works of the flesh*, if not that they are works of human beings whom, as I have said, [Paul] calls *flesh*? People do not become like the devil by having flesh, which the devil does not have, but by living according to themselves—that is, in a human way.

—from *On the City of God* 14*

301. *Those who belong to Christ have crucified their flesh with its vices . . .* † †**Ga 5:24**

In accord with our devotion, we who are about to celebrate the passion of the crucified Lord, which is now approaching, should make a cross for ourselves out of the sensual pleasures which we are to restrain. As the Apostle says, *Those who belong to Christ have crucified their flesh with its passions and cravings.* Christians ought always to hang on this cross, throughout their entire lives, which they lead in the midst of temptations. Not on this earth is the time for pulling out the nails, of which the psalm says, 'Pierce my flesh with nails by fear of you.'† 'Flesh' is fleshly cravings, the 'nails' are the precepts of righteousness. The fear of God pierces [the cravings] with [the precepts] and crucifies us as an offering acceptable to him. Hence the Apostle says, 'I appeal to you by the compassion of God to present your bodies as a living sacrifice, holy, pleasing to God.'†

†Ps 119:120. The Vulgate lacks 'with nails.'

†Rm 12:1

—from a sermon for Lent*

302. *Brothers and sisters, if anyone is detected in some transgression, you who are spiritual, instruct such a one in a spirit of gentleness.*† †**Ga 6:1**

'We know that the law is spiritual, but I am carnal.'† Does the carnal Apostle, then, who said to others, *You who are spiritual, instruct such a one in a spirit of gentleness*, address others as spiritual while he

†Rm 7:14

*300. *De Civ. Dei* 14.2–3; CC 48: 415,39–416,4; 417,34/41; 52–418,59 passim
*301. *Serm.* 205.1; PL 38: 1039

himself is carnal? But what did he say to those who were spiritual, since they were not yet safe, not yet in a state of heavenly and angelic perfection, not yet in the safety of their homeland, but remaining in the anxious circumstances of this pilgrimage? What did he say to them?

Certainly he called them *spiritual. You who are spiritual,* he said, *instruct such a one in the spirit of gentleness, taking note of yourself lest you too be tempted.* See how he has already called their life spiritual, but he is afraid of temptation for them—a weakness through which spiritual people could be tempted, not from the mind, but certainly from the flesh. They are spiritual because they live according to the Spirit, while still being carnal from their mortal part. The same persons are both spiritual and carnal. Here is the spiritual: 'With my mind I serve the law of God.' Here is the carnal: 'but with my flesh
†Rm 7:25 I serve the law of sin.'† Are the same ones both spiritual and carnal? The same. As long as they live here, so they are.

—from the second sermon on the letter to the Romans*

†**Ga 6:2** 303. *Bear one another's burdens.*†

Because the keeping of the old covenant involved fear, that the gift of the new covenant is love could not be more clearly indicated than in the passage where the Apostle says, *Bear one another's burdens, and in this way you will fulfill the law of Christ.* We take him to be referring to that *law of Christ* by which the Lord himself commanded us to love one another. [Jesus] put such great weight on his statement of the commandment that he said, 'By this everyone will know that you are my disciples, if you love one
†Jn 13:35 another.'† The obligation of this love is, *Bear one another's burdens*, but this obligation does not last forever. It will certainly lead to eternal happiness, in which no burdens we are commanded to bear for one another will exist..

—from *On Eighty-Four Questions**

---

*302. *Serm.* 154.5.7; PL 38: 836
*303. *De Div. Quest. LXXXIII* 71.1; CC 44 A: 200, 4/15

304. *All must test their own work, and then they will have glory in themselves and not in someone else.*† †**Ga 6:4**

Let us return to conscience, of which the Apostle says, 'Now our glory is this, the testimony of our conscience.'† Let us return †2 Co 1:12 to conscience, of which the same apostle says, *All must test their own work, and then they will have glory in themselves and not in someone else.*

All must test their own work, whether it flows from the vein of love, whether the branches of good deeds sprout from the root of love. *All must test their own work*, [Paul] says, *and then they will have glory in themselves and not in someone else*—not when someone else bears witness to them, but when their own conscience bears it. Inquire of your heart, and see what you have done and what you have sought there—your salvation, or windy human praise? Look within, for we cannot judge someone we cannot see.

—from homily six on the Letter of Saint John*

305. *All must carry their own burdens.*† †**Ga 6:5**

Unless you attribute different meanings to the word *burdens* you will doubtless suppose that [Paul] is contradicting himself in what he says, and this in a single passage where the words are so close together. After he had just said, *Bear one another's burdens*,† he said, *All must carry their own burdens*. But the *burdens* of sharing another's weakness are one thing, and those of rendering an account of our own actions to God are another. The former we share in bearing up with our brothers and sisters, the latter are personal and are borne by each alone.

†**Ga 6:2**. Augustine does not seem to be aware that in the Greek text the words are different.

—from *On the Harmony of the Gospels* 2.30*

306. *One who sows in the Spirit will reap eternal life from the Spirit. Let us not grow weary in doing good, for in due season we will reap.*† †**Ga 6:8–9**

*304. *In Ioh. Ep.* 6.2–3; PL 35: 2020–21 passim
*305. *De Cons. Ev.* 2.30.72; CSEL 43: 176,21–177,7

Although we ask some things in his name—that is, we ask in harmony with him as saviour and as teacher—he does not do them at the time when we ask; yet he does do them. We ask that his kingdom
†Jn 14:13; Mt 6:10 may come,† and it does not follow that he is not doing what we ask because we are not at once reigning with him in eternity. What we ask is delayed, not denied. Nevertheless, *let us not grow weary* in praying—like people sowing the seed—*for in due season we will reap.*

—from homily seventy on the Gospel of John*

†Ga 6:14 307. *Far be it for me to glory except in the cross of our Lord Jesus Christ.*†

[Paul] could have said, 'in the wisdom of our Lord Jesus Christ,' and he would have been speaking the truth. He could have said, 'in the majesty,' and he would have been speaking the truth. He could have said, 'in the power,' and he would have been speaking the truth. But he said *in the cross*. Where the worldly philosopher felt shame the Apostle discovered a treasure. By not despising a worthless wrapping he reached the treasure wrapped in it.

Far be it for me to glory, he said, *except in the cross of our Lord Jesus Christ.* You have supported an illustrious burden; everything you were looking for is there; and you have revealed what great thing was concealed there. What help [did it give]? *Through which*, he says, *the world has been crucified to me, and I to the world.* When would the world have been crucified to you if the one through whom 'the
†Jn 1:10 world came into being'† was not crucified for you?

†1 Co 1:31 And so, 'Let the one who glories, glory in the Lord.'† In which Lord? In Christ crucified. Where lowliness was is majesty, where weakness was is power, where death was is life. If you want to reach these latter do not despise the former. To glory in Christ's wisdom is no great thing; to glory in Christ's cross is a great thing. The reason the ungodly scoff at you is the reason the godly glory; the reason the proud scoff is the reason Christians glory.

Do not be ashamed of the cross of Christ. That is why you accepted this very sign on your forehead, as on the site of your

---

*306. *Tract. in Ioh.* 73.4; CC 36: 511,1/8

sense of shame. Think of your forehead so that you do not shrink away from another's person's tongue. The sign of the old covenant was circumcision in the hidden flesh; the sign of the new covenant is the cross on the observable forehead. There concealment, here revelation; that was beneath a veil, this on the face.

'Whenever Moses is read a veil lies over their hearts.' Why is this? Because they have not passed over to Christ. When you pass over to Christ every veil will be taken away, so that you who have your circumcision in a concealed place may bear the cross on your forehead. 'We, seeing with unveiled face the glory of the Lord as in a mirror,' [Paul] said, 'are being transformed into the same image from glory to glory, as by the Spirit of the Lord.'† You are not to attribute this to yourself, you are not to suppose that it belongs to you, and being ignorant of the righteousness of God and wanting to establish your own, fail to submit to God's righteousness.†

†2 Co 3:15–18

†Rm 10:3

Is anyone uncertain that Christ was foretold in that sign? The knife was of rock, 'and the rock was Christ.' The eighth day was the day of circumcision, and of the Lord's resurrection.† The Apostle, passing over from there, coming from there, passing over to Christ so that the veil may be taken away, knew the source of his glory. *Far be it for me to glory*, he said, *except in the cross of our Lord Jesus Christ.* What had he just said? *Even the circumcised do not keep the law, but they want you to be circumcised so that they may glory in your flesh.*†

†Jos 5:2–3; 1 Co 10:4; Gn 17:11–12; Lk 2:21; Mt 28:1–6; Mk 16:1–6; Lk 24:1–2; Jn 20:1

†Ga 6:13

What about you, Apostle? You transfer the sign to the forehead. '*Far be it for me to glory except in the cross of our Lord Jesus Christ,*' he says. 'Here I have what I was ignorant of. The new covenant has come; what was concealed has been revealed. For those who were sitting in the shadow of death, light has arisen.† What was concealed has been revealed; what was hidden is in the open. The Rock himself has come, has circumcised us all with his Spirit, and has fastened the sign of his humility on the foreheads of the redeemed.'

†Lk 1:79; Is 9:2

—from a sermon on [words of] the Apostle, 'Let the one who glories, glory in the Lord.'*

*307. *Serm.* 160.4–6; PL 38: 875–77 passim

†Ga 6:14 308. Let us too glory *in the cross of our Lord Jesus Christ, through which the world has been crucified to* us, *and* we *to the world.*† That we may not be ashamed of this cross, we have marked it on our very foreheads, that is, on the place we show shame.

—from a sermon on the Lord's passion*

---

*308. *Serm.* See *Sermones post Maurinos reperti*, ed. G. Morin, *Miscellanea Agostiniana* I [1930], 454,25/28; PL 39: 1724.

Saint Augustine's Commentary

the Letter of Paul to the Church at Ephesus

ALL THINGS ARE RESTORED IN CHRIST, those in heaven and those on earth, in him.† †**Eph 1:10**

All things in heaven are restored when what fell from there in the angels is restored from among human beings. Things on earth are restored when the human beings predestined for eternal life are renewed from their old state of corruption.

—from *Enchiridion* 62*

310. *In which we too have been renewed by chance.*† †**Eph 1:11**

'My chances are in your hands.'† As far as I can determine, †Ps 31:15
[the psalmist] has called the grace by which we are saved a 'chance.' Why did he call grace a 'chance'? Because in chance we have no choice, but everything depends upon the will of God. When we say, 'This person does,' or 'That one does not,' we are taking account of merits, and when we take account of merits we have choice, not chance. When God found us without merits, he saved us by the chance which was his will—because he willed it, not because we were worthy. 'By grace you have been saved through faith, and this is not from you; it is the gift of God.'† This chance is in a sense †Eph 2:8
God's secret will. Among humans it is chance, chance coming from the secret will of God with whom is no injustice. God shows no partiality,† but to you his secret justice is chance. †Rm 9:14; 2:11

—from the treatise on Psalm 30*

311. If unbelief is blindness, and faith enlightenment, whom did Christ find faithful when he came? The Apostle, born a member of the race of the prophets, says, *We too were once by nature children of wrath, like everyone else.*† If *children of wrath*, then children of †**Eph 2:3**
vengeance, children of punishment, children of hell. How was this *by*

---

*309. *Enchir.* 16.62; CC 46: 82, 34/39
*310. *En. in Ps* 30.2.13; CC 38: 211,11/18; 23/25; 28/31 passim. Augustine notices the oddity of his Latin translation. The obvious meaning of the Greek text is 'In whom we too have obtained an inheritance,' of the Vulgate, 'In whom we too are called by lot' or 'by chance.'

nature except that when the first human being sinned, vice implanted itself in us as a nature. If vice implanted itself in us as a nature, every human being is born mentally blind.

—from homily forty-one on the Gospel of John*

312. *Even when we were dead because of our sins, [God] brought us to life with Christ, by whose grace we have been saved.* What [Paul] expressed here as *[God] brought us to life with Christ* he expressed to the Corinthians as 'So that those who live may live no longer for themselves, but for him who died and rose on their behalf,' and what he says here, *by whose grace we have been saved*, he speaks of as something completed, because he holds it in hope. He says explicitly elsewhere, 'By hope we have been saved.'†

†**Eph 2:5**; 2 Co 5:15; Rm 8:24

This is why he goes on here, and counts as completed what is still in the future: *and he has raised us up together, and has made us sit together in the heavenly places in Christ Jesus.*† Christ is certainly already sitting *in the heaven places*, but we not yet. But because we now hold by a sure hope what is in the future, he said that we are *sitting together in the heavenly places*, not yet in ourselves, but already in him. And that we may understand that this is still in the future, he goes on and says, *So that he may show in coming ages the superabundant riches of his grace, in truth toward us in Christ Jesus.*†

†**Eph 2:6**

†**Eph 2:7**

—from *Against Faustus* 11*

313. *By grace you have been saved through faith.*†

†**Eph 2:8–10**

And that people may not immediately claim that faith for themselves, with the result that they fail to grasp that it is a divine gift, the same apostle—who says elsewhere that he obtained mercy in order to be faithful†—here added, *and this is not from you, but it is the gift of God; it is not the result of works, so that no one may become proud.* That we may not suppose that those who believe will be

†1 Co 7:25

*311. *Tract. in Ioh.* 44.1; CC 36: 381, 14/21
*312. *Contra Faust. Manich.* 11.8; CSEL 25: 326,30–327,19 passim

lacking in good works, he made another addition: *For we are his fashioning, created in Christ Jesus for the good works that God has prepared beforehand, that we may walk in them.* We are then made truly free when God fashions us—that is, forms us—not as human beings, which he has already done, but as good human beings. This he is now doing by his grace, that we may be 'a new creation in Christ,' in accord with what has been said: 'Create in me a clean heart, O God.'† God had already created [the psalmist's] heart, as far as the natural human heart is concerned. †2 Co 5:17; Ps 51:10

—from *Enchiridion* 31*

314. *For we are his workmanship, created in Christ Jesus for good works.*† **†Eph 2:10** This is grace. The words that follow, *that God has prepared beforehand, that we may walk in them*, is predestination. Predestination is the preparation for grace, while grace is the gift itself.

—from *To Prosper and Hilary**

315. *And to bring to light what is the plan of the mystery which has been hidden for ages in God who created all things, so that it may be made known to the principalities and powers in the heavenly places through the Church of the manifold wisdom of God.*† **†Eph 3:9–10**

This [mystery] was *hidden for ages in God*, yet in such a way *that it may be made known to the principalities and powers in the heavenly places through the Church of the manifold wisdom of God.* The Church was primordially in the place where, after the resurrection, this Church too is to be assembled so that we may be equal to the angels of God.† †Mt 22:30

—from the *Literal Commentary on Genesis* 5.23*

316. *For this reason I bend my knees before the Father of our Lord Jesus Christ, from whom all fatherhood in heaven and on earth takes its name,*

---

*313. *Enchir.* 9.30–31; CC 46: 66, 56/71
*314. *De Praedest. Sanc.* 10.19; PL 44: 974–75 passim
*315. *De Gen. ad Litt.* 5.19; CSEL 28, 1; 162, 9/19

that he may grant you, according to the riches of his glory, to be strengthened through his Spirit in your inner being, and that Christ may dwell in your hearts through faith.†

†**Eph 3:14–17**

Deservedly will the hearts of those who are satisfied live forever. Christ, who for now dwells in their hearts by faith, and afterwards by sight as well, is life; [now] they 'see through a mirror, in a riddle, but then face to face.'†

†Ps 22:26; 2 Co 5:7; 1 Co 13:12

We are now practicing charity in the good works of love, which reaches out in every possible direction in order to provide help—and this is *breadth*.† At present it bears adversity with forbearance, and perseveres in what it holds true—and this is *length*. All this it does in order to secure the eternal life promised it on high—and this is *height*. Charity exists in the hidden place where we are to some extent *grounded and rooted*, and where we do not scrutinize the reasons for God's will—by whose grace we are saved, 'not as a result of the works of righteousness we have done, but according to his mercy.' 'Of his own will he begot us by the word of truth,' and this will of his is concealed. Alarmed, in a sense, at the depth of the secret, the Apostle cries out, 'O the depth of the riches of the wisdom and knowledge of God! How inscrutable are his judgments and unsearchable his ways! For who has known the mind of the Lord?'†—and this is *depth*.

†The italicized words are from **Ephesians 3:18**.

†Eph 2:8–9; Tt 3:5; Jm 1:18; Rm 11:33–34

From this comes the passage from the Apostle you listed among others for explanation. *For this reason*, he says, *I bend my knees before the Father of our Lord Jesus Christ, from whom all fatherhood in heaven and on earth takes its name*. 'For what reason?' you ask. [Paul] had just said, *Because of this I pray [you] not to be enfeebled by my afflictions for you*.† This then is what he wants for them—that they not be enfeebled by the Apostle's afflictions, which he was enduring for them. This is why he was bending his knees before the Father. That they may not have reason to be enfeebled, he goes on to ask *that he may grant you, according to the riches of his glory, to be strengthened with power through his Spirit*. These are the riches of which he says, 'O the depth of the riches!' They have concealed causes, where we have no previous merits. 'What have we that we have not received?'†

†**Eph 3:13**

†1 Co 4:7

Then he goes on, adding what he asks for them. *In your inner being,* he says, *may Christ dwell in your hearts through faith.* This is the life of hearts, by which we live forever, from the beginning in faith, to the goal which is sight.

That rooted and grounded in love, he says, *you may have the power to comprehend, with all the saints.* This is fellowship in a divine and heavenly commonwealth. From this source the poor are satisfied, those who do not seek their own interests but those of Jesus Christ—that is, they do not pursue their own advantage, but they consider the common good, where everyone's salvation lies. Of the bread with which such people are satisfied, the Apostle says in a certain place, 'We, being many, are one bread, one body.'† †Ps 22:26; Ph 2:21; 1 Co 10:17

What, then, are we to *comprehend*? *What is the breadth*—as I have already said, good-will extends even to the point of loving our enemies; *and length*—so that we put up with annoyances patiently for the sake of the breadth; *and height*—so that on account of these things we hope for an eternal reward, which is in the heights above, not something temporary and without meaning; *and depth*—whence God's freely-given grace issues, in accord with the secret and hidden [nature] of his will. There we are *rooted and grounded*—*rooted* in terms of husbandry, *grounded* in terms of building. Since this does not come from human nature, the same apostle says in another place, 'You are God's husbandry, God's building.' All this is accomplished when, in this our pilgrimage, 'faith works through love.'† †1 Co 3:9; Ga 5:6

In the age to come, charity, perfect and full, with no evils to bear, does not believe with faith what it does not see, or desire with hope what it does not possess, but it will contemplate the immutable sight of truth forever. Its unending peaceful occupation will be to praise what it loves and to love what it praises. Of this [Paul] then says, *to know also the love of Christ that surpasses knowledge, so that you may be filled with all the fullness of God.*† †**Eph 3:19**

This mystery reveals the form of the cross. He who died when he willed died as he willed. He did not choose the kind of death he chose without a purpose—in this too he was the master of *breadth and length and height and depth.* In the beam fixed horizontally at the top is *breadth*; this refers to good works, because the hands are stretched there. *Length* is obvious in what extends from that beam to the ground. There he is in a sense stationed—that is, he persists and perseveres, which is an attribute of forbearance. *Height* is in that part of the beam that remains above the one fixed horizontally—that is, at the head of the crucified one—because the expectation of those who sincerely hope is above. The part of the beam that does not appear, that is fixed and hidden, but from which everything rises, signifies the *depth* of freely-given grace. There the talents of many—those being used to try to fathom [this mystery]—are ground to pieces, so that at the last they may be told, 'Who are you, O human being, to talk back to God?' The hearts of the satisfied poor will then live forever, the hearts, that is, of the humble who are on fire with love, who seek not their own advantage,† but who rejoice in the fellowship of the saints.

†Rm 9:20; Ps 22:26; Ph 2:21

—from *On the Grace of the New Covenant*, to Honoratus*

†**Eph 3:19**

317. *So that you may be filled with all the fullness of God.*†

Some people have understood the *fullness of God* that the Apostle speaks of in such a way as to suppose that we will be altogether what God is. 'If we will possess anything less than God has,' they say, 'and will be in any way inferior, how will we be *filled with all the fullness of God*? Because we will be filled, we will indeed be his equals.' I know that you turn away and abhor this error of the human mind, and you are right to do so. Also toward the end of the book:

'Happy are the pure in heart, for they will see God'—not when he will appear to them as a body out of some intervening space, but when he will come to them and make his home with them.† Thus they will be *filled with all the fullness of God* not when they themselves will be fully God, but when they will be perfectly filled by God.

†Mt 5:8; Jn 14:23

—from *To Paulina, On Seeing God**

*316. *Ep.* 140.25.62–26.64; CSEL 44: 207,23–208,19; 209,2–212,6 passim. Honoratus was a catechumen who was afterwards ordained a priest.

*317. *Ep.* 147.15.36, 23.53; CSEL 44: 309,17/26; 329,23–330,2 passim

318. *Making every effort to preserve the unity of the Spirit in the bond of peace—one body and one Spirit.*† †**Eph 4:3–4**

The Holy Spirit deigned to manifest himself in the tongues of all nations † so that those included within the unity of the Church, which speaks with the tongues of all, may understand that they possess the Holy Spirit. *One body* says the apostle Paul, *one body and one Spirit.* Take note of our members—one body is made up of many members and one spirit enlivens all the members. See how by my human spirit, which makes me a human being, I unite and give life to all my members! I order my members to move—I direct my eyes to look, my ears to hear, my tongue to speak, my hand to work, my feet to walk. My members' duties are various, but the unity of the spirit embraces them all. Many orders are given, many things are done; one gives the orders, one is served. What our spirit—that is, our soul—is to our members, the Holy Spirit is to the members of Christ, to the body of Christ, 'which is the Church.'† †Ac 2:1–11 †Col 1:24

And so that we will not think of a dead body, the Apostle says *one body* to indicate that it is *one* whole *body*. But, I ask you, is this body alive? It is alive. What gives it life? *One spirit.* If a member is severed from the body, does the spirit follow it? Yet, we still acknowledge it to be a member. So too in the case of those separated from the Church. You ask them about the sacrament, and find out. You ask about baptism, and find out. You ask about the Creed, and find out. This is the outward form. I am asking about the life. Unless you are enlivened by the Spirit, bragging outwardly about the form is useless.

—from a sermon on the holy day of Pentecost*

319. *To each of us grace is given according to the measure of Christ's gift.* To show that *Christ's gift* is the Holy Spirit, [Paul] immediately added, *Therefore [the psalmist] says, 'He ascended on high, he took captivity captive, he gave gifts to people.'*† †**Eph 4:7–8** (Ps 68:18)

---

*318. *Serm.* 268.2; PL 38: 1232–33 passim

It is well known that when the Lord Jesus ascended into heaven after his resurrection from the dead he gave the Holy Spirit. Filled [with the Spirit], those who had believed began to speak in the tongues of all nations.† †Ac 2:1–11

No one should be disturbed because [Paul] said *gifts* and not 'gift,' since he was quoting a text from a psalm. The psalm reads thus: 'You have ascended on high, you have taken captivity captive, you have received gifts in people.'† †Ps 68:18 Many manuscripts, especially Greek ones, have it thus, and we also have it like this in a translation from the Hebrew. The Apostle said *gifts*, not 'gift,' as the prophet did; but whereas the prophet said, 'You have received them in people,' the Apostle preferred to say that *he gave them to people.* This was so that we may draw the fullest meaning from the two texts, one prophetic, the other apostolic, since each possesses divine authority.

Each is true, both that *he gave to people* and that 'he received in people.' *He gave to people* as the head to its members; the same one 'received in people,' in his members. On account of his members he called out from heaven, 'Saul, Saul, why are you persecuting me?' and of his members he said, 'When you did it for one of my least ones, you did it for me.'† †Ac 9:4; Mt 25:40 Christ himself, then, both *gave* from heaven and 'received' on earth.

But, in addition, both the prophet and the Apostle said *gifts* for this reason, that through the gift that is the Holy Spirit held in common by all the members of Christ many *gifts* that are unique to each person are divided among them. *And he gave some to be apostles, some prophets, some evangelists, some pastors and teachers*. See why he called them *gifts*—as he says elsewhere, 'Are all apostles? Are all prophets?' and so on.† †**Eph 4:11**; 1 Co 12:29

—from *On the Trinity* 15.17*

320. *And he gave some to be apostles, some prophets, some evangelists, some pastors and teachers.*† †**Eph 4:11**

Concerning the prophets, the Apostle said that God *gave some* in the Church *to be apostles, some prophets*. I take it, as you yourself have

*319. *De Trin.* 15.19.34; CC 50 A: 509,30–510,57; 511,68/72

written, that in this place he means the *prophets* of whom Agabus was one,† not those who prophesied that our Lord was going to come in the flesh. We find *evangelists* who we do not read were apostles, like Mark and Luke. *Pastors and teachers*, whom you especially wanted me to distinguish, I suppose to be the same, as you thought as well, so that we do not take some to be *pastors* and others *teachers*. When he had mentioned *pastors* first he added *and teachers* so that *pastors* would understand that teaching is one of their duties. This was why he did not say 'some pastors' and 'some teachers' as he had distinguished the earlier ones by saying *some apostles, some prophets, some evangelists*. These, as being one thing, he embraced under two names, *some pastors and teachers.*

†Ac 11:27–28

—from *Questions*, to Paulinus, bishop of Nola*

321. [Paul] added here, *For the perfection of the saints in the work of ministry, in the building up of the body of Christ.* This is the house which, as the psalm chants, is built after the captivity,† since the body of Christ is being built of those rescued from the devil who was holding them captive. This house is called the Church. The one who overcame the devil 'took this captivity captive,' and to keep [the devil] from dragging down into eternal punishment with himself those who were going to be the members of the sacred head, [Christ] bound him first with the bonds of righteousness, then with those of power. The devil himself is called the 'captivity' which the one who 'ascended on high' and 'gave gifts to people'—or 'received gifts in people'—'took captive.'†

†**Eph 4:12;** Ps 95:1 Vulgate

†Eph 4:8; Ps 68:18

—from *On the Trinity* 15.19*

322. *Until we all attain to the unity of faith and the knowledge of the Son of God, to human maturity, to the measure of the age of the fullness of Christ.*†

†**Eph 4:13**

*320. *Ep.* 149.2.11; CSEL 44: 358,12–359,6 passim. Paulinus was bishop of Nola in Italy.
*321. *De Trin.* 15.19.34; CC 50 A: 511,72/83

If we say that larger bodies are to be reduced to the size of the Lord's body, much of many people's bodies will perish,
†Lk 21:18 although he himself promised that not a hair was going to perish.† I conclude, therefore, that we will all receive the physical size we had in the prime of life, if we die in old age, or the size we were going to have, if we died early. What the Apostle said of *the measure of the age of the fullness of Christ* we should take either to refer to something else—that is, that *the measure of his age* will be completed when the perfection of all the members is added to him as their head among the Christian people—or, if this was said of the resurrection of bodies, we should take it as saying that the bodies of the dead will rise in neither less nor more than their youthful form, but at the age and strength we know that Christ reached while here on earth. Even the most learned people of the present time define 'youth' as about thirty years of age. Past this age a person declines into a burdensome and senile period. This is why Paul did not say 'to the measure of the body,' or 'to the measure of the stature,' but *to the measure of the age of the fullness of Christ*.

—from *On the City of God* 22.15*

323. *Some to be pastors and teachers, for the perfection of the saints . . . in the measure of every part, promotes the body's growth in building itself up*
†Eph 4:11–16 *in love.*†

See what a *perfect man* is—the head, and a body made up of all the members who will be perfected in their own time. Additions are made to this body every day, while the Church—which is told,
†1 Co 12:27 'Now you are the body of Christ and his members'†—is being built up. *In accord with the operation*, [Paul] says, *in the measure of every part.* As there is a *measure of every part*, then, so is there *a measure of the fullness* of the whole body which is made up of all its members. *To the measure of the age of the fullness of Christ* is said of this. He also recalls this *fullness* in the place where he says of Christ, 'And he gave

*322. *De Civ. Dei* 22.15; CC 48: 834, 5/24

him as head over all things for the Church, which is his body and the fullness of the one who fills all in all,'† †Eph 1:22–23

—from the same book, chapter 18*

324. *Be renewed in the spirit of your mind, and put on the new self, which has been created according to God in the righteousness and holiness of truth.*† **†Eph 4:23–24**

Created according to God is expressed in another place as 'in the image of God.'† By sinning [humanity] lost *the righteousness and holiness of truth.* For this reason the image became disfigured and discolored. It recovers this image when it is reformed and renewed. †Gn 1:27

[Paul] did not want us to take his words *in the spirit of your mind* as referring to two things—as though 'mind' was one thing and 'the spirit of the mind' another. Every mind is a spirit, but not every spirit is a mind. God too is spirit†—God cannot be renewed because he cannot grow old. We also speak of a spirit in a person which is not mind—mental images in the likeness of bodies pertain to it. [Paul] says of it to the Corinthians, 'If I pray in a tongue my spirit prays but my mind is unproductive.'† He means that what is said is not understood; it could not even be said unless we had the image of a sound in our minds before we emitted the sound from our mouths. A human soul is also called a spirit; hence, in the gospel, 'And having bowed his head he gave up his spirit.'† The departure of the soul indicates the death of the body. And a little farther on: †Jn 4:24 †1 Co 14:14 †Jn 19:30

Because the spirit is spoken of in so many ways, [Paul] chose to speak of *the spirit of the mind,* [meaning] that *spirit* which is called *mind.* So too the same apostle says, 'In stripping off the body of the flesh.'† Surely he did not want us to understand two things, as though 'the flesh' was one thing and 'the body of the flesh' another. Because 'body' refers to many things that have no flesh—many 'heavenly bodies and earthly bodies'† are without flesh—he said 'the body of the flesh' [meaning] the body that is flesh. Thus he [calls] that spirit that is mind *the spirit of the mind.* †Col 2:11 †1 Co 15:40

—from *On the Trinity* 14.16*

*323. *Ibid.* 22.18; CC 48: 836,6–837,21; 31/38

*324. *De Trin.* 14.16.22; CC 50 A: 451,7–452,26; 453,34/42

325. The *old self* is not the body and the *new self* the soul, as some people have supposed, but the body is the outer self and the soul is the inner self. Oldness and newness are found internally. When the Apostle said *put off the old self* and *put on the new* † he was not telling us to lay aside the body but to change our lives for the better. He taught this subsequently. Wanting to explain his words he said, *So then, putting away lying, speak the truth, each of you, to your neighbor.*†

†**Eph 4:22, 24** (Col 3:9–10)

†**Eph 4:25**

—from a sermon on the Lord's passion*

326. No one should think that truth is to be spoken to a Christian and a lie to a pagan. Speak with your neighbor—every person is your neighbor. We are all neighbors from the circumstance of our earthly birth, and otherwise brothers and sisters by our hope in a heavenly inheritance. You should consider all people your neighbors, even before they are Christians—you do not know what kind of people they will be in God's sight. One who is now a Jew, a heretic, or a pagan, may perhaps, by God's mercy, be so converted to the Lord as to be worthy to have the first place among the saints!

Be angry, and do not sin.† If you are angry with your servants because they have committed a fault, be angry with yourself so that you do not commit one. *Do not let the sun go down on your anger.* Understand this in terms of time. If anger suddenly overtakes a Christian as a result of the condition and weakness of mortality that we bear, it must not be retained long, and carried over to the next day. Cast it from your heart before the visible light sets, so that the invisible light will not leave you.

†**Eph 4:26** (Ps 4:4 LXX)

But we can take this in another and better way. Our 'sun of righteousness'† and truth is Christ; his truth enlightens the human soul. The angels rejoice at him, but because of human weakness the eyes of the heart, although they blink before his piercing rays, must be cleansed by the commandments for us to contemplate him. When this sun begins to dwell in us by faith, do not let him see the great anger that is born in you, so that *the sun goes down on your*

†Ml 4:2 (3:20)

*325. *Serm.* See PL 39:1724

anger—that is, Christ leaves your mind, because he does not choose to dwell with your anger.

—from a sermon on this text*

327. I read, *Be angry, and do not sin,*† and how I was moved, my God! I had by then learned to be angry with myself for the past, in order that I may not sin for the rest of my life. †**Eph 4:26** (Ps 4:4 LXX)

—from *Confessions* 9*

328. *Do not give room to the devil.*† †**Eph 4:27**

God tempts in order to teach. The devil tempts in order to deceive—yet unless the person being tempted gives room, the ineffectual and ridiculous temptation is rejected. For this reason the Apostle says, *Do not give room to the devil.* People give room to the devil as a result of their cravings. Humans do not see the devil they are fighting with, but they have a ready remedy—let them overcome themselves inwardly, and they triumph over him outwardly.

—from a sermon on Abraham when he was tempted by God†* †Gn 22:1–14

329. *And do not grieve the Holy Spirit of God, with which you were sealed for the day of redemption.*† †**Eph 4:30**

The substance of the Holy Spirit, which makes him what he is, cannot be grieved. He possesses eternal and unchangeable happiness—or rather, he is eternal and unchangeable happiness itself. Since, however, he dwells in the saints so as to fill them with the love which demands that people rejoice instantaneously in the progress and the good deeds of believers, [this love] also demands that they be grieved by the backsliding and sins of those

*326. *En. in Ps* 25.2.2–3; CC 38: 142,1–143,7 passim
*327. *Confess.* 9.4 (10); CC 27: 138,65/67
*328. *Serm.* 2.3.3; PL 38: 29

in whose faith and devotion they were rejoicing. This grief is praiseworthy because it comes from the love that the Holy Spirit pours into us. For this reason the Spirit himself is said to be grieved by those who behave in such a way, so that the saints are grieved by their deeds for no other reason than that they possess the Holy Spirit. By this gift they are so good that evil persons sadden them, especially those they knew or believed were good. This grief is not only not blameworthy, but we must particularly praise and commend it.

—from the *Literal Commentary on Genesis* 4.10*

†**Eph 4:31** 330. *Let clamor and blasphemy be put away from you.*†

Blasphemy occurs when false statements are made concerning God himself. This is why to blaspheme is worse than to swear falsely. In swearing falsely God is made a witness to a falsehood, but in blaspheming false statements are made concerning God himself.

—from *To Consentius, Against Lying**

331. *Be aware of this, understanding that no fornicator or unclean or greedy person—which is idolatry—has an inheritance in the kingdom of Christ*
†**Eph 5:5** *and of God.*† I ask who sins more gravely, one who unwittingly falls into heresy, or one who wittingly does not give up greed, that is, idolatry? According to the rule which lays down that the sins of those with awareness are graver than sins of ignorance, greed with knowledge prevails in wickedness—unless perhaps the gravity of the wickedness involved in heresy does what a person with awareness does in greed, [in which case] a heretic who sins unwittingly is on a par with a greedy person with awareness.

—from *On the One Baptism* 4*

*329. *De Gen. ad Litt.* 4.9; CSEL 28, 1: 105,12–106,3
*330. *Contra Mend.* 20.39; CSEL 41: 524,4/7.
*331. *De Bapt. Contra Donat.* 4.5.7; CSEL 51: 229,14/17; 20–230,3

332. *Cleansing her [the Church] by the washing of water in the word, that he may present to himself a glorious Church, having no spot or wrinkle or anything of the kind; but that she may be holy and without blemish.*† †**Eph 5:26–27**

This is the bride of Christ, *having no spot or wrinkle.* Do you want to have no spot? Do what is written: 'Wash yourselves, make yourselves clean, remove the evils from your hearts.'† Do you want to have no wrinkle? Stretch yourself on the cross. You need not only to wash yourself but also to be stretched in order to be without spot or wrinkle. Washing removes sins; stretching produces a desire for the age to come. This is why Christ was crucified. †Is 1:16

Listen to Paul himself, after he was washed: '[Christ] saved us,' he said, 'not because of the works of righteousness which we have done, but according to his mercy, through the washing of rebirth.' Listen to him after he was stretched: 'Forgetful of what is behind,' he said, 'stretched out toward what is ahead, according to my purpose I pursue the prize† of the heavenly call in Christ Jesus.' Rightly, then, is he without any spot of iniquity, and without the wrinkle of a divided heart, as a good and faithful friend of the bridegroom; he had betrothed [himself] 'to one husband, to present [himself] as a chaste virgin to Christ,'† without spot or wrinkle.

—from a sermon on the three types [of disciples]*

†*palmam*, the palm branch awarded to a victor, symbol of a martyr's eternal reward (Vulgate, *bravium*).
†Tt 3:5; Ph 3:13–14; Mt 25:21; Jn 3:29; 2 Co 11:2

333. 'Then,' through his mercy, 'will the righteous' who are fully and perfectly cleansed 'shine like the sun in the kingdom of their Father'; then will the Church be wholly and completely without *spot or wrinkle or anything of the kind*, because then will it be truly *glorious*.† Since [Paul] said not only *that he may present to himself a Church having no spot or wrinkle or anything of the kind*, but added *glorious*, he indicated clearly enough when it will be without *spot or wrinkle or anything of the kind*—then, of course, when it will be *glorious*. Now, among such evils, such scandals, such a mix of the worst people, and such abuse from the godless, we are not to call

†Mt 13:43; **Eph 5:27**

*332. *Serm.* 341.11.13; PL 39:1501. See section 132, 388.

it *glorious* simply because kings are subject to it. In this is a more perilous and a greater temptation. Then, rather, will it be *glorious* when the Apostle's words come about: 'When Christ, your life, appears, then you also will appear with him in glory.'†

†Col 3:4

—from *On the Perfection of Human Righteousness*, to the bishops Paul and Eutropius*

334. *A man will leave father and mother and be joined to his wife, and they will be two in one flesh. This is a great mystery. I am speaking of Christ and the Church.*†

†**Eph 5:31–32** (Gn 2:24)

Does anyone not recognize that Christ—'who, though he was in the form of God, did not regard equality with God as something to be grasped, but emptied himself, taking the form of a servant'†—left his Father in this way, and that he also left his mother, the synagogue of the Jews, which clung in a carnal way to the old covenant, and was joined to his wife, the holy Church, so that in the peace of the new covenant the two may be one flesh? Though with the Father he was the God through whom we were made, he became partaker [of our nature] through his flesh, that we may be the body of which he is the head.†

†Ph 2:6–7

†Jn 1:3, 10; Eph 4:15–16; 5:23; Col 1:18

—from Against Faustus 12*

335. [The psalmist] is going to say some things in this psalm which seem inappropriate to Christ, to the pre-eminence of our head. And yet Christ is speaking, because Christ is in the members of Christ. That you may be sure that the head and his body are one Christ, he himself says, when speaking of marriage, 'They will be two in one flesh. So they are no longer two, but one flesh.'†

†Mt 19:5–6

Is he saying this of any sort of marriage? Listen to the apostle Paul. *And they will be two in one flesh,* he says. *This is a great*

*333. *De Perf. Iust. Hom.* 15.34–35; CSEL 42: 35,16–36,5. Paul and Eutropius were Augustine's fellow bishops in North Africa.
*334. *Contra Faust. Manich.* 12.8; CSEL 25: 337,2/14

mystery—that Christ and his Church are one person. *I am speaking of Christ and the Church.*† One particular person comes into existence, then, as if from two—from head and body, from bridegroom and bride. The prophet Isaiah also commends the wonderful and pre-eminent unity of [Christ's] person. Christ, speaking in him, says, 'He bound a wreath upon me as a bridegroom, and he adorned me with an adornment as a bride.'† He calls himself both bridegroom and bride. Why does he do this, if not because *they will be two in one flesh*? If they are *two in one flesh*, why should the two not speak as one? In Christ the Church speaks, and in the Church Christ speaks, the body in the head, and the head in the body.

†**Eph 5:31–32** (Gn 2:24)

†Is 61:10. Augustine's text scarcely corresponds to the Vulgate.

—from the treatise on Psalm 30*

336. *For your struggle is not against flesh and blood.*† †**Eph 6:12**

Human enemies, of whatever sort they may be, are not to be hated. When the evil hate the evil who cause them suffering, the number of evil persons is doubled. The good must love the evil even when they suffer, so that only one of them is evil. Consequently the apostle Paul, when advising us how we must be on guard against our enemies, tells God's servants who endure tribulations, dissensions, depravity, and the enmity of other human beings, *Your struggle is not against flesh and blood*—that is, not against human beings—*but against the principalities and powers and rulers of the world*. Of what world? That of heaven and earth? Far from it. The Ruler of this world is none other than its creator. But what does he mean by *world*? Those who love the world.

Accordingly he goes on and explains what he means: *the world of this darkness*. Of what *darkness* if not that of the unfaithful and ungodly? When the ungodly and unfaithful have become godly and faithful the same apostle addresses them in this way, 'Once you were darkness, but now you are light in the Lord.'† †Eph 5:8

You are struggling *against the spiritual powers of evil in the heavenly places*, he says, against the devil and his angels. You do not see your

*335. *En. in Ps* 30.1.4; CC 38: 193,2/23 passim

enemies, and you overcome them. 'Rescue me from the hands of
†Ps 31:15 my enemies, and from those who persecute me!'†

—from the treatise on Psalm 30*

†Eph 6:12 337. [Paul] called them *rulers of the world*† because they rule those who love the world. They are not ruling the world as if they are the rulers of heaven and earth—he is referring to sinners as *the world*.
†Jn 1:10 'And the world did not know him.'† Those who do not know Christ rule such a world.

—from the treatise on Psalm 77*

†Eph 6:16 338. *In all things taking the shield of faith.*†

'Take hold of arms and shield, and rise up to help me!' To see God armed on our behalf is a magnificent spectacle. And what is his shield, what are his arms? 'Lord,' [the psalmist] says, 'you have
†Ps 35:2; 5:12 surrounded us as with the shield of your good will.'†

And so that you may not suppose that a shield is always a shield, and a breastplate is always a breastplate, we see that the same apostle
†1 Th 5:8 referred in one place to 'the breastplate of faith'† and in another to *the shield of faith*. The same faith, then, can be both breastplate and shield—a shield because it intercepts and repels the weapons of the enemy, a breastplate because it does not allow your inner parts to be pierced.

—from the treatise on Psalm 34*

339. *Our struggle is not against flesh and blood*—surely because when humans persecute you the devil is acting through them, and before your enemies can injure you in the body they slay themselves in

*336. *Ibid.* 30.3.2; CC 38: 213,6/8, 13/29
*337. *En. in Ps* 76.7; CC 39: 1057, 11/15
*338. *En. in Ps* 34.1.2; CC 38: 300,3/7; 301,19/28 passim

the heart. *Our struggle is not against flesh and blood*—humans against humans, who are flesh and blood—*but against principalities and powers, the rulers of this darkness.*† As Christ governs and guides those who are light, so does the devil draw and incite to every kind of evil those who are darkness. †**Eph 6:12**

Therefore the Apostle urges us not to pray against evil people but against the devil who operates with them, and to do whatever we can to get the devil expelled and the people freed. When an armed man seated on a horse comes from the opposite side toward someone engaged in battle, the person is not angry with the horse but with the horseman. He wants to do all he can to strike the horseman and take possession of the horse. We must behave this way toward wicked people. We must work with all our strength, not against them, but against the one who is inciting them. Then, when the devil is overcome, the unfortunate person whom he had begun to possess may be set free.

—again, from a sermon on the same text*

*339. *Serm.* See PL 39: 1733–34

Saint Augustine's Commentary

the Letter of Paul to the Church at Philippi

PAUL AND TIMOTHY, *servants of Christ Jesus.*†

Just as there are two kinds of fear which produce two kinds of fearful people, so there are two kinds of servitude which produce two kinds of servants. There is a fear which perfect love casts out, and another, chaste fear, enduring forever.† †**Ph 1:1**

†1 Jn 4:18; Ps 19:9

Servitude exists in the fear that love casts out, and has to be cast out along with the fear. The Apostle linked the two things—that is, servitude and fear—when he said, 'For you did not receive a spirit of servitude again in fear.' The Lord too had in mind a servant connected with this kind of servitude when he said, 'I no longer call you servants, because a servant does not know what the master is doing.' This is surely not the servant characterized by chaste fear, who is told, 'Well done, good and faithful servant; enter into the joy of your master,' but the servant characterized by the fear that has to be cast out by love, of whom he says in another place, 'The servant does not have a permanent place in the household, but the son has a place there forever.'†

†Rm 8:15; Jn 15:15; Mt 25:23; Jn 8:35

Accordingly, since he has given us power to become children of God† we are not servants but children. In some wonderful and indescribable—but real—way we can then be servants who are not servants. We are servants with the chaste fear that belongs to the servant entering into the joy of the master, but not servants with the fear that must be cast out, the fear belonging to the servant who does not have a permanent place in the household.

†Jn 1:12

—from homily eighty-two on the Gospel of John*

341. *Some proclaim Christ through defiance, not sincerely, intending to raise up trouble against my chains.*† †**Ph 1:17**

These were hirelings who disliked the apostle Paul. Why did they dislike him except that they were looking for temporal advantages? But notice what he adds: *What does it matter while in every way, whether in pretense or in truth, Christ is proclaimed. In this I rejoice, yes, and will continue to rejoice.*† Christ is the truth†—let hirelings proclaim the †**Ph 1:18** †Jn 14:6

*340. *Tract. in Ioh.* 85.3; CC 36: 539,5/9; 540,12/29 passim truth *in pretense* and the children proclaim it *in truth.* The children are waiting patiently for the eternal inheritance of their Father; the hirelings want the temporal pay of their employer in a hurry. As for me, let me have less of the human glory that I see that hirelings envy, but let the tongues of both hirelings and children spread abroad the divine glory of Christ!

—from homily forty-seven on the Gospel of John*

342. We see those who have proclaimed something holy and pure in an impure way. Why does the Apostle rejoice? Not in their evil, but in the good of Christ's name.

—from *Against the Letter of Petilianus**

343. *[Do] nothing through contention or vainglory, but in humility regard*
†Ph 2:3 *others as better than yourselves.*†

We ought not to make this evaluation in such a way that we do not really do so but only pretend that we do. Instead, let us genuinely consider the possibility that others have some hidden qualities that may make them superior to us, even if our good qualities, which seem to make us superior to them, are not hidden. These thoughts, which crush pride and increase love, make our brothers' and sisters' burdens such that we can endure them not only calmly but even with great willingness.

Nothing makes us expend our energies in willingly bearing the burdens of others, as we are obliged to do, except the thought of how much our Lord bore for us. This led the Apostle to urge, *each of you not looking to your own interests, but to the interests of others. Let the same mind be in you that was in Christ Jesus, who, though he was in the form of God, did not regard equality with God as something to be grasped,*
†Ph 2:4–7 *but emptied himself, taking the form of a servant . . .* † As far as this is

*341. *Ibid.* 46.6; CC 36: 401,38–402,50
*342. *Contra Litt. Petil.* 2.80.180; CSEL 52: 111,13/20 passim. Petilianus, a Donatist, was bishop of Cirta in North Africa.

concerned, in that 'the Word became flesh and dwelt among us,' and being without sin assumed our sins, he paid no heed to his own interests but to ours. So we too should willingly 'bear one another's burdens'† in imitation of him. †Jn 1:14; Ga 6:2

—from *On Eighty-Four Questions**

344. [Heretics] say that the Son is less than the Father because it is written that the Lord himself said, 'The Father is greater than I.'† †Jn 14:28 The truth, however, shows that in this way the Son is less even than himself. How did the one who *emptied himself, taking the form of a servant,*† not become less even than himself? †**Ph 2:7** He did not take on *the form of a servant* in such a way as to lose *the form of God*. If then he took on *the form of a servant* in such a way as not to lose *the form of God*—since the same only-begotten Son of the Father is both in *the form of a servant* and in *the form of God*—in *the form of God* equal to the Father, in *the form of a servant* 'the mediator between God and humanity, Christ Jesus, himself human'†—can anyone fail to †1 Tm 2:5 see that in *the form of God* he too is greater than himself, and in *the form of a servant* he is less than himself?

Being made in human likeness, and in condition found human. God's Son, then, is by nature equal to God the Father, and *in condition* less. In *the form of a servant* which he took on he is less than the Father; in *the form of God* in which he existed even before he took it on, he is the Father's equal.

—from *On the Trinity* 1.7*

345. A *condition*† is something that happens to us so as to change our condition. Nevertheless there are differences. Certain things that happen to us are not changed by us so as to produce a condition, but they change us while in themselves remaining whole and constant. For example, when wisdom 'happens' to a person,

†*Habitus*. Augustine is reflecting on **Philippians 2:6–7** here.

*343. *De Div. Quaest. LXXXIII* 71.5.3; CC 44A: 204,95–205,103; 202,59–203,74
*344. *De Trin.* 1.7.14; CC 50: 45,13/25; 46,34/38

wisdom is not changed, but it changes the person, making the foolish wise. Certain things, however, happen in such a way as both to change and be changed. For example, food loses its character and is changed into our bodies, and at the same time we are refreshed by the food, changed from weakness and sickness into strength and good health.

A third type occurs when what happens is changed, and both produces a condition and is in some way shaped by what produces the condition. An example is clothing. When put on it receives a shape it did not have while off, while the body remains in its own state, both when clothed and when stripped. There can also be a fourth type, when what happens to produce a condition neither changes the thing that happens nor is changed by it. An example is the ring on a finger.

When the Apostle, then, was speaking of God's only-begotten Son, with regard to his divinity—according to which he is most truly God—he spoke of *equality with* the Father. He did not have to seize it, as *something to be grasped*—that is, as if it belonged to someone else—if he always continued in that *equality*, and did not choose to clothe himself with humanity and to appear to human beings as a human.

But he emptied himself, not changing his own form but *taking the form of a servant.* He was not converted or transformed into a human, with the loss of his unalterable immutability, but, although by accepting genuine humanity he himself, the one who accepted it, *was made in human likeness,* [he did not do this] for himself, but for those for whom he appeared as a human being. *And in condition he was found human*—that is, by having humanity *he was found human.* Those with unclean hearts could not find him *human*, and they could not see the Word with the Father except by [his] accepting something they could see, something that could lead them to the inner light.

This *condition* is not of the first type, for the abiding human nature did not affect the divine nature. Nor is it of the second type, for the human did not change the divine, nor was it changed by it. Nor is it of the fourth type, for he did not assume the human nature in such a way as neither to change the divine nor be changed by it. Rather it is of the third type, for he so assumed [a human nature] as to be ineffably changed, in both a more excellent and more intimate way, than a garment when a human person puts it on.

And so by the word *condition* the Apostle has adequately indicated what he meant by *made in human likeness.* [Christ] did not become human by a change in shape but by a change in *condition* when he put on a human nature. By uniting and adapting this to himself in some way, he joined it to his immortality and eternity. The *condition* that consists in the perception of wisdom and knowledge the Greeks call *hexis*, while that in accord with what we refer to as 'clothed' or 'armed' they call *schema.* From this we understand that the Apostle spoke of this latter type of *condition*, since in the Greek texts *schemati* is written, which we have in Latin as *habitu.* This word demands that we understand that the Word was not changed by the assumption of a human nature, just as a body is not changed by being clothed.

—from *On Eighty-Four Questions**

346. When the Apostle was commending [Christ's] obedience *to the point of death*, it was not enough for him to say that he *became obedient to the point of death*—not just any kind of death, but he added *even the death of the cross.*† No worse death existed among all the kinds of †**Ph 2:8**
death. When the most intense pains torment a person we use the word *cruciatus*, from *crux*, a cross. The crucified, hanging on a tree, fastened hand and foot to the wood by nails, were killed by a slow lingering death. They lived a long time on the cross, not because they chose a longer life, but because death itself was stretched out so that the pain would not end too quickly.

[Christ] willed to die for us. We are saying too little—he deigned to be crucified. By the worst death he slew all death. To the uncomprehending Jews it was the worst; but the Lord chose it. He was to have that very cross as his sign; that very cross—a trophy, as it were, over the vanquished devil—he was to put on the foreheads of believers, so that the Apostle may say, 'Far be it for me to glory except in the cross of our Lord Jesus Christ.† †Ga 6:14

—from homily thirty-three on the Gospel of John*

---

*345. *De Div. Quaest. LXXXIII* 73.1–2; CC 44A: 209,18–212,75 passim
*346. *Tract in Ioh.* 36.4; CC 36: 326,36/42; 44/54 passim

†Ph 2:12 347. *Work out your salvation with fear and trembling.*†

It is astonishing that when the crucified Christ is proclaimed, two people listen: one despises it, the other rises higher. Let those who despise it impute this to themselves; let those who rise higher not claim this for themselves, lest their pride forfeit what their humility deserved. Even those already walking in the way of righteousness lose their way if they attribute this to themselves and to their own strength. Therefore holy Scripture, teaching us humility, tells us through the Apostle, *Work out your and their salvation with fear and trembling*. And, to keep people from attributing anything to themselves because he said *work out*, he immediately added, *for it is*
†Ph 2:13 *God who is at work in you, both to will and to work for his good pleasure.*†

It is God who is at work in you. Therefore, make a valley with fear, and receive the rain. Furrows are filled, ridges remain dry. Grace is rain. Why are you surprised if 'God resists the proud, but gives grace to the humble'? *With fear and trembling*, then—that is, with humility.
†Jm 4:6=1 P 5:5 (Pr 3:34); Rm 11:20 'Do not be high-minded, but fear';† 'fear' so that you may be filled; 'do not be high-minded' lest you dry up.

—from the sermon on 'Unless you eat my flesh and drink
†Jn 6:54 (53) my blood, you will not have life in you'† *

†Ph 2:21 348. *All of them are seeking their own interests, not those of Jesus Christ.*†

†Jn 10:12 Who is a 'hireling'?† The apostle Paul describes some of those in the Church who have been set over others as *seeking their own interests, not those of Jesus Christ*. What does *seeking their own interests* mean? It means not loving Christ freely, not seeking God for God's own sake. It means pursuing temporal advantages, being avid for gain, coveting honors from others. When those set over others love these things and serve God for their sake, whoever is like this is a hireling. They cannot count themselves among the children. Of such as these
†Mt 6:5, 12 the Lord says, 'Truly I tell you, they have received their reward.'†

—from homily forty-three on the Gospel of John*

---

*347. *Serm.* 131.3.3; PL38: 730 passim
*348. *Tract in Ioh.* 46.5; CC 36: 400,11/20

349. *We are the circumcision, serving the Spirit of God.*† †Ph 3:3

That the Holy Spirit is not a creature is made perfectly clear in the place where we are told not to serve a creature but the Creator—not in the way we are told to 'serve one another through love,' which is *douleuein* in Greek, but in the way we serve God alone, which is *latreuein* in Greek—hence those who pay to images the service owed to God are called 'idolaters.' With regard to this service it is said, 'You shall worship the Lord your God, and him only shall you serve.'† This is expressed more precisely in the Greek scriptures, for they have *latreuseis*. †Rm 1:25; Ga 5:13; Mt 4:10 (Dt 6:13)

In addition, if we are forbidden to serve a creature with this kind of service—since 'You shall worship the Lord your God, and him only shall you serve,' for which reason the Apostle abhors those who 'worshipped and served a creature instead of the Creator'—the Holy Spirit is certainly not a creature, since all the saints pay service of this kind to the Spirit. As the Apostle says, *We are the circumcision, serving the Spirit of God*—which is *latreuontes* in Greek.

Many, even of the Latin manuscripts, have it thus: 'We who serve the Spirit of God,' as do all, or almost all, the Greek ones. In some Latin copies, however, we do not find 'we serve the Spirit of God' but 'we serve God in the spirit.' But can those mistaken in this, who refuse to credit a weightier authority, also find a variant in the manuscripts for this text: 'Do you not know that your bodies are a temple within you of the Holy Spirit, whom you have from God'?† †1 Co 6:19

—from *On the Trinity* 6*

350. *If anyone else seems to have confidence in the flesh, I have more: circumcised on the eighth day.*† **†Ph 3:4–5** (Gn 17:12; Lv 12:3)

In the ancient mysteries, the circumcision of baby boys was commanded to be done *on the eighth day*, since Christ, in whom the putting off of the sin of the flesh—represented by circumcision—took place † rose on the Lord's day. After the seven days, this is the eighth. †Col 2:11

—from a letter in reply to the queries of Hilary*

*349. *De Trin.* 1.6.13; CC 50: 42,112–44,135
*350. *Ep.* 157.3.14; CSEL 44: 462,1/5

351. *Because of the surpassing knowledge of Christ Jesus my Lord, for whose sake I have suffered the loss of all things, and I regard them as dung, in order that I may gain Christ.*†

†**Ph 3:8**

Paul had abandoned everything pertaining to the Jews that they held to be evil, primarily that 'being ignorant of God's righteousness, and seeking to establish their own, they have not submitted to God's righteousness'; next, that after the passion and resurrection of Christ, when the mystery of grace 'according to the order of Melchizedek' had been given and made manifest, they still supposed that the ancient mysteries were to be celebrated, not as customary and festive, but as necessary for salvation—yet if they had never been necessary the martyrdom of the Maccabees † in their defense would have been fruitless and vain; and finally this, that the Jews persecuted the Christian preachers of grace as enemies of the law.

†Rm 10:3; Ps 110:4=Heb 5:6 et al; Heb 6:20; 2 M 7:1 ff.

These and other errors and sins of the same kind [Paul] says that he condemns and regards *as dung* in order to *gain Christ*. He did not mean the observances of the law, if they were celebrated in the way of their ancestors, as he himself celebrated them. They were not to be regarded as necessary for salvation, as the Jews supposed they were to be celebrated. Nor were they to be celebrated with the deceptive pretense he had rebuked in Peter.†

†Ac 16:1–3; Ga 2:11–13

—from a letter to the priest Jerome*

352. Those who suppose that they are fulfilling the precepts of the law by a decision of their own will apart from the Spirit of grace want to establish their own righteousness, not to accept the righteousness of God. This is why the Apostle says, *That I may be found in him, not having a righteousness of my own that comes from the law, but a righteousness that comes from faith, a righteousness from God.*† Why does he call the *righteousness that comes from the law* his own, and reject it, but not *the righteousness from God that comes from faith*? Is the law not *from God*? Who except an infidel would say this? No,

†Rm 10:3; **Ph 3:9**

*351. *Ep*. 40.4.6; CSEL 34: 75,12–76,12

he is calling the *righteousness that comes from the law* 'his own.' He means the righteousness that leads people to suppose that the law is sufficient for them to carry out the divine commandments, trusting in their own strength.

[Paul] says that the *righteousness from faith* is therefore *from God.* God imparts a measure of faith to each person, and belief is connected with faith. God is at work in us even 'to will,' just as he was at work in the seller of purple cloth whose heart God opened to listen eagerly to what was said by Paul. For this reason we are not to say that even the Jews who believed in Christ, among whom was Paul, are altogether heirs *from the law*, but are rather [heirs] 'from the promise.' This was why it was said, 'In Isaac shall your descendants be called, because it is not the children of the flesh who are the children of God, but the children of the promise are counted as descendants.'† †Ph 2:13; Ac 16:14; Rm 4:13; Ga 3:18, 29; Rm 9:7–8

—from *Against Julian* 2*

353. *I press on to take possession, because Jesus Christ has taken possession of me.*† **†Ph 3:12**

The new life is begun now by faith and lived by hope. A time will come when death will be swallowed up in victory, when the last enemy will be destroyed, when we will be changed and made equal to the angels. We have now been taken possession of in fear by faith, but then we shall be taken possession of in love by sight. 'As long as we are in the body, we are away from the Lord, for we walk by faith, not by sight.'† †1 Co 15:54, 26, 51; Lk 20:36; 2 Co 5:6–7

Accordingly, the Apostle, who says *to take possession* as *Jesus Christ has taken possession of me*, is clearly admitting that he has not taken possession. *Brothers and sisters*, he says, *I do not consider that I have taken possession.*† **†Ph 3:13** Yet because our hope, based on the promise, is sure, when he said 'we have been buried with him by baptism into death,' he added 'so that, just as Christ rose from the dead by the glory of the Father, so we too may walk in newness of life.'† †Rm 6:4 We are

*352. *Contra Sec. Iul. Resp.* 2.158; CSEL 85,1: 280,21–281,41

walking in the reality of labor but in the hope of rest, in the flesh of oldness but in the faith of newness.

—from a letter to Januarius on the reason for Easter*

354. Beloved, as each of you can, 'make vows to the Lord your God, and perform them,' whatever each of you can. Let none look back,† none take delight in their former interests, none be diverted from what is ahead to what is behind; let all run until they arrive—we are running not with feet but with desire. In this life none should say that they have reached their goal. Who can be as perfect as Paul? And yet he says, *Brothers and sisters, I do not consider that I have taken possession; but one thing [I do]: forgetful of what lies behind, and stretched out toward what lies head, according to my purpose I pursue the prize of the heavenly call in Christ Jesus.*† You see Paul still running—and do you presume that you have already reached your goal?

†Ps 76:11; Lk 9:62

†**Ph 3:13–14**

—from the treatise on Psalm 70*

355. 'For a thousand years in your sight are like yesterday when it is past.' So must everything that comes to an end with time be taken as past. Hence the Apostle's purpose is ahead of him—*forgetting what lies behind*, where we are to understand all the things of time, and *stretching out toward what lies ahead*,† which is a longing for what is eternal.

†Ps 90:4; **Ph 3:13**. Here Augustine's text agrees with the Vulgate.

—again, from the treatise on Psalm 89*

356. 'Lord, make me know my end'—the end, not the course that is failing me; that end which, as he ran, the Apostle kept his eye

*353. *Ep*. 55.14.26; CSEL 34: 199,3–200,1. Januarius was a layman about whom nothing is known.
*354. *En. in Ps* 83.4; CC 39: 1149,21/31. Psalm 70 in the reference is an error for Psalm 83 (Hebrew 84).
*355. *En. in Ps* 89.5; CC 39: 1246,1/2; 1247,8/12

on. He was admitting his own imperfection as he sought something different elsewhere. *One thing [I do]*, he said; *forgetful of what lies behind, and stretched out toward what lies ahead, according to my purpose I pursue the prize of the heavenly call in God.*† *According to my purpose*, not my achievement, *I pursue the prize of the heavenly call of God in Christ*. [Christ] is the end. This is what Juduthun wanted, to become known to himself while he was still here on earth, that he may know what he was lacking. Then, by a kind of sprinkling of the Lord's drops coming from the cloud of the scriptures, he may come like a deer to the fountain of life, see light in that light, and be hidden in God's countenance from the disturbance of human beings.†

†Ps 39:4; **Ph 3:13–14**

—in the explanation of Psalm 38*

†Ps 39 title; Ps 42:1; Ps 36:9; Ps 31:20

357. *According to my purpose I pursue the prize of the heavenly call.* [Paul] described himself as stretching out, and as pursuing *according to* his *purpose*. He felt he was too little to contain 'what eye has not seen, nor ear heard, nor has it ascended into the human heart.'† This is our life, to be exercised by desiring. But a holy desire exercises us only to the extent that we cut off our desires from the love of the world.

†**Ph 3:14**; 1 Co 2:9

—from homily four on the Letter of John*

358. *Let those of us then who are perfect adopt this attitude.*†

†**Ph 3:15**

Let as many of us then who are perfect adopt this attitude—that is, let as many of us who are running perfectly *adopt this attitude*. We are not yet perfect, so as to arrive at the point to which we are still running in a perfect way. Thus 'when what is perfect comes, what is partially so may be destroyed'—that is, when it is no longer partial but complete. Reality itself—not what is believed and hoped, but what is seen and possessed—will succeed to faith and hope at once. Love, which is the greatest of these three,† is not to be taken away, but increased and fulfilled, as it contemplates what it used to believe

†1 Co 13:10, 13

*356. *En. in Ps* 38.5–6; CC 38: 406,30–407,1; 35/3; 10/13; 19/20; 28/30; 34/37
*357. *In Ioh. Ep.* 4.6; PL 35: 2009

and attains what it used to hope for. In this fullness of love will the commandment be fulfilled, 'You shall love the Lord your God with
†Mt 22:37; Mk 12:30; Lk 10:27 (Dt 6:5) all your heart, and with all your soul, and with all your mind.'†

As long as any of the carnal covetousness which is to be curbed by self-restraint remains, we do not love God entirely, 'with all our soul.' The flesh does not covet apart from the soul, even though we say that the flesh covets because the soul covets carnally. At that time will the righteous be without any sin at all, because no law in
†Rm 7:23 their members will be at war with the law of their minds;† then will they truly love God will all their heart, with all their soul, and with all their mind, which is the first and greatest commandment. Why is this degree of perfection enjoined on human beings even though no one can possess it in this life? People do not run well if they do not know where they are running. And how would they know if no commandments pointed it out?

—from *On the Perfection of Human Righteousness*, to the bishops Paul and Eutropius*

359. *If you think differently about anything, even this God has revealed to you. Nevertheless, whatever the stage we have reached, that we may be in*
†Ph 3:15–16 *accord let us continue on the same course.*†

If we *continue on the course we have reached, God has revealed even this* to us—not only what we do not know but should know, but even if we *think differently about anything. We have reached* the way of faith—let us keep to it tenaciously. It leads to the chamber of the King,
†Est 2:16; Col 2:3 'in whom are hidden all the treasures of wisdom and knowledge.'† We must keep walking, making progress, and growing, in order that our hearts may be capable of receiving those things we cannot now receive. If the last day finds us making progress, we will learn there what we have been unable to learn here.

—from homily fifty on the Gospel of John*

*358. *De Perf. Iustit. Hom.* 8.19; CSEL 42:15,15–18,12. Augustine is trying to account for the contradiction between verse 12 (where Paul says he is 'not yet perfect') and verse 15 ('as many as are perfect') of Philippians 3.
*359. *Tract in Ioh.* 53.7; CC 36: 455, 9/15; 18/21

360. I hope from God's mercy that he will make me persevering in all the truths that I am sure of. If I *think differently about anything*,† that too he will reveal to me, whether by hidden inspirations and admonitions, or by his own unmistakable words, or by discussions with my friends. †**Ph 3:15**

—from *On the Holy Trinity* 1.3*

361. *Let your requests be made known in God's presence.*† †**Ph 4:6**

We should not take this to mean that they are to *be made known* to God, who knew them even before they came to exist. They are to *be made known* to us *in God's presence* by our patient endurance, not in the presence of human beings by our ostentatious display. Or perhaps they are even to *be made known* in the presence of the angels, who are *in God's presence*, that in some way they may offer them to God, and consult with him about them. Then they can report to us, either openly or secretly, what they recognize to be his will, which must be fulfilled. The angel said to [Tobias], 'When you [and Sarah] were at prayer, I offered your prayer in the sight of the splendor of God.'† †Tb 12:12 (LXX)

—to Proba, on praying to God*

362. *And may the peace of God, which surpasses all understanding, guard your hearts.*† †**Ph 4:7**

Now let us see, with the help the Lord grants, what the saints—when their flesh no longer lives carnally, but spiritually—are going to be doing in their immortal and spiritual bodies. There is *the peace of God, which*, as the Apostle says, *surpasses all understanding*. What *understanding*, if not ours—or perhaps even that of the holy angels? It does not [surpass] God's too. If, then, the saints are going to live in *the peace of God* they will surely be living in that peace that *surpasses all understanding*. We cannot doubt that it surpasses ours.

*360. *De Trin.* 1.3.5; CC 50: 33,41–34,45
*361. *Ep.* 130.9.18; CSEL 44: 61, 3/13.

If it also surpasses that of the angels—so that the one who said *all understanding* seems not to have excepted them—we must take the saying to mean that we cannot know, as God knows, *the peace of God* which belongs to God himself.

—from *On the City of God* 22.29*

363. *I rejoice in the Lord exceedingly that now at last your concern for me*
†Ph 4:10 *has blossomed again.*†

In those who bestow gifts, the fruit is not in what they give, but in the spirit in which they give it. I see the obvious source of the joy of the one who served God and not his belly. I see it and I wish him great joy. [Paul] had received from the Philippians what
†Ph 3:19, 4:18 they had sent through Epaphroditus.†

But still I see the source of his joy. He is nourished from the source of his joy, because he is speaking in the truth. *I rejoice richly,* he says, *in the Lord, because now at last your thought for me has sprung up again; indeed, you were thinking of me, but you were weary.* They had grown weak from that long-lasting weariness, and the fruit of their good works had, so to speak, withered. He rejoices for them since they are springing up again, not for himself because they are relieving his needs.

This was why he went on and said, *I am not saying that I lack anything; I have learned to be content in whatever state I am. I know how to have little, and I know how to have plenty. In any and all circumstances*
†Ph 4:11–12 *I have been satisfied . . .* †

What is the source of your joy, then, O great Paul? What is the source of your joy, of your nourishment? What nourishes you? Happiness? Let us listen to what follows. *Nevertheless,* he says, *you*
†Ph 4:14 *have done well in sharing my distress.*† This is the source of his joy, this nourishes him, that they *have done well*, not that his need has been relieved. He is the one who says to you, 'You gave me room when
†Ps 4:1 I was in distress,'† because he knows how to have plenty and how to suffer poverty in you who strengthen him.

---

*362. *De Civ. Dei* 22.29; CC 48: 856, 1/4; 8–857,17

You also know, he says, *O Philippians, that in the early days of the gospel, when I left Macedonia, no church communicated with me in the matter of giving and receiving, except you alone. You even sent to Thessalonica once and again for my needs.*† He now rejoices that they have returned to these good works, and is happy that they have begun to spring up again, as when the fruitfulness of a field revives. †**Ph 4:15–16**

Is it because of his *needs* that he rejoices, since he said that *you sent for my needs? This* was not his reason. And how do we know? Because he goes on to say, *Not that I seek the gift, but I seek the fruit.*† I have learned from you, my God, to distinguish between *gift* and *fruit*. The *gift* is the thing itself, what the person who supplies these necessary things gives, like money, food, drink, clothing, shelter, assistance. The *fruit* is the good and upright will of the giver. The *gift* is to receive a prophet, to receive a righteous person, to offer a cup of cold water to a disciple. The *fruit* is to do this in the name of the prophet, in the name of the righteous person, in the name of the disciple. Elijah was fed with *fruit* by a widow who knew that she was feeding a man of God. He was fed with a *gift* by the raven. [The raven] did not feed the spirit but the body of Elijah, who may have perished from lack of such food.† †**Ph 4:17**

†Mt 10:41–42; 1 K 17:6–15

—from *Confessions* 13*

*363. *Confess.* 13.26 (39–41); (CC 27: 265,2–267,38; 45/51)

Saint Augustine's Commentary

the Letter of Paul to the Church at Colossae

HE HAS RESCUED US *from the power of darkness, and transferred us into the kingdom of the Son of his love.*† †**Col 1:13**

The words *the Son of his love* mean nothing else than 'his beloved Son,' and, finally, than 'the Son of his own substance.' The Father's love, which is in his inexpressibly simple nature, is nothing else than his own nature, and therefore *the Son of his love* is no one else than the one born of his substance.

—from *On the Trinity* 15.19*

365. *He is the image of the invisible God, the first-born of all creation.*† †**Col 1:15** (Pr 8:22–31)

The Catholic faith, which distinguishes between the Creator and the creation, experiences no difficulty in understanding the difference between these two words.† It interprets 'only-begotten' in accord with the Scripture, 'In the beginning was the Word, and the Word was with God, and the Word was God'. It takes *first-born of all creation* in accord with the Apostle's words, 'So that he may be the first-born among many brothers,'† those the Father begot for himself, not by an equality of substance but by the adoption of grace, to associate with one another as brothers and sisters. And a little farther on:

†*unigenitus* (Jn 1:14, 18) and *primogenitus.*

†Jn 1:1; Rm 8:29

. . . in order that Jesus Christ may be both the 'only-begotten' in that he is the Word of God, God with God, unchangeable and eternal in equal degree, one who did not 'think that equality with God was something to be grasped,' and may also be *the first-born of all creation,* in that *in him all things in heaven and on earth, things visible and invisible, were created.*† †Ph 2:6; **Col 1:16**

—from *Against the Letter of the Manichaean, Secundinus**

366. *Because [God] was pleased that all fullness should dwell in him, and through him to reconcile in himself all things.*† †**Col 1:19–20**

---

*364. *De Trin.* 15.19.37; CC 50A: 514, 162/69 passim
*365. *Contra Secund. Manich.* 5.7; CSEL 25: 911,26–912,6; 915,23–916,1.

By that unique sacrifice in which the Mediator was immolated—the one prefigured by the many victims under the law—peace is made between things heavenly and earthly, and things earthly and heavenly, *because*, as the Apostle says, *[God] was pleased that all fullness should dwell in him, and through him to reconcile in himself all things, whether things on earth or things in heaven, by making peace through the blood of his cross*. This peace, as Scripture says, 'surpasses all understanding.' We can know it only when we reach it. How is peace made with heavenly things unless [it is made] with us—that is, by their coming into harmony with us? Peace always exists there [in heaven], between all the intelligent creatures among themselves, and also with their Creator. This peace, as is said, 'surpasses all understanding'—ours, surely, not theirs who 'continually see the face of the Father.'†

†Ph 4:7; Mt 18:10

—from *Enchiridion* 62*

367. *And I am completing in my flesh what is lacking in Christ's sufferings for the sake of his body, which is the Church*.†

†**Col 1:24**

Whether I say 'head and body,' or whether I say 'bridegroom and bride,' you are to understand a unit. That is why the Apostle, while still Saul, heard, 'Saul, Saul, why do you persecute me?'—because [Christ's] body is joined to the head. Christ's preacher was suffering from others what he himself had done as a persecutor,† and so he asked that *I may complete in my flesh what is lacking in Christ's afflictions*, indicating that what he was suffering was connected to *Christ's afflictions*. We cannot take this as referring to the head, which being now in heaven suffers nothing of this kind, but as referring to the body, that is, to the Church. This body, with its head, is one Christ.

†Ac 9:4, 8:3, 9:1–2; 1 Co 15:9

—from the sermon on the three types [of disciples]*

368. [Paul] did not speak of 'my' *afflictions* but of *Christ's* because he was a member of Christ. In his own persecutions, of the kind Christ

*366. *Enchir.* 16.62; CC 46: 82,40–83,53
*367. *Serm.* 341.10.12; PL 39: 1500

had necessarily to suffer in his whole body, he too was *completing* his own share of *Christ's afflictions*.† †Col 1:24

—from homily one hundred five on the Gospel of John*

369. *In whom are hidden all the treasures of wisdom and knowledge*.† †Col 2:3

Who can know how deeply the Apostle knew these treasures, how much of them he had penetrated, and how many of them he had reached? Yet for myself—according to what is written, 'To each of us is given a manifestation of the Spirit for use. To one is given through the Spirit the utterance of wisdom, to another the utterance of knowledge according to the same Spirit'†—if the †1 Co 12:7–8 difference between these two things is that *wisdom* is attributed to divine realities and *knowledge* to human, I, and with me all who believe in him, acknowledge both in Christ. When I read, 'The Word became flesh and lived among us,'† I understand in †Jn 1:14 'the Word' the true Son of God, and recognize in 'the flesh' the true Son of Man, and both joined together into the one person of God and man by an inexpressible abundance of grace. And a little farther on:

Therefore Christ is our *knowledge*, and the same Christ is also our *wisdom*. He implants faith concerning temporal realities within us, and presents the truth concerning those of eternity. Through him we go to him; through knowledge we proceed to wisdom; yet we do not fall away from one and the same Christ, *in whom are hidden all the treasures of wisdom and knowledge*.

—from *On the Trinity* 13.19*

370. *Be on guard that no one deceives you through philosophy and empty deceit, according to human tradition, according to the elements of this world, and not according to Christ*.† †Col 2:8

*368. *Tract in Ioh*. 108.5; CC 36: 618, 16/19
*369. *De Trin*. 13.19.24; CC 50A: 415,14–416,1; 50–417,55

What then is Juno? Juno, they say, is the air. For a long time now he has been inviting us to worship the sea in Neptune and to worship the earth in an image of Tellus; now he is inviting us to worship the air. These are *the elements* that make up this world. The apostle Paul alerts us to this in his letter. *Be on guard,* he says, *that no one deceives you through philosophy and empty deceit, according to the elements of this world.* He was alluding to the people who explain idols as though with considerable common sense. And so when he said *through philosophy*, he said in the same place *according to the elements of this world*, not as though advising us to be on guard against those who are in some sense or other worshipers of images, but against apparently more learned interpreters of the signs.

—from a sermon against the pagans, on January first*

†Col 2:9 371. *For in him the whole fullness of divinity dwells bodily*†—not *bodily* [in a literal sense], because God is incorporeal. Either [Paul] used the word figuratively, as if [God] dwells incorporeally—that is, by prefiguring signs—in a temple made by human hands (for he calls all these observances, in an equally figurative way, 'shadows of things to come'; God most high, as Scripture says, 'does not dwell in temples made by human hands'). Or he says *bodily* because God dwells in Christ's body, which he took from the Virgin, just as he dwells in a temple. Hence when he had told the Jews who were asking for a sign, 'Destroy this temple, and in three days I will raise it up,' the evangelist, subsequently explaining what this meant, said, 'He said this of the temple of his body.'†

†Col 2:17; Heb 10:1; Ac 17:24; Jn 2:19, 21

—from *On the Presence of God*, to Dardanus*

†Col 2:11 372. *In stripping off the body of the flesh.*†

*370. *Serm.* 197.1.6; PL 38: 1023–24
*371. *Ep.* 187.13.39; CSEL 57: 116,9/23. Dardanus was the prefect of the Province of Gaul.

Surely [Paul] did not want us to understand two things, as though 'the flesh' was one thing and *the body of the flesh* another. Because *body* refers to many things that have no flesh—many 'heavenly bodies and earthly bodies' are without flesh—he said *the body of the flesh,* [meaning] the body that is flesh. Thus he [calls] that spirit that is mind 'the spirit of the mind': 'Be renewed in the spirit of your mind.'† †1 Co 15:40; Eph 4:23

—from *On the Trinity* 14.16*

373. *And you, when you were dead in trespasses and the uncircumcision of your flesh, [God] made you alive together with him.*† **†Col 2:13**

[Paul] called 'the uncircumcision' what is represented by the foreskin—that is, carnal trespasses, of which we must be stripped.

—from *To Paulinus**

374. What does circumcision of the flesh represent if not the stripping off of the mortality which we bear from our carnal generation? This is why the Apostle says, *Becoming free of the flesh, he made an example of the principalities and powers.*† He said he was freed *of the flesh*—we take *flesh* in this passage to be the mortality of the flesh, on account of which the body is appropriately named *flesh.* That mortality which will not exist in the immortality of the resurrection is appropriately called *flesh.* **†Col 2:15**

He made an example of the principalities and powers. By this mortality the envious diabolical *powers* held sway over us. [Christ] is said to have *made an example* of them because he provided an example in himself, our head, which will be fully realized in the final resurrection in his entire body—that is, the Church—which is to be delivered from the power of the devil.

—from *Against Faustus* 16*

---

*372. *De Trin.* 14.16.22; CC 50A: 453,36/42. Repeats the last part of section 324.
*373. *Ep.* 149.2.26; CSEL 44: 372,13/15. Paulinus was bishop of Nola.
*374. *Contra Faust. Manich.* 16.29; CSEL 25: 474,20–475,1; 21/26 passim

†Col 2:15 375. *He made an example of the principalities*†—that is, he gave them as an example, that as *he had become free of the flesh* he may show that his followers were to be freed of the fleshly vices by which [*the principalities*] held sway over them.

—from *To Paulinus*★

376. *Therefore do not let anyone condemn you in matters of food and drink or of observing festivals, the new moon, or sabbaths—which is a shadow of*
†Col 2:16–17 *what is to come.*†

When [Paul] says *Do not let anyone condemn you in matters of food* he is declaring that these things no longer need to be observed. When he says *which is a shadow of what is to come* he is showing how they had to be observed at the time when those things that have now dawned for us as manifest were being proclaimed as still *to come* through such shadowy shapes.

—from *Against Faustus* 6★

377. *Do not let anyone disqualify you, insisting on self-abasement and*
†Col 2:18 *worship of angels, things not seen . . .* †

When [saying] these words we must have a certain expression on the face and in the tone of voice. [Paul] set down the words of those who say, *Do not handle, Do not taste,* in mockery, since 'to the pure
†Col 2:21; Tt 1:15 all things are pure.'† He perceived that they should guard against the concern with meaningless observances in the name of knowledge [that is shown] by those called philosophers, and by Judaism. They
†Col 2:17; Heb 10:1 were to abandon the 'shadows of things to come'† since Christ, their light, had already come.

—from *To Paulinus*★

★375. *Ep.* 149.2.26; CSEL 44: 372,21–373,2 passim
★376. *Contra Faust. Manich.* 6.2; CC 25: 286, 6/14
★377. *Ep.* 149.2.23; CSEL 44: 369,3/5; 11/16; 22–370,3 passim

378. *If you have risen with Christ, seek the things that are above.*† †**Col 3:1**

We have not yet risen as Christ has, but still, on account of the hope that we have in him, [Paul] has asserted that we have already risen with him. Hence he also says, 'He saved us according to his mercy by the washing of rebirth,' as if salvation had already been bestowed. In another place he says explicitly, 'By hope we have been saved.'† †Tt 3:5; Rm 8:24

—from *Against Faustus* 11*

379. The change that will be free of corruption will be that of the saints. It will belong to those who now possess the resurrection of the spirit. Of this resurrection the Apostle says, *If you have risen with Christ, seek the things that are above, where Christ is, seated at the right hand of God. Set your minds on things that are above, not those that are earthly, for you have died, and your life is hidden with Christ in God.*† As †**Col 3:1–3** we die according to the spirit and rise according to the spirit, so later we die according to the flesh and rise according to the flesh. This is the first death—not doing what you used to do, not believing what you used to believe. People used to serve idols, they have come to know the one God: they have died to idolatry, they have risen in faith. People were drunkards, they are sober: drunkenness has died, sobriety has risen. All the deeds we characterize as evil bring about a kind of death in us.

—from a sermon on the resurrection of the dead*

380. Then will our desire lack nothing, when God will be all in all.† Such an end has no end. No one dies there where no one †1 Co 15:28 arrives—unless they die to this world, not by the death common to all, in which the soul forsakes the body, but by the death of the

---

*378. *Contra Faust. Manich.* 11.7; CSEL 25: 324,12/25 passim
*379. *Serm.* 362.20.23; PL 39: 1627 passim

elect, in which the heart is set on high even while still remaining in the mortal flesh.

Of this kind of mortality the apostle Paul said, *For you have died, and your life is hidden with Christ in God*. Perhaps 'love is strong as
†**Col 3:3**; Sg 8:6 death'† refers to this. Love of this kind brings it about that while we are still in this corruptible flesh we die to this world and our *life is hidden with Christ in God*. In fact, this love is itself our death to the world, our life with God. If death occurs when the soul leaves the body, how can it not be a death when our love leaves the world? 'Love,' then, 'is strong as death.' What is stronger than what
†Jn 16:33 overcomes the world?†

—from homily sixty-two on the Gospel of John*

381. *Put to death your members that are on earth: fornication, impurity,*
†**Col 3:5** *lust . . .* †

We first rise in faith when these members have been put to death. As death according to the spirit precedes resurrection according to the spirit, so will death according to the flesh precede the resurrection which will be according to the flesh.

—from a sermon on the resurrection of the dead*

†**Col 3:5** 382. *And greed, which is idolatry.*†

'Neither the greedy, nor the rapacious, will possess the kingdom
†1 Co 6:10 of God.'† Paul is comparing greed to idolatry. *And greed*, he says, *which is idolatry*. Blessed Cyprian has so extended the meaning in a
†Letter 55.27. Cyprian addresses his correspondent as Antonianus. letter to Antony † that he did not hesitate to compare the greedy to the sin of those who during the time of persecution had declared in writing that they were going to offer incense. And a little farther on:

And yet, since it is perfectly clear that to sin wittingly is much more serious than to sin unwittingly, I wish that someone would tell me which of these is worse—one who falls into heresy without

*380. *Tract. in Ioh.* 65.1; CC 36: 491, 36/50
*381. *Serm.* 362.20.23; PL 39: 1627 passim

being aware of how great an evil it is, or one who does not give up greed while being aware of how great an evil it is. I can also put it thus: if someone unwittingly rushes into heresy, and someone else wittingly does not keep away from idolatry, [the latter is committing the greater evil], since the Apostle says, *and greed, which is idolatry.*

—from *On the One Baptism* 4*

383. *Strip off the old self with its practices, and put on the new, which is being renewed in knowledge of God according to the image of the one who created it, where there is no male and female, Jew and Greek, . . .* †

†**Col 3:9–11**. Bede conflates this passage with phrases from Ga 3:28.

If we are being renewed in the spirit of our mind, and it is the new self *which is being renewed in knowledge of God according to the image of the one who created it,* no one can doubt that humans were not made in the image of the one who created them with respect to the body, or to just any part of the soul, but with respect to the reasoning soul, which is capable of the *knowledge of God.* With respect to this renewal we are also becoming children of God through Christ's baptism, and as we put on the new self we are surely putting on Christ through faith.

Who then would exclude women from this community, since they are fellow heirs with us of grace? The same apostle says in another place, 'For you are all children of God through faith in Christ Jesus. Whoever among you were baptized in Christ have put on Christ. There is neither Jew nor Greek, there is neither slave nor free, there is neither male nor female; for you are all one in Christ Jesus.' Have female believers, then, lost their bodily sex? But they are being renewed in the image of God there where there is no sex—'human beings were made in the image of God' there where there is no sex, that is, in the spirit of their minds.†

†Ga 3:26–28; Gn 9:6; Eph 4:23

—from *On the Trinity* 12.7*

*382. *De Bapt. Contra Donat.* 4.3.6–7; CSEL 51: 227, 7/13; 229, 2/9 (Cyprian, *Ep.* 55.27; CSEL 3,1: 644,1–645,19). This excerpt resembles section 331.
*383. *De Trin.* 12.7.12; CC 50: 366,80–367,97. The last line also occurs in section 187, 276.

384. Just as after the fall into sin humanity *is being renewed in knowledge*
†Col 3:10 *of God according to the image of the one who created it*,† so in creation itself, before it could grow old through trespass, it was created where it may again be renewed in the same knowledge.

—from the *Literal Commentary on Genesis* 3.11*

385. And so renewal and reformation of the mind comes about
†Col 3:10 according to God or *according to the image* † of God. We say 'according to God' in case we should suppose that it comes about according to another creature; we say *according to the image* of God so that we can grasp the fact that the renewal comes about in that very thing where God's image is—that is, in the soul. We should not, then, understand *according to the image of the one who created it* as if the image according to which it is being renewed is something else, not the very thing that is being renewed.

—from *On the Trinity* 14.16*

386. 'The Lord has sworn and will not repent. You are a priest forever according to the order of Melchizedek.' Those who read [Scripture] know what Melchizedek brought out when he blessed
†Ps 110:4; Gn 14:18–19 Abraham,† and if they already partake of it they see a sacrifice of this kind now offered to God throughout the whole world. God's oath is a rebuke to the skeptical, and the fact that God will not repent is an indication that he will not change this priesthood.

—from *Against the Opponent of the Law* 1*

---

*384. *De Gen. ad Litt.* 3.20; CSEL 28,1: 87, 15/19
*385. *De Trin.* 14.16.22; CC 50A: 453,52/56; 454, 64/66
*386. *Contra Adv. Leg. et Prophet.* 1.20.39; CC 49: 70,1071–71,1078

Saint Augustine's Commentary

the First Letter of Paul to the Church in Thessalonika

PAUL, SILVANUS, AND TIMOTHY, to the church of the Thessalonians.† †1 Th 1:1

'God has taken his place in the synagogue of the gods.'† †Ps 82:1 We use the word 'synagogue' specifically of the Jews, though it can also be called a 'church.' The apostles never called our gatherings a synagogue but always a church, either to distinguish the two, or because of a difference between *congregatio* (gathering)—whence 'synagogue'—and *convocatio* (assembly)—whence 'church.' Even flocks are 'gathered,' while 'assembled' is used of those who employ reason, as do human beings.

—in the explanation of Psalm 81*

388. *I became an infant among you, like a nurse tenderly caring for her own children.*† †1 Th 2:7

[Paul] did not say 'mother.' Mothers are sometimes either more indulgent or less loving toward their children. When they bear them they hand them over to others to be nursed. Again, if he had said only *like a nurse tenderly caring* and had not added *for her own children* it may seem that they were taken for nursing as if some other woman had borne them. He called himself *a nurse* because he was nourishing them, and he called them his *own children* because he bore them. He said, 'My children, for whom I am again in the pain of childbirth until Christ is formed in you.'† †Ga 4:19 He bears them just as he bears the Church, from his womb, not from his seed.

—from a sermon on the three types [of disciples]*

389. *For this reason, in all our need and affliction we have been encouraged, brothers and sisters, about you through your faith.*† †1 Th 3:7. The alternative meaning of the Latin is that *we have encouraged [these] brothers and sisters about you through your faith.*

Whether *brothers and sisters* is in the vocative or the objective case is unclear; neither of these is against the faith. These cases are not the same in Greek, however, and so when we look into it we

---

*387. *En. in Ps* 81.1; CC 39: 1135,6; 1136,16/24
*388. *Serm.* PL 39: 1732. See sections 132, 332.

declare it to be in the vocative—that is, 'O brothers and sisters!' If the translator had chosen to say, 'For this reason, brothers and sisters, we have encouragement in you,' the correspondence would have been less exact, but the meaning would have been less in doubt. Or if 'our' was added—anyone who heard, 'For this reason, our brothers and sisters, we have been encouraged about you,' would scarcely be uncertain. But this is rather risky.

—from *On Christian Doctrine* 3*

390. *For the Lord himself, with a commandment, with an archangel's voice, and with God's trumpet, will descend from heaven, and the dead in Christ will rise first. Then we who are alive, who are left, will be caught up in the clouds together with them to meet Christ; and so we will always be with*
†1 Th 4:16–17 *the Lord.*†

These words of the Apostle show with perfect clarity the future resurrection of the dead, when Christ will come to judge the living and the dead.

But it is commonly asked whether those whom Christ will find alive on earth—represented by the Apostle and those living in his own time—will never die at all, or whether they are going to pass with wonderful rapidity through death to immortality at the very time in which they *will be caught up in the clouds to meet Christ in the air* along with those who are rising [from the dead]. We must not say that in that moment when they are being carried on high through the air they cannot both die and be brought back to life.

We must not take [Paul's] words, *and so we will always be with the Lord*, to mean that we will always remain with the Lord *in the air*. Surely not even he will remain there, but will pass through it as he comes. People go to meet someone coming, not remaining. But *so we will be with the Lord*—that is, being possessed of everlasting bodies we will be with him wherever he is. To this view, however—by which we judge that even those whom the Lord will find alive here will both suffer death and receive immortality in that brief

*389. *De Doct. Christ.* 3.4.8; CC 32: 82, 4/13

interval—the Apostle seems to urge us when he says that 'in Christ all will be made alive,' since in another passage he says expressly of the resurrection of bodies, 'What you sow does not come to life unless first it dies.'† †1 Co 15:22, 36

—from *On the City of God* 20.20*

391. *Admonish the restless, encourage the faint-hearted, help the weak; see that none of you repays evil for evil.*† **†1 Th 5:14–15**

When people see someone living an evil life—and perhaps providing something for the Church—and do not admonish that one, they are running away in spirit. What is running away is spirit? Being afraid. Fear is inner flight. Why are they afraid? Because they are hirelings. They are afraid that the one [they admonish] may take the admonition badly, and not give what is customary. '[Hirelings] see the wolf coming'—that is, the devil breaking the neck of the one living the evil life—and run away in spirit.† Filled with fear, they †Jn 10:12–13 withhold the helpful admonition. Those who are shepherds and who care for the sheep do not let such a one go. They do what the Apostle says, *Admonish the restless, encourage the faint-hearted*, and so on. No shepherds, then—or those who call themselves shepherds—should suppose that they are not repaying *evil for evil* when instead they are repaying evil for good. Scoundrels, sinners though they are, give of their possessions to the Church. Those who withhold admonishment from them are repaying evil for good.

But all this must be done out of love. Sometimes people consider that those who admonish them are their enemies, and so when [Paul] had said, *Admonish the restless*, he added, *encourage the faint-hearted*. Perhaps they begin to lose heart and to be upset over the admonition. Then you must offer encouragement. *Help the weak* so that they will not fall through weakness. If weakness causes them to falter, love must take them to its breast.

And when [Paul] had said these things, he added in the last place, *see that none of you repays evil for evil*. Therefore admonishment

*390. *De Civ. Dei* 20.20; CC 48: 733,8–734,35

is not an evil, even if it may seem so. What does a good sheep say when admonished by its overseer? 'The righteous one has corrected
†Ps 141:5 me in mercy.'†

—from a sermon on the words, 'If any want to come after me,
†Mt 16:24 let them deny themselves'†*

†1 Th 5:19 392. *Do not quench the Spirit*†—not that he can be quenched, but as far as it is in their power, they are rightly called his quenchers who act as if they want him quenched.

—from a letter to Boniface*

393. *And may your spirit and soul and body be kept sound and blameless*
†1 Th 5:23 *on the day of our Lord Jesus Christ.*†

To be sinless, which in this life is said solely of the Only-
†1 P 2:22; 1 Jn 3:5 begotten,† is one thing; to be *blameless*, which even in this life can be said of many righteous persons, is another. A certain measure of a good life, which allows no just blame even in this human milieu, does exist. Who justly blames those who wish ill to no one, who give reliable counsel to those they can, and who retain no desire for revenge in return for wrongs inflicted by anyone so as to say truthfully, 'as we also forgive our debtors'? And yet by the fact that
†Mt 6:12 people say, 'Forgive, as we also forgive,'† they declare that they are not sinless.

—from *On the Perfection of Human Righteousness*, to Paul and Eutropius*

*391. *Serm.* PL 39: 1732–33
*392. *Ep.* 98.3; CSEL 34: 523, 12/14. Boniface was a fellow bishop in North Africa.
*393. *De Perf. Iust. Hom.* 9.24; CSEL 42: 25,4/14.

Saint Augustine's Commentary

the Second Letter of Paul to the Church in Thessalonika

WE ASK YOU, BROTHERS AND SISTERS, through the coming of our Lord Jesus Christ and of our being gathered together in him, not to be quickly shaken in mind or alarmed, either by spirit or by word or by letter, as though sent from us, to the effect that the day of the Lord is already here. Do not let anyone deceive you in any way, because, unless the apostate comes first . . . † †2 Th 2:1–12

We cannot doubt that [Paul] was speaking of the Antichrist, and that the day of judgment—which he calls *the day of the Lord*—will not come unless the one he calls *the apostate* comes first—an *apostate* from the Lord God, of course. And if this can be justly said of all the ungodly, how much more of [the Antichrist]!

But *in* which *temple of God* he is going to take his seat is uncertain, whether in the ruins of the temple King Solomon built, or in the Church. The Apostle would not call the temple of any idol or demon *the temple of God*. Hence, some people want us to take the Antichrist in this passage not as the ruler himself but, in a sense, as his entire body—that is, the multitude of human beings associated with him, together with himself, their ruler. Then they think that we would express the Greek more accurately if we say *he takes his seat* not *in the temple of God* but *as the temple of God*, as if he was himself the temple of God, which is the Church. In the same way we say that a person sits 'for a friend,' that is, 'as a friend,' and other common expressions of this kind.

[Paul] says, *And you know what is now restraining him*—that is, *you know* what the delay is, the reason for his detention—*so that [the Antichrist] may be revealed in his own time*. He said that they knew, and so he chose not to speak of it explicitly. We, who do not know what he knew, and who are unable to arrive, even with an effort, at what the Apostle means, we have the desire but not the ability [to arrive at his meaning], especially because what he added makes this passage even more obscure.

Now what does this mean? *The mystery of lawlessness is already at work; only let the one who is now restraining it restrain it until it is removed from their midst. And then the lawless one will be revealed*. Some suppose that this was said of the Roman Empire, and that the apostle Paul chose not to write it explicitly lest he incur the false accusation that he wished evil to the Roman Empire, whereas people were hoping that it was eternal; by his words, *the mystery of lawlessness is already at work*, he wanted us to understand Nero, whose deeds already seemed to be those of the Antichrist. What the Apostle says, *only let the one who is now restraining it restrain it until it is removed from their midst*, we may not unreasonably believe he was saying of the Roman Empire, as though he meant, 'only let the one who is now Emperor continue to be so until he is removed from their midst,' that is, removed from his position. *And then the lawless one will be revealed.* No one doubts that this is the Antichrist.

Some suppose that the words, *you know what is restraining him*, as well as *the mystery of lawlessness is at work*, were said of wicked and hypocritical people, who are in the Church until they reach such a large number that they can constitute a great people for the Antichrist, and that this is *the mystery of lawlessness* which seems to be concealed. The Apostle is encouraging believers to persevere in the faith they hold by saying, *only let the one who is now restraining it restrain it until it is removed from their midst*—that is, until *the mystery of lawlessness*, which is now concealed, *is removed from the midst* of the Church.

They are of the opinion that what John says in his letter, 'They went out from us, but they did not belong to us,'† pertains to this mystery, *whose presence, according to the working of Satan, is in all power and signs and lying wonders, and in every kind of wicked deception for those who are perishing.* Then will Satan be unbound, and through him the Antichrist will work *in all* his *power*, wonderfully, indeed, but dishonestly. People are often uncertain whether they are called *signs and lying wonders* because he is going to deceive our mortal senses through illusions, not doing what he appears to be doing, or because these occurrences, even if they are true wonders, will attract to a lie those inclined to believe that they can only be done by divine influence, being unaware of the devil's power.

†1 Jn 2:19

But whatever the basis, those who deserve to be deceived will be deceived by these *signs* and *wonders*, *because they did not receive the love of the truth, that they may be saved.* And the Apostle did not hesitate to add, *For this reason God will send them a power that deludes people, so that they may believe the lie. God will send* it since God will permit the devil to do these things; [God] does this by his just judgment, although [the devil] does it by his lawless and malign intention.

So that all who have not believed the truth, [Paul] says, *but gave their assent to iniquity, may be judged*. Those who have been judged, then, are going to be deceived, and those who have been deceived are going to be judged. Those who have been judged will be deceived by the hidden just judgments of God, which are justly hidden; by them, from the beginning of sin, he has never ceased judging the rational creation. Those who have been deceived will be judged in a last and manifest judgment by Jesus Christ. He who was judged with perfect injustice is going to judge with perfect justice.

—from *On the City of God* 20.13*

395. *Take note of those who do not obey what we say in this letter, and have nothing to do with them*.† †**2 Th 3:14**

We, brothers and sisters, we keep aloof from our brothers and sisters as a rebuke, and do not associate with them. We associate with pagans rather than with those close to us if we see that they are living wickedly, in order that they may be discomfited and freed from their faults. As the Apostle says, *Take note of those who do not obey what we say in this letter, and have nothing to do with them. Do not regard them as enemies, but admonish them as brothers and sisters.*

We often do this for the sake of healing—and yet we frequently eat with many strangers and ungodly people. What does [the psalmist] say? 'With those with haughty eyes and greedy hearts I did not eat.'† Godly hearts have their meal, proud hearts their †Ps 101:5 meal. He spoke of 'greedy hearts' on account of the food of a proud heart. What feeds a proud heart? The proud are envious; it cannot be otherwise. Pride is envy; it cannot avoid producing it, and always exists along with it. All the proud are envious. If they are envious, they feed on the misfortunes to others. This is why the Apostle says, 'If you bite and devour one another, take care that

*394. *De Civ. Dei* 20.19; CC 48: 730, 5/10; 731,26–732,58; 64–733,126 passim

†Ga 5:15 you are not consumed by one another.'† You see people devouring [one another]; do not eat with them, keep away from such a meal. They are not satisfied with rejoicing over the misfortunes of others because their hearts are greedy.

—from the treatise on Psalm 100*

*395. *En. in Ps* 100.8–9; CC 39: 1413,42–1414,12

Saint Augustine's Commentary

the First Letter from Paul to Timothy

PAUL, AN APOSTLE OF CHRIST JESUS by the command of God our Saviour.† †**1 Tm 1:1**

You chose what is weak in the world to shame the strong, and you chose what is low in the world and despised, and things that are not, though they may seem to be, to reduce to nothing those that are.† †1 Co 1:27–28

And yet even this 'least of your apostles,' by whose tongue you uttered these words, chose to be called Paul in place of his previous name of Saul. This was in testimony to the great victory that took place when Paulus the proconsul, with his pride overcome through [Paul's] efforts, was sent out beneath the easy yoke [of Christ] as a subject of the Great King.† The enemy is more completely overcome in one on whom he has a stronger hold and through whom he holds more people. He has a stronger hold on the proud because of their noble rank, and through them he holds many people by reason of their authority. †1 Co 15:9; Ac 13:7–12; Mt 11:30

—from *Confessions* 8*

397. *They should not concern themselves with Jewish fables and endless genealogies, which furnish questions rather than the edification of God, which is [realized] in faith.*† †**1 Tm 1:4**

[The opponent] supposes that the Apostle called the divine utterances of the law and the prophets 'profane and old wives' tales' and *endless genealogies* because he said, 'Avoid profane and old wives' tales,'† and in another place, *Do not concern yourselves with Jewish fables and boundless genealogies that furnish questions rather than edification.* Who but a completely blind heretic would make such a mistake? Why did the Apostle not do this himself if he judged that these were old wives' tales? Why does he tell the Galatians, 'Tell me, you who want to be under the law, have you not heard the law? It is written that Abraham had two sons, one from a slave woman and one from a free woman. This is an allegory. These women are two covenants.'† †1 Tm 4:7 †Ga 4:21–24

He is not aware that the Jews have certain traditions of their own in addition to the law and the prophets. They do not have them in

*396. *Confess.* 8.4.(9); CC 27: 118,13–119-23

writing, but they keep them in their memories and pass them on one to another orally. They call them *deuterosin*,† where they even dare to say and believe that God created two wives for the first man. From them they weave two genealogies which are, as the Apostle says, truly boundless, producing absolutely fruitless questions.

†The word seems to mean 'Jewish traditions' here (perhaps as a translation of Mishnah?).

—from *Against the Opponent of the Law and the Prophets* 2*

†1 Tm 1:5

398. *The aim of the commandment is love that comes from a pure heart, a good conscience, and sincere faith.*†

When people recognize that *the aim of the commandment is love that comes from a pure heart, a good conscience, and sincere faith*, and will refer their whole understanding of the divine Scriptures to these three, they may approach the interpretation of these books without anxiety. When he said *love* [Paul] added *from a pure heart* so that we would love nothing but what should be loved. He joined with it *a good conscience* with reference to hope—people troubled by a bad conscience despair of attaining what they believe and love. In third place he says *and sincere faith*. If our faith is without falsehood, then we do not love what should not be loved, and by living uprightly we hope for it, so that in no way can our hope be deceived.

—from *On Christian Doctrine* 1*

†1 Tm 1:8

399. *We know that the law is good, if one uses it lawfully.*†

In this is help from the letter [of the law] for those who are predestined. By giving commands but not assistance it warns the weak to have recourse to the spirit of grace. For those who use the law *lawfully* it *is good*—that is, profitable. On the other hand, in itself 'the letter kills,'† because by commanding good and not bestowing love—which alone wills the good—it makes them guilty of transgression.

†2 Co 3:6

—from *Against Julian* 1*

---

*397. *Contra Adv. Leg. et Prophet.* 2.1.1–2; CC 49: 87,4/14; 21–88,27
*398. *De Doct. Christ.* 1.40.44; CC 32: 31,1–32,12
*399. *Contra Sec. Iul. Resp.* 1.94; CSEL 85,1: 109,76–110,82

400. The law that threatens those who do not fulfill what it commands brings them under itself. These people are under the law, not under grace. *The law is good, if one uses it lawfully.* What does using the law *lawfully* mean? It means acknowledging one's illness through the law, and seeking divine help for healing, since 'if a law had been given that could give life, righteousness would come entirely from the law,' and a Saviour would not be needed, Christ would not come, and he would not seek the lost sheep by his own blood.† †**1 Tm 1:8**; Ga 3:21; Lk 15:4

—from the fourth sermon on the letter to the Romans*

401. *Being aware that the law is not laid down for the righteous but for the unrighteous and disobedient, the ungodly and sinners . . .* † †**1 Tm 1:9–11**

The Apostle says that *the law is not laid down for the righteous but for the unrighteous and disobedient*, and so on to the place where he says in conclusion, *and whatever else is contrary to the sound teaching that conforms to the glorious gospel of the blessed God, which he entrusted to me.* Was the person who said, 'Lay down for me a law, O Lord,' the kind of person for whom blessed Paul says that the law was laid down? By no means. If he was such he would not have said immediately before, 'I have run the way of your commandments, when you enlarged my heart.'† †Ps 119:33, 32

Why then does he pray that the Lord lay down a law for him, if it *is not laid down for the righteous*? It *is not laid down for the righteous* in the way it was laid down for a stubborn people 'on tablets of stone' and not 'on fleshly tablets of the heart'—in accord with the old covenant from Mount Sinai which bears children into slavery, not in accord with the new covenant. Scripture says of this new covenant through the prophet Jeremiah, 'Behold, the days will come, says the Lord, and I will bring about for the house of Israel and for the house of Judah a new covenant, not like the covenant I drew up for their ancestors on the day I took them by the hand to bring them out of the land of Egypt, because they did not remain faithful to my covenant, and I forsook them, says the Lord. But this is the

---

*400. *Serm.* 156.3.3; PL 38: 851 passim. Part of section 274 is repeated here.

covenant I will make with the house of Israel after these days, says the Lord, by giving my laws in their minds, and I will write them on their hearts.'†

†2 Co 3:3; Ga 4:24; Jer 31:31–33. Here Augustine's text differs from the Vulgate.

You see how [the psalmist] does not want the Lord to lay down a law for him as it was laid down 'on tablets of stone' *for the unrighteous and disobedient* who belonged to the old covenant, but as it is given in minds and written on hearts for the holy children of the free woman—that is, of Jerusalem on high†—for the children of the promise, the children of an eternal inheritance—by the Holy Spirit, as by the finger of God.

†Ga 4:26

—from the treatise on Psalm 118*

402. *The saying is reliable and worthy of full acceptance, that Jesus Christ came into this world to save sinners.*†

†**1 Tm 1:15**

To save sinners, [Paul] says, *of whom I am the first.* Were there no sinners before Paul? Certainly: Adam before all the others—and the earth destroyed by the flood was filled with sinners†—and how many after them! How are [Paul's words] *I am the first* true, then?

†Gn 3:6–7; 6:11–12, 17

He called himself *first* not in the series of sinners but in the seriousness of the sin. He was considering the seriousness of his sin, and so he called himself *the first* of sinners, just as among lawyers, for example, some are called first. [A lawyer] is first, not from having more years since beginning to practice, but for surpassing all the rest since the beginning.

Let the Apostle tell us in another passage why he is *the first* of sinners. 'I am the last of the apostles,' he says, 'unworthy to be called an apostle, because I persecuted the Church of God.'† No one was fiercer among persecutors, and therefore no one was more *the first* among sinners. *But I have obtained mercy*, he says; and he explains the reason he obtained mercy: *So that in me*, he says, *Christ Jesus may display the utmost patience for the instruction of those who are going to believe in him for eternal life.*†

†1 Co 15:9

†**1 Tm 1:16**

Christ, he says, will grant pardon to all the sinners who turn to him. Mercy even descends on his enemies, and first he chose me,

*401. *En. in Ps* 118.11.1; CC 40: 1695,4–1696,30

his fiercest enemy, so that since he healed me none of the rest would despair. The one who healed me sent me to you and said to me, 'Go to the despairing and tell them what you had, what I healed in you, how quickly I healed you. I called from heaven—with one word I struck and cast you down, with another I raised you up and chose you, with a third I filled you and sent you forth, with a fourth I set you free and crowned you. Go, speak to the sick, cry aloud to the despairing: *The saying is reliable and worthy of full acceptance, that Christ Jesus came into the world to save sinners . . .*'

Again, he says *of whom I am the first*, not because he sinned before others but because he sinned more than the rest. Just as among the skilled we call a doctor inferior in age but superior in skill *the first*, a carpenter *the first*, an architect *the first*, so does the Apostle call himself *the first* of sinners. No one persecuted the Church more grievously.

—from a sermon on the same text*

403. *To the King of the ages, immortal, uncorrupted, the only blessed God, honor and glory to the ages of ages. Amen.*† †**1 Tm 1:17**.**

In the sense that things we call 'visible' are seen, 'no one has ever seen God,' 'or can see him,' since 'he dwells in inaccessible light,'† and his nature is *invisible* just as it is *incorruptible*. The Apostle has established this in a related passage, saying, *To the King of the ages, invisible, incorruptible*. As he is now *incorruptible*, and will not afterwards be corruptible, so is he *invisible* not only now but always. God is not seen in a place, but by 'the pure in heart'. He is not sought by bodily eyes, nor encompassed by sight, nor grasped by touch, nor heard when speaking, nor perceived in his approach. 'The only-begotten Son, who is in the Father's bosom,'† soundlessly makes known the nature and substance of the Godhead, and for this reason he also invisibly reveals it to the deserving and apt.

†Jn 1:18; 1 Jn 4:12; 1 Tm 6:16

†Mt 5:8; Jn 1:18

*402. *Serm.* 176.3.3–4.4; PL 38: 951–52 passim
**Augustine seems to be familiar with Latin versions that attribute immortality, incorruption, and invisibility to God; the Greek text says *aphthartos* and *aoratos*, of which the first means both *immortal* and *incorruptible*, and the second *invisible*. He is commenting on 1 John 3:2, 'we shall see him as he is.'

These are the eyes of which the Apostle says 'with the eyes of your heart enlightened,' and of which [the psalmist] says, "Enlighten my eyes, that I never sleep in death.' 'The Lord is the Spirit,' hence 'anyone who is united to the Lord is one spirit [with him].'† Consequently, anyone who can see God invisibly can be united to God incorporeally.

†Eph 1:18; Ps 13:3; 2 Co 3:17; 1 Co 6:17

—from *On Seeing God*, to Paulina*

404. Since we ordinarily call bodies 'visible,' we say that God is *invisible*† so that we will not believe him to be corporeal. He will not deprive pure hearts of the contemplation of his substance, since this great and supreme reward is promised to those who worship and love the Lord. The Lord himself said this when he appeared visibly to bodily eyes and promised that the pure of heart would see his invisible self. 'Those who love me will be loved by my Father, and I will love them and reveal myself to them.'† Of course his nature and the Father's are equally *invisible*, just as they are equally *incorruptible*. This nature, as was said above, the Apostle continually asserted is the divine substance, commending it to people, as far as he could, by his preaching.

†Col 1:15; **1 Tm 1:17**

†Jn 14:21

—again, from the same book*

405. *First of all, then, I urge that supplications, prayers, intercessions, and thanksgivings be made.*†

†**1 Tm 2:1**

Much can be said about this, which no one should disapprove. I choose to understand by these words what the whole, or almost the whole, Church does. *Supplications* we take to be the words used in the celebration of the mysteries, before we start to bless what is on the Lord's table; *prayers*, when it is blessed and sanctified and broken for distribution—almost the entire Church closes this

*403. *Ep.* 147.15.37; CSEL 44: 311,8–312,2.
*404. *Ibid.* 20.48; CSEL 44: 323,9/20

whole petition with the Lord's prayer; *intercessions*—or as your manuscripts have it, *requests*—are made when the assembly is blessed, for then through the laying on of hands the bishops, as advocates, offer those in their charge to the most merciful Power. When this is completed, and the great sacrament has been partaken of, a *thanksgiving* concludes the whole. This the Apostle also commends last in this passage.

My special reason for mentioning these things was that, after they have been briefly described and explained, no one may suppose that what follows could be overlooked: *for everyone, for kings and all who are in high positions, so that we may lead a quiet and peaceable life in all godliness and love,*† and that no one would judge, given the weakness of human thought, that [*supplications, prayers, intercessions, and thanksgivings*] were not to be made on behalf of those from whom the Church was suffering persecution, since Christ's members were to be assembled from every sort of human being. †**1 Tm 2:1–2**

Hence [Paul] adds, *This is good and is acceptable in the sight of God our Saviour, who wills that everyone be saved and come to the knowledge of the truth.*† And that no one may say that a way of salvation can consist in leading a good life and worshipping the one almighty God without sharing in the body and blood of Christ, [Paul] says, *For there is one God, and one mediator between God and humanity, Christ Jesus, himself human.*† This is so that we will take his words, *[God] desires all humans* † to be saved, as being granted only through a mediator who is not God, which the Word always was, but through *Christ Jesus, himself human*, since 'the Word became flesh and lived among us.'† †**1 Tm 2:3–4** †**1 Tm 2:5** †Translated *all humans* here, rather than *everyone*, to make the point that humans must be saved in a human fashion. †Jn 1:1, 14

—from *Questions*, to Paulinus, Bishop of Nola*

406. Almighty God, whether through the mercy 'he shows to whom he wills,' or the judgment by which 'he hardens whom he wills,' does nothing unjustly, nor does he do anything except

*405. *Ep.* 149.2.15–17; CSEL 44: 362,6/16; 363,10–364,12

†Rm 9:18; Ps 135:6 what he wills, and 'whatever he wills he does.'† Therefore because we hear and read in the sacred books that he *wills that everyone be*
†**1 Tm 2:4** *saved*,† although it is certain that not everyone is saved, yet we must not set any limits to the will of the supremely mighty God. Instead we must understand what is written, *who wills that everyone be saved*, as saying that no one is saved unless [God] wills it to happen. Not that there is a human being whom [God] does not will to be saved, but that no one is saved unless God wills it. Therefore we must ask him to will it, because what he wills must take place. The Apostle had praying to God in mind when he said this. That is how we
†Jn 1:9 understand the words in the gospel, 'who enlightens everyone'†—not that anyone is not enlightened, but that no one is enlightened except by him.

Who wills that everyone be saved was not said because there is anyone whose salvation he does not will—he was unwilling to do
†Mt 11:21 miraculous deeds among those he said would repent if he did so†—but because we are to interpret *everyone* as the whole human race in all its variations. The Apostle had charged that prayers be said *for everyone*, and especially added *for kings and all who are in high positions*, whom we may suppose to shrink from the humility of the Christian faith through disdain and worldly pride. Then as he said, *This is good*
†**1 Tm 2:2, 3** *in the sight of God our Saviour*†—that is, that we pray on behalf of such as these—he added at once, to take away despair, *who wills that everyone be saved and come to the knowledge of the truth*. God, then, has judged this to be good, that by the prayers of the humble he would deign to grant salvation to the lofty—something surely we have already seen fulfilled.

—from *Enchiridion* 105*

407. *For there is one God, and one mediator between God and humanity,*
†**1 Tm 2:5** *Christ Jesus, himself human*.†

What does *one God* mean? The Father alone, the Son alone, the Holy Spirit alone? But of course, the Father, the Son and the

---

*406. *Enchir*. 26.102–103; CC 46: 104,50–105,19; 30/39

Holy Spirit, *one God*. Therefore *one God, and one mediator between God and humanity, Christ Jesus, himself human.*

Had [Paul] said 'one God, and one mediator between God and humanity,' we would have taken Christ Jesus to be a kind of lesser God. He would be excluded from the divine nature of the Trinity if 'there is one God, and one mediator between God and humanity, Christ Jesus'—as if he is not the God who is said to be one. But because the Father, the Son and the Holy Spirit exist in the unity of God, the divine nature preserves the unity, humanity takes on mediation, and by this mediation the whole mass of the human race, which was estranged from God by Adam, is reconciled to God.

—from a sermon on the birthday of John the Baptist*

408. *I want, then, the men to pray in every place, lifting up pure hands.*† †**1 Tm 2:8**

'And in your name I will lift up my hands.'† And so, lift up †Ps 63:4
hands in prayer! Our Lord lifted up his hands on the cross for us, and his hands were extended for us. His hands were extended on the cross so that our hands may be extended in good works, since his cross brought us mercy. See how he lifted up his hands, and offered himself as a sacrifice to God for us, and by that sacrifice all our sins were wiped away! Let us too lift up our hands to God in prayer—our hands, being lifted up to God, will not be balked if they are employed in good works.

What do those who lift up hands do? Where are we commanded to pray to God with uplifted hands? The Apostle says, *lifting up pure hands, without anger and quarreling*. This is so that when you lift up your hands to God, your works may come to your mind. Those hands that are lifted up so that you may obtain what you want, those same hands you think to employ in good works, so that they may not be ashamed to be lifted up to God.

—from the treatise on Psalm 62*

---

*407. *Serm.* 293.7–8; PL 38: 1333
*408. *En. in Ps* 62.13; CC 39: 801,8–802,23

†**1 Tm 2:13–14**

409. *Adam was made first, then Eve . . .* †

'A man ought not to cover his head, since he is the image and glory of God; woman, however, is the glory of man.' This is not because the female soul cannot receive the same image, since [Paul] says that in that grace 'there is neither male nor female.'† Perhaps [Eve] had not yet received what comes with the knowledge of God, and with her husband's guidance and management she had been going to receive it gradually.

†1 Co 11:7; Ga 3:28

The Apostle had a purpose in saying that *Adam was formed first, then Eve; and Adam was not deceived, but the woman was deceived and became a transgressor*—that is, through her the man too transgressed. [Paul] also calls [Adam] a transgressor where he says, 'after the pattern of the transgression of Adam, who is an image of the one who was to come,' yet he denies that he was deceived. When questioned [Adam] did not say, 'The woman whom you gave to be with me deceived me and I ate,' but 'she gave me [fruit] from the tree,' he said, 'and I ate'—whereas she said, 'The serpent deceived me.'†

†Rm 5:14; Gn 3:12–13

So with Solomon, a man of very great wisdom. Are we to suppose that he believed the worship of idols of some use? Yet he had not the strength to resist the love of the women who were drawing him to this evil.† He was doing what he was aware should not be done, in order not to make the women by whom he was being ruined unhappy and so deprive himself of their deadly delights.

†1 K 11:4

So too with Adam. After the woman had been deceived and ate from the forbidden tree, and gave to him so that they may eat together,† he did not want to make her unhappy. He believed that she could waste away without his solace if she should be estranged from him, and may altogether perish because of this disaffection. [Adam] was not overcome by any carnal craving—he had not yet experienced this in a law in his members resisting the law in his mind.† [He was, however, overcome] by the kind of friendly good will that often leads us to offend God in order not to make a friend into an enemy. That he should not have done so the just outcome of the divine sentence made clear.

†Gn 3:6

†Rm 7:23

Therefore he was deceived in some other way. I do not think that he could have been deceived at all by the snaky guile that deceived the woman. The Apostle has called it 'deception' in the proper sense when what was being urged was taken to be true when it was false—that is, that God forbade [Adam and Eve] to touch the tree because he was aware that if they touched it they would be like gods, as if the one who had made them human begrudged them divinity!

—from the *Literal Commentary on Genesis* 11.44*

410. *Whoever desires the office of overseer desires a noble task.*† †1 Tm 3:1

In what we do we should not prize honor and power in this life, since everything under the sun is vain,† but the task itself that we accomplish through the honor and power, if it is done properly and helpfully—that is, if it contributes to that salvation which is God's intention. This is why the Apostle says that *whoever desires the office of overseer desires a noble task.* He wanted to explain what the word† *office of overseer* is—it names a *task*, not an honor. The word is Greek, and derives from the fact that those set over others 'oversee' those they are set over, showing concern for them. *Skopos* means attention, and so if we wish we can translate *episcopein* by 'oversee.' Thus we can understand that those who like to preside over others, not to profit them, are not overseers.

†Qo 1:2–3 Vulgate

†*Episcopatus*—it can also be translated 'office of bishop.'

No one is forbidden to strive to know the truth, for that is bound up with praiseworthy leisure. Ambition for the higher position without which a people cannot be governed, however, even if it can be held and administered as it should be, is unseemly. On account of this the love of truth seeks holy leisure, the constraint of love undertakes holy activity.

—from *On the City of God* [19].19*

411. *Now an overseer must be irreproachable.*† †1 Tm 3:2

So it is, and who would deny it? But since *an overseer must be irreproachable*, is it right for a Christian to be reproachable? The word *episcopus* is Greek; we can say *overseer* or 'visitor.' We are *overseers*, but with you we are Christians. We get our special name from 'visiting,'

*409. *De Gen. ad Litt.* 11.42; CSEL 28,1: 377,6–378,17

*410. *De Civ. Dei* 19.19; CC 48: 686,17–687,35 passim

†*Unctio*, Latin for the Greek *chrisma*, anointing. Christ is 'the anointed one.'

and we all get our common name from 'anointing.'† If our anointing is universal, so is our wrestling-match. Why do we 'visit' if we see no good in you?

—from a sermon on the kind of person an overseer ought to be, and when Paul reproached Peter*

†**1 Tm 3:2**

412. *An overseer must be irreproachable, the husband of one wife.*†

Those who have taken this more narrowly have judged that one who as a catechumen or pagan had another wife should not be ordained. This is a question of the sacrament, not of sin. In baptism all sins are forgiven. The one who said, 'If you take a wife, you have not sinned, and if a virgin marries, she does not sin'; 'Let him do what he wills; he does not sin; let her marry,'† has made perfectly clear that marriage is not a sin. But because of the sanctity of the sacrament, just as a woman, a catechumen who has lost her virginity, cannot become a consecrated virgin after her baptism, so it does not seem unreasonable that a person who has had more than one wife has not committed a sin but has forfeited a certain standard to the sacrament, something not necessary to the merit of a good life but to the seal of ecclesiastical ordination. For this reason, as the several wives of our ancestors represented our future churches of all nations brought under one husband, Christ, so our bishop, *the husband of one wife*, represents the unity of all nations brought under Christ.

†1 Co 7:28, 36

—from *On the Good of Marriage**

413. *Rebuke sinners in the presence of all, so that the rest also may have fear.*†

†**1 Tm 5:20**

We must take this of sins that are not secret lest we suppose that the Apostle was speaking against the Lord's statement. [Jesus]

*411. *Serm.* PL 39: 1734
*412. *De Bono Coniug.* 18.21; CSEL 41: 214,8–215,5

said, 'If your brother sins against you, rebuke him between you and him alone.'† †Mt 18:15

—from *On Rebuke and Grace*★

414. *Godliness combined with contentment is great gain.*† **†1 Tm 6:6**

'We know that all things work together for good for those who love God.'† They have lost all they used to have. Does this include †Rm 8:28 their faith? Their godliness? The blessings of the inner self, which is rich in God's sight? These are the resources of Christians, and to those who possess them the Apostle says, *Godliness combined with contentment is great gain. We brought nothing into this world, but neither can we take anything out of it. Possessing food and covering, with them we are content. Those who want to become rich fall into temptation . . . and they have involved themselves in many sorrows.*† **†1 Tm 6:6–10**

In the case of those whose earthly riches were destroyed in the sack [of Rome], if they had possessed them in the spirit they learned from the one who was outwardly poor but inwardly rich—that is, if they used the world as if not using it—they would have been able to say with a person who was seriously tried but not overcome, 'Naked I came from my mother's womb, naked shall I return to the earth; the Lord gave, the Lord has taken away; as it has pleased the Lord, so has it been done.'† As a good servant he counted his Lord's will †1 Co 7:31; Jb 1:21 itself as great abundance— by attending on it his soul would grow, and not be saddened by having to leave behind while yet alive those things he was soon going to have to leave behind when he died.

Vacillating persons who, although they did not prefer these earthly goods to Christ, yet clung to them with a certain amount of attachment, perceived by losing them how greatly they sinned by loving them. They grieved to the extent that they had *involved themselves in sorrows*, as I reminded you that the Apostle said. When the Apostle said, *Those who want to become rich fall into temptation*, and so on, clearly in regard to riches he is finding fault with the craving, not with the possession. Concerning this he charged elsewhere,

★413. *De Corrept. et Gratia* 16.49; PL 44: 946

Charge the rich of this world not to be high-minded, nor to trust in the uncertainty of riches, but in the living God, who abundantly provides us with all things for our enjoyment. They are to do good, to be rich in good
†**1 Tm 6:17–19** *works, to give readily, to share . . .* †

—from *On the City of God* 1.10*

415. [Paul] does not say 'those who are rich,' but *those who want to*
†**1 Tm 6:9** *become rich fall into temptation, and a trap, and many harmful desires*†—by wanting to become so, not by being so. Therefore he speaks of *desires*. Desire exists in those who want to attain something. No one desires what is already possessed. Greed cannot be satisfied. In people with many possessions we must not speak of desire for the thing they possess but for the thing they do not possess. By wanting to be rich they desire, they are inflamed, they thirst—and like those with the disease of dropsy, the more they drink the thirstier they are.

—from a sermon on the same text*

†**1 Tm 6:10** 416. *The root of all evils is greed.*†

Scripture set down that pride is the beginning of all sin when
†Si 10:13 (15) it said, 'The beginning of all sin is pride.'† What the Apostle says, *The root of all evils is greed*, supports this statement, if we take *greed* in a general sense to mean that by which people, on account of their exceptional worth and a certain love of their own interests, desire more than is reasonable. In a particular sense *greed* is what we more commonly call 'love of money.' By this word the Apostle, indicating the general by the particular, wanted us to understand all kinds of *greed* when he said that *the root of all evils is greed*. This caused the fall of the devil—who did not love money, of course, but his own power.

—from the *Literal Commentary on Genesis* 11.11*

---

*414. *De Civ. Dei* 1.10; CC 47: 10,4–11,40 passim
*415. *Serm*. 177.6; PL 38: 956 passim
*416. *De Gen. ad Litt*. 11.15; CSEL 28,1: 347,1/7; 12/17

417. We sometimes ask how these two statements can agree: *The root of all evils is greed*, and, 'The beginning of all sin is pride.'† If pride is the beginning of all sin, then pride is *the root of all evils*. Undoubtedly *the root of all evils is greed*. We find greed present in pride, for humanity has exceeded its bounds. What is being greedy? To go beyond what is enough. Adam fell through pride. 'The beginning of all sin is pride,' it says. Was it by greed? What is greedier than one for whom God could not be enough?

†**1 Tm 6:10**; Si 10:13 (15)

—from homily eight on the Letter of Saint John*

418. 'Turn my heart to your testimonies and not to greed.' God deals with us by means of his testimonies so that we may worship him without recompense. *Greed, the root of all evils*,† hinders this. [Paul] calls it here by a Greek word meaning *greed* in general, that which makes a person desire more than enough. The Greek word *pleon* means 'more'; *hexis* is a condition, from the verb meaning 'to possess.' Therefore from 'possessing more' we have the word *pleonexia*, which some commentators on this passage have translated 'profit' and others 'utility'—but those [who say] *greed* do better.

†Ps 119:36; **1 Tm 6:10**. Some liberty has been taken with the lines that follow.

The Apostle says, *The root of all evils is greed*. In Greek, however, from which the words have been translated into our language, we do not read in the Apostle's text *pleonexia*, as in this psalm, but *philarguria*, a word meaning 'love of money.' By this word we must take the Apostle to have been indicating the general by the particular—that is, greed universally, which truly is *the root of all evils*, by love of money. The first human beings would not have been deceived by the serpent and heaved [out of paradise] if they had not wanted to possess more than they had received and to be more than they had been created to be. [The devil] had promised them this, telling them, 'You will be like gods.'† They were, then, overthrown by *pleonexia*. Wanting to possess more than they had received, they lost what they had received.

†Gn 3:5

—from the treatise on Psalm 118*

*417. *In Ioh. Ep.* 8.6; PL 35: 2038–39
*418. *En. in Ps* 118.11.6; CC 40: 1698,10/11; 16–1699,37

419. *Some people, desiring this, have strayed from the faith and have*
†1 Tm 6:10 *involved themselves in many sorrows.*†

If you choose to tie up your heart by love of money you involve yourself *in many sorrows*, and where will [these words] be, *But as for*
†1 Tm 6:11 *you, man of God, flee these things?*† He does not say 'leave them behind and abandon them' but *flee*—as from an enemy. You were seeking to flee with gold—flee from gold! In this case, if you are unwilling to be a servant, be a fugitive.

You have heard what you are to flee, and you also possess what you are to pursue. *Pursue righteousness, faith, godliness, love.* Let these make you rich. These riches are inside. No thief has access to them, unless an evil will provides an opening.

—from a sermon on the same text*

420. *To keep the commandment without stain, blameless, until the coming of our Lord, which he who is blessed and sole Sovereign, the King of kings*
†1 Tm 6:14–15 *and Lord of lords, will manifest in his own times.*†

If [Paul] had said, *which* the Father, *who is blessed and sole Sovereign, the King of kings and Lord of lords, will manifest in his own times, he who alone has immortality*—even then we should not take the Son to be excluded from this. The Son himself, speaking elsewhere with the voice of wisdom—he is 'the wisdom of God'—says, 'I
†1 Co 1:24; Si 24:5 (8) alone have traversed the circuit of heaven';† he has not separated the Father from himself. How much less necessary, then, for us to take the words *who alone has immortality* of the Father apart from the Son, since [Paul says], *to keep the commandment without stain, blameless, until the coming of our Lord Jesus Christ, which he who is blessed and sole Sovereign, the King of kings and Lord of lords, will manifest in his own times, he who alone has immortality and dwells in unapproachable*
†1 Tm 6:14–16 *light.*† In these words neither the Father nor the Son nor the Holy Spirit is specifically named, but the *blessed and sole Sovereign, the King of kings and Lord of lords.*, which is the one sole true God, the Trinity itself.

---

*419. *Serm.* 177.3–4; PL 38: 955 passim

Unless perhaps what follows will upset this interpretation, since [Paul] has said *whom no one has seen or can see*. This too we can take as relating to Christ in his divine nature, which the Jews did not see, although they saw and crucified his flesh. Divinity cannot in any way be seen by human sight, but it is seen by that sight which makes those who already see by it not human but more than human. Rightly then do we understand that the triune God itself is the *blessed and sole Sovereign*, manifesting *the coming of our Lord Jesus Christ in his own times*.

—from *On the Holy Trinity* 1.6*

421. *And he dwells*, [Paul] says, *in unapproachable light*.† **†1 Tm 6:16**

[The psalmist] says here, 'With my lips I have declared all the judgments of your mouth.' Perhaps God's judgments have been called inscrutable to people because they cannot scrutinize them by their own powers. But why can they not [scrutinize them] by the gift of the Holy Spirit—they on whom the Lord deigns to bestow this gift? We also say of God that *he dwells in unapproachable light*, and yet we hear, 'Come to him, and be enlightened.'† The problem †Ps 119:13; 34:5
is surely solved in this way, that he is unapproachable by our own powers, but we can come to him by his own gifts.

—in the explanation of Psalm 118*

422. *Charge the rich of this world not to be high-minded*.† **†1 Tm 6:17**

Charge the rich, Paul says, *of this world*, since there are also the 'rich of God,' and they are not truly rich unless they are rich of God. Such was Paul, who said, 'I have learned to be content in whatever state I am.'† †Ph 4:11

Nor to trust in the uncertainty of riches. Do you love gold? Make certain, if you can, that you are not afraid of losing it. Have you gathered a fortune? Provide yourself, if you can, with security.

---

*420. *De Trin*. 1.6.10–11; CC 50: 39,36–40,63 passim
*421. *En. in Ps* 118.6.1–2; CC 40: 1679,2/3; 1680,15/22

But in the living God, who abundantly provides us with all things for our enjoyment. If *all things*, how much more himself! And truly *for our enjoyment* he himself will be *all things*. It seems to me that *who abundantly gives us all things for our enjoyment* is not said except of himself. Use seems to be one thing and enjoyment another. We use things from necessity; we enjoy them from delight. [God] gives us temporal things to use, himself to enjoy. If [he gives us] himself, why does [Paul] say *all things* unless because it is written, 'So that
†1 Co 15:28 God may be all in all'?†
†1 Tm 6:18 *They are to be rich in good works* so that they *give readily*.† Be rich for this reason, to give readily. The poor want to give and cannot—with them is difficulty, with you ease. That you are rich works to your advantage, because when you want to do something you do it at once. *They are to give readily, to share.* Do they lose anything? They are to *store up for themselves the treasure of a good foundation for*
†1 Tm 6:19 *the future*.†

—from a sermon on the same text*

*422. *Serm*. 177.7–10; PL 38: 957–59 passim

Saint Augustine's Commentary

the Second Letter from Paul to Timothy

IF WE DO NOT BELIEVE, *he remains faithful—he cannot deny himself.*† †**2 Tm 2:13**

[John] said, 'They could not believe.'† Here we must understand that they would not. In the same way it was said of the Lord our God, *If we do not believe, he remains faithful—he cannot deny himself.* Of the Almighty it is said that *he cannot*! Therefore as the fact that the Lord *cannot deny himself* is praise of the divine will, so the fact that 'they could not' is blame of the human will. †Jn 12:39

—from homily fifty on the Gospel of John*

424. *And their talk spreads like a cancer. Among them are Hymenaeus and Philetus, who have wandered around the truth by claiming that the resurrection has already taken place.*† †**2 Tm 2:17–18**

Let us therefore hold fast to both resurrections, the spiritual and the bodily. What the Apostle said refers to the spiritual one: 'If you have risen with Christ, seek the things that are above'; and in another passage, 'Rise, you who sleep, and arise from the dead, and Christ will enlighten you.' On the other hand, his words, 'But someone asks, How do the dead rise? With what kind of body do they come?'† refer to the bodily one. †Col 3:1; Eph 5:14; 1 Co 15:35

Those, then, *who have wandered around the truth* have not altogether denied the resurrection. If they denied it in every respect they would be wandering away from the truth, not *around the truth.* Because they *have wandered around the truth* they have confessed one but denied the other. They have said *that the resurrection has already taken place*, so that no resurrection of the body was to be hoped for, *and have overthrown the faith of some.*

—from a sermon on the resurrection of the dead*

425. *They have overthrown the faith of some.*† †**2 Tm 2:18**

[Paul] did not say 'of everyone'—and if he were to say 'of everyone' we would have to understand this as 'everyone belonging

*423. *Tract. in Ioh.* 53.9; CC 36: 456, 6/12
*424. *Serm.* 362.20.23–21-24; PL 39: 1627–28 passim

to the city of Babylon,' which he holds to be condemned along with the devil. Yet he said *the faith of some.* And as if we were asking him, 'And who is able to resist them?' he added at once, *But God's firm foundation stands, bearing this inscription: The Lord knows those who are his.* This is 'the world that shall not be shaken': *The Lord knows those who are his.*†

†**2 Tm 2:19**; Ps 93:1

And what inscription does it bear? *And let everyone who calls on the name of the Lord depart from wickedness.* Let them only *depart from wickedness*; they cannot depart from the wicked, because the chaff is mixed with the wheat until the winnowing takes place.† What am I saying, brothers and sisters? Even on the threshing floor itself a marvel takes place concerning the wheat: it parts from the chaff when it is stripped, and does not part from the threshing floor when it is threshed. When will it be altogether separated? When the winnower comes. As yet the threshing floor is in the entire world—to make progress you must live among the wicked. You cannot depart from the wicked; *depart from wickedness.*

†Mt 3:12, 13:29–30

—from the treatise on Psalm 92*

426. *Let everyone who calls on the name of the Lord depart from wickedness.*†

†**2 Tm 2:19**

If they do not depart from wickedness they do not belong to the kingdom of Christ, even though they call on Christ's name. *The Lord knows those who are his.* People should not delude themselves about a word. If they want the Lord's name to benefit them, let those who call *on the name of the Lord depart from wickedness.*

—from a sermon on blasphemy against the Holy Spirit*

427. *In a great house are utensils not only of gold and silver but also of wood and clay; some are for honor, others for shame.*†

†**2 Tm 2:20**

The Apostle also speaks of certain people *who had wandered around the truth* and were overthrowing *the faith of some*, whose *talk*

*425. *En. in Ps* 92.5; CC 39: 1295,22/40 passim
*426. *Serm.* 71.2.4; PL 38: 446–47 passim

was spreading like a cancer.† When he said that they were to be avoided he is indicating that they were in the one *great house*, but as *utensils for shame*—I suppose because they had not yet departed. Or, if they had already departed, why does he say that they were in the same *great house* along with the honorable *utensils*? Perhaps it is on account of the sacraments themselves, which have not been altered even in the separate gatherings of the heretics. He says that they all belong to one *great house*, but with different degrees of merit—some people *for honor*, others *for shame*.

†**2 Tm 2:18, 17**

If any cleanse themselves from such things, they will be utensils for honor, sanctified, useful to the Lord, ready for every good work.† What does cleansing oneself from such things mean if not what [Paul] had just said: *Let everyone who calls on the name of the Lord depart from wickedness*?† And so that none would suppose that, as being in the one house, they could perish along with such as these, he told them earlier with great care, *The Lord knows those who are his*—those, that is, who by departing from wickedness cleanse themselves from the utensils made *for shame*, so as not to perish with those whom they are compelled to tolerate in the *great house*.

†**2 Tm 2:21**

†**2 Tm 2:19**

—from *On the One Baptism* 3*

428. [The number of the just, of whom Scripture says,] *The Lord knows those who are his*, are themselves 'the garden enclosed, the fountain sealed, the well of living water, the paradise with fruit of the orchard.' Certain persons from this number live spiritually and enter on the 'supereminent way' of love. When they 'instruct a person detected in some transgression in a spirit of gentleness' they 'take note lest they too be tempted.'† When perhaps they too are detected, the disposition of love is somewhat repressed in them, though not extinguished, and, rising up and burning brightly again, it is restored to its former course. They have learned to say, 'My soul has slumbered from weariness; strengthen me by your words.' When they 'think differently about anything' this too God will reveal to

†**2 Tm 2:19**; Sg 4:12, 15, 13; 1 Co 12:31; Ga 6:1

*427. *De Bapt. Contra Donat.* 3.19.26; CSEL 51: 218,13/23; 219,7/17

them, as they live in the burning flame of love, and do not break
†Ps 119:28; Ph 3:15; Eph 4:3 'the bond of peace.'†

—from *On the One Baptism* 5*

429. *The Lord's servant must not be contentious, but be gentle toward*
†**2 Tm 2:24** *everyone, an apt teacher, patient.*†

The holy man Cyprian was not only taught, he was also teachable. He himself so understood the character the Apostle describes in his praise of a bishop that he said that this too should be valued in a bishop—not only should he teach with knowledge, but he should
†*Letter* 74 also learn with patience.†

—from *On the One Baptism* 4*

†**2 Tm 3:5** 430. *Having an appearance of godliness but denying its power.*†

You have just heard, as the lesson was being read, that Simon the magician was baptized but did not put aside his evil disposition. He possessed the form of the sacrament; the power of the sacrament he did not have. Listen to what the Apostle says about the ungodly: *Having the form of godliness*, he says, *but denying its power.* What is the *form of godliness*? The visible sacrament. What is the *power* of godliness? Invisible love. Listen to the *power* of godliness: 'If I speak with the tongues of humans and of angels, but do not have love, I
†Ac 8:9–23; 1 Co 13:1 have become like sounding bronze . . .'†

—from a sermon [delivered] on the octave of Easter*

431. *I charge you, in the presence of God and of Christ Jesus, who is to*
†**2 Tm 4:1** *judge the living and the dead.*†

That Christ's will judge the living and the dead we can take in two ways. We can understand *the living* to be those not yet dead in

---

*428. *Ibid.* 5.27.38; CSEL 51: 294,16/28
*429. *Ibid.* 4.5.7; CSEL 51: 228,18/22 (Cyprian, *Ep.* 74; CSEL 3,2: 807,16/19)
*430. *Serm.* PL 39: 1727

this world but whom his coming will find still alive in this flesh, and *the dead* to be those who have left or will leave their bodies before he comes; or, [we may understand] *the living* to be the righteous, and *the dead* the unrighteous, since the righteous too are going to be judged.

—from *Enchiridion* 54*

432. *As for me, I am already being immolated, and the time of my departure has come.*† †2 Tm 4:6

[Paul] said that he was *being immolated*, not that he was dying. This was not because a person being immolated does not die, but because not everyone who dies is immolated. Immolation is death for God—the word denotes sacrifice. Everything sacrificed is slaughtered for God. The Apostle understood this: to whom he owed his blood in suffering. He for whom his Lord's blood was shed became a debtor to his blood. That one man shed his blood, and pledged us all [to do the same].

—from a sermon on the birthday of the apostles Peter and Paul*

433. *I am already being immolated.* What does *I am being immolated* mean? I will be a sacrifice. Whose sacrifice, if not God's? 'Precious in the sight of the Lord is the death of his saints.'† *As for me*, [Paul] says, *I am already being immolated.* I am safe. I have a priest on high who is offering me to God. I have the very priest who was earlier a victim for me. †2 Tm 4:6; Ps 116:15

I am already being immolated, and the time of my departure has come. He means *departure* from his body. The body is a kind of agreeable fetter; a human is bound, and does not want to be set free. Yet the one who was saying that 'my desire is to depart and be with Christ'† was thankful that these fetters were finally to be removed, that the fetters of his bodily members were to be removed, †Ph 1:23

---

*431. *Enchir.* 14.55; CC 46: 79,118/23
*432. *Serm.* 299.3; PL 38: 1368

and that he was to receive the garments and adornments of the eternal virtues.

I have fought the good fight, I have finished the course, I have kept
†2 Tm 4:7–8 *the faith; as to the rest, a crown of righteousness remains for me.*† You are right to hurry, right to rejoice that you are to be immolated—*a crown of righteousness remains for* you! The bitterness of suffering still awaits him, but the thought of the one who is going to suffer passes beyond it. He is thinking of what is beyond—not the means of his going, but where he is going; and as he is thinking with great love of where he is going, he scorns with great fortitude the means of his going.

—from another sermon on the birthday of the same apostles*

434. *I have fought the good fight, I have finished the course, I have kept*
†2 Tm 4:7 *the faith.*†

'The Lord loves mercy and truth.' At first [Paul] says, 'I, who was formerly a blasphemer, a persecutor, and a man of violence,
†Ps 83:12 Vulgate; 1 Tm 1:13; 1 Co 15:10 have obtained mercy.' 'By the grace of God I am what I am.'† Later, as he was approaching his passion, he says *I have fought the good fight, I have finished the course, I have kept the faith; as to the rest, a crown of righteousness remains for me.* The one who bestows mercy keeps truth. How does he keep truth? *[A crown of righteousness] which the Lord,*
†2 Tm 4:8 *a righteous judge, will give me on that day.*† He has granted pardon, he will give a crown. He is the grantor of pardon, the debtor of a crown.

The Lord will give me, Paul says, *on that day*. What will he give you except what he owes you? How does he owe it to you? What have you given him? 'Who has first given to him, and recompense will
†Rm 11:35 be made him?'† The Lord made himself a debtor, not by receiving but by promising. We do not say to him, 'Give what you have received,' but 'Give what you have promised.' He expended mercy on me, [Paul] says, to make me innocent—'I who was formerly a blasphemer and a man of violence'—but by his grace I have become

*433. *Serm.* 298.2.3–3; PL 38: 1366 passim

innocent. Can the one who first expended mercy deny his debt? 'He loves mercy and truth.'

—in the explanation of Psalm 83*

435. So that he would not seem to be glorying overmuch, as though he was unique, and to be appropriating the Lord for himself, [Paul] says, *and not only to me, but also to all who long for his appearing.*† He †2 Tm 4:8
could not suggest better and more succinctly what people ought to do in order to be worthy of *a crown of righteousness.* We must not all of us expect to shed our blood—martyrs are few, but believers are many. Are you unable to be immolated like Paul? You can keep the faith. By keeping the faith you *long for his appearing.* If you are afraid of the Lord's coming, you do not *long for his appearing.* The Lord Christ is now hidden. Our future Judge, who was unjustly accused before a judge, will justly appear at his own time. If you keep the faith, and truly long for his appearing, you should await *a crown of righteousness* without anxiety.

—from a sermon on the birthday of the apostles Peter and Paul*

436. *Alexander the coppersmith has done me much harm. The Lord will repay him according to his deeds.*† †2 Tm 4:14

To those who reflect without much care or sense many other parts of Scripture appear to contradict the Lord's precept in which he urges us to love our enemies, to do good to those who hate us, and to pray for those who persecute us.† In the prophets we find †Mt 5:44
many invocations of evil against their enemies. These we judge to be curses—for example, 'May his children be orphans, and his wife a widow.' Even of our Lord it is written that he cursed the cities that did not accept his word.† The Apostle, too, spoke thus against †Ps 109:9; Mt 11:20–24
a certain person: *The Lord will repay him according to his deeds.*

*434. *En. in Ps* 83.16; CC 39: 1159,2–1160,3; 19/27; 30/39
*435. *Serm.* 299.4–5; PL 38: 1369–70 passim

These passages can be easily explained. In his invocation of evil the prophet sang of what was going to be—not as one praying for what he wanted, but in the spirit of one who saw it beforehand. So too the Lord; so too the Apostle—in their words too we do not find what they wanted but what they foretold. When the Lord says, 'Woe to you, Capernaum,' he only says that some evil is going to befall them because of their lack of faith; the Lord did not pray for this by ill-will but perceived it by divinity. And the Apostle does not say, 'May the Lord repay,' but, *The Lord will repay him according to his deeds*. These are the words of someone foretelling evil, not invoking it.

But the words of the apostle John make the question more urgent. 'Those aware that a brother or sister is committing a sin that is not deadly will ask, and God will give life to the one whose sin is not deadly. There is, however, a deadly sin. I do not say that anyone should pray for it.'† I suppose that a brother or sister's sin is deadly when, after coming to the knowledge of our Lord Jesus Christ, they attack the fellowship, and are stirred up by the flames of resentment against the very grace by which they were reconciled to God. 'A sin that is not deadly' exists if people do not direct their love away from a brother or sister, but through some weakness of spirit they fail to perform the duties required of the fellowship. This is why the Lord said on the cross, 'Father, forgive them, for they do not know what they are doing.' As they had not yet become sharers in the grace of the Holy Spirit, they had not yet entered the company of the holy fellowship. And blessed Stephen, in the Acts of the Apostles, prays for those who are stoning him†—they had not yet believed in Christ, and were not contending against the common grace. The apostle Paul, as I see it, does not pray for Alexander because he was already a brother, and had committed a deadly sin by attacking the brotherhood—that is, the sin of resentment.

†1 Jn 5:16

†Lk 23:34; Ac 7:60

For those, however, who had not sundered love but had surrendered to fear he prays that it be forgiven them. This is what he says: *Alexander the coppersmith has done me much harm. The Lord will repay him according to his deeds. You, too, avoid him, for he strongly resisted our words*. Then he adds for whom he does pray: *At my first defense no one was there to defend me, but everyone abandoned me; may it not be counted against them!*† †**2 Tm 4:14–16**

This difference in their sins distinguishes Judas, who betrayed [Christ], from Peter, who denied him—not that we should not forgive a person who repents, lest we come into opposition to the Lord's statement in which he tells us always to forgive a brother or sister who asks a brother or sister for forgiveness. The ruin of [Judas's] sin, however, is so great that he cannot submit to the humiliation of asking [for forgiveness] even if his bad conscience should compel him both to acknowledge his sin and to declare it.† †Mt 18:21; Lk 17:3–4; Mt 27:4

—from *On the Lord's Sermon on the Mount* 1*

437. I was saying that the works of mercy are signified and prefigured allegorically by the fruits of the earth, which the fruitful earth provides for the necessities of this life. Such an 'earth' was the devout Onesiphorus, to whose household you gave mercy because he often refreshed your [servant] Paul, and was not ashamed of his chain.† †2 Tm 1:16, 4:19 But how [Paul] grieves for certain 'trees' which have not given him the fruit due him when he says, *At my first defense no one was there to defend me, but everyone abandoned me; may it not be counted against them!*† †**2 Tm 4:16** These [fruits] are due to those who minister spiritual doctrine through their understanding of the divine mysteries.

—from *Confessions* 13, commenting on the beginning of Genesis†* †Gn 1:29

*436. *De Serm. Dom. in Monte* 1.21.71–74; CC 35: 79,1732/39; 80,1744/57; 81,1773/77; 82,1791–84,1819

*437. *Confess.* 13.25 (38); CC 27: 265,11/22

Saint Augustine's Commentary

the Letter from Paul to Titus

IN THE HOPE OF ETERNAL LIFE that God, who does not lie, promised before the eternal times.† †Tt 1:2

I admit that I do not know what ages passed before the human race was created. Yet, I do not doubt that no creature at all is coeternal with the Creator. The Apostle spoke of *eternal times*, [referring] not to future times but, what is surprising, to those that are past. This is what he says: *In the hope of eternal life that God, who does not lie, promised before the eternal times; in his own times he revealed his Word.* See how he spoke of *eternal times* that existed before, yet were not coeternal with God; before *the eternal times* [God] not only existed, but he also promised the *eternal life* that *he revealed in his own times*—that is, in appropriate times.

What else was this than his Word? This is eternal life. But how did he make this promise, since surely he made his promise to human beings who did not yet exist *before the eternal times*? Is it not that what was to be *in his own times* had already been determined by predestination in his eternity, and in his very Word that is coeternal with him?

—from *On the City of God* 12*

439. The Apostle calls earlier *times* in the distant past *eternal*—we read in Greek *pro chronon aionion*. Writing to Titus he refers to *the hope of eternal life that God, who does not lie, promised before the eternal times.*† Since, however, the *times* seem to have a beginning back with †Tt 1:2
the foundation of the world,† how are they *eternal*, unless he called †Eph 1:4
eternal those that have no time before them?

—from *A Reply to the Questions of the Priest Orosius**

440. *One of them, their very own prophet, said.*† †Tt 1:12

I am not surprised that an uneducated person thinks that the Apostle's statement, *One of them, their very own prophet, has said,*

---

*438. *De Civ. Dei* 12.17; CC 48: 373,1/16
*439. *Ad Oros. Contra Prisc. et Orig.* 5.6; CC 49: 170,143/49

'Cretans are always liars, evil beasts, lazy gluttons.' This statement is true, refers to the prophets of the Jews. He does not know that this was said by a certain Epimenides, who was a Cretan, in whose books it is found. This man is not among the Lord's prophets, nor does [the saying] belong among the utterances—which [Paul] says were entrusted to the Jews—of God, who does not lie.

—from *Against the Opponent of the Law and the Prophets* 2*

†Tt 3:5

441. *He saved us, according to his mercy, through the washing of rebirth.*†

Does anyone fail to understand that a hope of future salvation has been given us in the washing of rebirth, and not yet salvation itself, which is only promised? And yet, because our hope is certain, [Paul] said that *he saved us*, as though salvation had already been given us.

—from *Against Faustus* 11*

*440. *Contra Adv. Leg. et Prophet.* 2.4.13; CC 49: 100,427–101,434
*441. *Contra Faust. Manich.* 11.7; CSEL 25: 324,17/22

Saint Augustine's Commentary

the Letter from Paul to the Hebrews

TO WHICH OF THE ANGELS did [God] ever say, 'You are my Son; today I have begotten you'?† †**Heb 1:5** (Ps 2:7)

Although prophecy may seem to have spoken of that day on which Christ Jesus was born in his human nature, we must interpret *today*, since it signifies the present—and in eternity nothing is past, as if it has ceased to be, or future, as if it does not yet exist, but only present, since whatever is eternal always exists—in a divine sense in accord with the words, 'Today I have begotten you.' In these words the most authentic and catholic faith proclaims the eternal begetting of the Power and Wisdom of God, who is the only-begotten Son.

—in the explanation of Psalm 2*

443. *And to the angels he says, 'He makes his spirits angels.'*† †**Heb 1:7** (Ps 104:4)

'He makes his spirits angels'—that is, he makes those who are by nature spirits to be his angels by laying on them the duty of carrying messages. The being called *angelos* in Greek is represented by the Latin word *angelus*, and translated by 'messenger.' As to whether as a consequence of this [God] added bodies to them—since he says, 'and his ministers a burning fire'—or his ministers have to burn with love as with spiritual fire, is not clear.

—from *On the City of God* 15.23*

444. 'And he makes his ministers a blazing fire.' We read that a fire appeared in a thorn-bush. We also read that fire was sent from above and accomplished what was commanded.† It ministered, then, when it accomplished [what was commanded]. When it [merely] existed, it was in its natural state. When it did what it was bidden, it accomplished a ministry. †Ps 104:4; Ex 3:2; Ac 2:3–4

—in the explanation of Psalm 103*

---

*442. *En. in Ps* 2.6; CC 38: 5,2/10
*443. *De Civ. Dei* 15.23; CC 48: 488,4/11
*444. *En. in Ps* 103.1.15; CC 40: 1488,16/20

†**Heb 1:8** (Ps 45:6)

445. *To the Son [God says], 'Your throne, O God, is from age to age.'*†

'Your throne, O God, is from age to age.' The throne of the Jewish kingdom was temporal; it belonged to those who were under the law. [Christ] came 'to deliver those who were under the law.' Why is the throne now 'from age to age'? Because it is God's. 'The scepter of your kingdom is a scepter of uprightness.'† The 'scepter of uprightness' makes people upright. They were bent, they were misshapen, they wanted to govern themselves, they loved themselves, they were fond of their evil deeds, and they did not subject their own wills to God but wanted to bend God's will to their own cravings.

†Ps 45:6

Sinners and unfair persons are often angry with God because it does not rain, and do not want God to be angry with them because it does rain.† God's will is uniform, yours is bent. Be upright toward it—do not choose to bend it to yourself. Do you want to be united with him? Set yourself right and his scepter which rules you will be a 'scepter of uprightness.' 'Ruler' comes from 'ruling.' No one rules who is not right. This is why our king is King of the upright. As he is a priest for sanctifying us, so is he a ruler by ruling us.

†The Latin text of this sentence is uncertain.

Listen to another psalm: 'How good God is to Israel, to the upright in heart.' See the 'scepter of uprightness': 'You have loved justice and hated wickedness.' Draw near that scepter. Let Christ be your king. Let him rule you with that scepter, not break you. That scepter is iron, it does not bend. What has been said of it? 'You will rule them with a scepter of iron.'† Some he rules, others he crushes. He rules the spiritual, crushes the carnal.

†Ps 73:1, 45:7, 2:9

'Therefore God, your God, has anointed you with the oil of gladness beyond your companions.'† 'Therefore he has anointed you'—that you may love justice and hate wickedness. And see how he says, 'God, your God, has anointed you.' In Latin we think that the same case of the word is repeated. In Greek, however, a distinction is perfectly clear: one is the name of what is addressed, and the other of the one who does the addressing. 'He has anointed you, God.' 'O you [who are] God, your God has anointed you.'

†Ps 45:7

When you hear 'anointed,' understand Christ. 'Christ' comes from 'chrism.' The name by which we call Christ expresses 'anointing.' God has been anointed by God. What oil has he used if not spiritual oil? Visible oil is used as a sign, invisible oil as a mystery; the spiritual oil is within. God has been anointed for us, and sent to us—God himself, in order to be anointed, was human, but he was human in such a way that he was God still. We could not, then, express Christ's name more explicitly than by saying 'the anointed God.' As he was 'handsome beyond the children of men,' so was he anointed 'with the oil of gladness beyond his companions.'† Who are his 'companions' if not the 'children of men,' since he is the Son of Man? †Ps 45:2, 7

—from the treatise on Psalm 101*

446. *And the heavens are the work of your hands; they will perish.*† **†Heb 1:10–11** (Ps 102:25–26)

In the letter of the apostle Peter as well, where the world of that time was said to have been 'deluged with water and perished,' we see clearly enough what part of the world was signified by the whole, to what extent it was said to have 'perished,' and what heavens were 'stored away,' to be 'reserved for fire until the day of judgment and destruction of the godless.' And when he says a little later, 'The day of the Lord will come like a thief; on that day the heavens will pass away with great violence, the elements will be melted by heat, and the earth and the works in it will be burned up,' and then adds, 'Since all these things are to perish, what sort of persons ought you to be?'† we can understand the heavens that are going to perish [to be those] he said have been 'stored away and reserved for fire,' and take the elements that are going to be melted [to be those] that exist, stormy and unstable, in this lowest part of the world. This is when he said that those heavens have been 'stored away,' while the higher [heavens], in whose firmament the constellations are set, are safe and remain in their own integrity. †2 P 3:6–7, 10–11

Even the text of Scripture, 'the stars are to fall from heaven'†—apart from the fact that this can with greater probability be taken a different way—shows that those heavens themselves will remain, if the stars are really to fall from them. The expression may either be †Mt 24:29

*445. *En. in Ps* 44.17–19.21; CC 38: 505,1/18; 25–506,8; 507,2/23; 509,3/7 passim. Psalm 101 in the reference is an error for Psalm 44 (Hebrew 45).

figurative, which is more believable, or something more wonderful than happens now will take place in this lowest heaven—something like the 'star' in Vergil that 'shot down, leaving a trail of dazzling light' and 'buried itself in the woods of Ida.'†

†*Aeneid* 2.694, 696

—from *On the City of God* 20.24★

447. *But to which of his angels has he ever said, 'Sit at my right hand until I make your enemies a footstool for your feet'?*†

†**Heb 1:13** (Ps 110:1)

A footstool for your feet means one under your feet, since a footstool goes under the feet. He said, 'The Lord said to my Lord.' David heard this, he heard it in the spirit. When and where he heard it we have not heard it, but we believe him when he says and writes that he heard it.

We know that Christ sits at the Father's right hand after his resurrection from the dead and ascension into heaven.† This has already occurred. We did not see it, but we believed it. Hence too, by the fact that Christ was David's son he became David's Lord also. What was born of David's seed was so honored that it was also David's Lord.

†Mk 16:19

What enemies are made a footstool for his feet? Those to whom, as they imagine vain things, is said, 'Why have the nations raged, and the people imagined vain things?'† They were enemies, whoever they were; they will be under his feet, either as adopted or as overcome.

†Ps 2:1

—from the treatise on Psalm 109★

448. 'God was pleased, through the foolishness of preaching, to save those who believe.' The Apostle says that he who is among the little ones knows no one 'except Christ Jesus, and him crucified.' This preaching is needed for a long time, until all enemies are put beneath his feet†—that is, until all the world's pride yields and is made subject

†1 Co 1:21; 2:2; **Heb 1:13** (Ps 110:1)

★446. *De Civ. Dei* 20.24; CC 48: 744,32–745,53 (Vergil, *Aen.* 2.694, 696)
★447. *En. in Ps* 109.7.9; CC 40: 1606,11/27; 1609,8/16 passim

to his humility, which I consider is meant by the word feet. This has in large part already happened, and we see it happening daily.

—from *On Eighty-Four Questions* 69*

449. *Someone has testified in a certain place, saying, 'What are human beings that you are mindful of them, or the children of humans, that you visit them?'*† †**Heb 2:6–8** (Ps 8:5–8)

We can inquire what the difference between 'humans' and 'the children of humans' is. If no difference existed, [the psalmist] would not have set down 'the children of humans' separately. This we should keep in mind, that every child of a human is a human, although we cannot take every human to be a child of a human. Adam was indeed a human, but not the child of a human.

From this we may now consider and distinguish what the difference between a 'human' and the 'child of a human' is in this passage. Then we can indicate those who bear 'the image of the earthly one, [Adam],' who is not the child of a human, by the word 'human,' while we call those who bear 'the image of the heavenly one' children of humans instead. The former is called the 'old self,' the latter the 'new self';† the new, however, is born of the old, since spiritual regeneration is begun by the change of an earthly and temporal life. Therefore the latter is characterized as a 'child of a human.' †1 Co 15:47, 49; Eph 4:22, 24

The 'human' in this passage is earthly, the 'child of a human' is heavenly. The former is separated far from God, whereas the latter is in God's presence. Therefore [God] 'is mindful of' the former as of people situated far off, but 'visits' the latter—being present to them, [God] enlightens them with his countenance. 'Salvation is far from sinners,' and, 'The light of your countenance has been impressed upon us, O Lord.'† †Ps 119:155, 4:6

The 'children of humans' were first visited by that divine Human born of the virgin Mary. Because of the weakness of the flesh which the Wisdom of God deigned to bear, and the humiliation of

*448. *De Div. Quaest. LXXXIII* 69.9; CC 44A: 193,201/208

the passion, [the psalmist] rightly says of him, 'You have made him a little less than the angels.' He adds to this, however, the splendor in which he rose and ascended into heaven: 'You have crowned him with glory and honor, and set him over the works of your hands.' Since the angels too are the work of God's hands, we take it that the only-begotten Son has been set even over the angels—this one we hear and believe was made a little less than the angels by the humiliation of his carnal generation and passion.

'You have subjected everything,' [the psalmist] says, 'beneath his feet.' When he says 'everything' he excludes nothing. And that we may not be allowed to take this any other way, the Apostle charges us to believe thus when he says, 'This does not include the one
†1 Co 15:27 who made everything subject to him.'† To the Hebrews he makes use of the testimony of this psalm when he wants it understood that 'everything' is so subjected to our Lord Jesus Christ that nothing should be excluded.

—in the explanation of Psalm 8*

450. *Therefore, as the Holy Spirit says, 'Today if you hear his voice, do*
†Heb 3:7–11 *not harden your hearts.'*†
(Ps 95:7–11)

'We are his people and the sheep of his pasture. Today if you hear his voice.' O my people, O people of God! God addresses his people, not only those he will reject, but also all his people: 'Today if you hear his voice, do not harden your hearts.' Once you heard his voice through Moses and you hardened your hearts. He spoke through a herald when you hardened your hearts. Now he speaks in person—let your hearts become soft.

'Do not harden your hearts as you did in that bitter experience, according to the day of temptation in the wilderness.' You surely recall, brothers and sisters, that the people tempted the Lord and received chastisement. 'Do not,' then, 'harden your hearts as you did in that bitter experience, according to the day of temptation in

*449. *En. in Ps* 8.10–12; CC 38: 53, 2/25; 54,1–55,6 passim

the wilderness, when your ancestors tempted me.' Do not let people such as these be your ancestors. Do not imitate them.

'They put me to the test and saw my works.' I did wonders before them by the hand of Moses and they became more and more hardened. 'For forty years I was close to this generation.' What does 'I was close' mean? I made myself present in signs and good works, not on one day, not on two, but, 'for forty years I was close to this generation. And I said, They always go astray in their hearts.' Forty years represents 'always,' since the number forty indicates the fullness of the ages. 'And they did not recognize my ways . . .'

Great terror [is here]. We began with exultation, but the psalmist ended with great fear. God is great. How much more may he have sworn? 'He swore to them in his anger that they would not enter into his rest.' And yet some must enter into his rest. Since they have been rejected, we will enter into his rest! But how do those who enter, those who have been chosen, who have not resisted with a hardened heart, enter? The truth is, 'the Lord will not reject his people.'

—from the treatise on Psalm 94*

451. *You have become such as need milk, not solid food.*† †**Heb 5:12**

The Church is a mother and her breasts are the two covenants of the divine scriptures. Let us suck from them the milk of all the mysteries accomplished in time for our eternal salvation, so that, being nourished and strengthened, we may come to eat this food: 'In the beginning was the Word, and the Word was with God, and the Word was God.'† Our milk is Christ in humility. Our food is the same Christ, equal to the Father. He nourishes you with milk so that he may feed you with bread. To touch Jesus spiritually with the heart is to recognize that he is equal to the Father. †Jn 1:1

—from homily three on the Letter of John*

*450. *En. in Ps* 94.11–15; CC 39: 1340,32–1342,33 passim
*451. *In Ioh. Ep.* 3.1; PL 35: 1998

452. *See what kind of person [Melchizedek] is! Even Abraham the patriarch gave him a tenth part of the first-fruits . . . and, as we must say, even Levi, who receives tithes, paid tithes on account of Abraham, for he was still in*
†**Heb 7:4–10** (Gn 14:20) *the loins of his ancestor.*†

If this is valid at such a distance [in time], how much does Christ's priesthood surpass the Levitical priesthood? Christ as priest was prefigured by the one who collected tithes from Abraham [that is, Melchizedek], in whom a tithe was imposed on Levi, while certainly no tithe was imposed on Christ. If a tithe was imposed on Levi because he was in Abraham's loins, it was not imposed on Christ because he was not in Abraham's loins.

On the other hand, if we take Levi to have been in Abraham not
†Rm 1:3 according to the spirit but only 'according to the flesh,'†Christ too was there from Abraham's seed 'according to the flesh,' and on him therefore a tithe was imposed. What, then, is the great difference we advance between the priesthood of Christ and of Levi? Melchizedek imposed a tithe on Levi, since he was in Abraham's loins—where Christ was, hence it was imposed on them equally. Unless we must take it that in a certain sense Christ was not there. But who would deny that he was there 'according to the flesh'? Therefore he was not there according to the spirit. Christ's spirit, then, was not from the transmission of the transgression of Adam; otherwise, it too would have been there.

Some come forward here who defend the transmission of souls and say that their opinion is confirmed if everyone agrees that Levi was in Abraham's loins even according to the spirit. Melchizedek collected tithes from him in Abraham, so that Christ may be distinguished from him in that payment of tithes. Since no tithe was imposed on him, and yet he was in the loins of Abraham 'according to the flesh,' it follows that he was not there according to the spirit, and therefore the conclusion is that Levi *was* there according to the spirit.

This does not greatly concern me, since at present I am more ready to continue listening to what is said by both parties than to confirm the opinion of either. Meanwhile, by this testimony I want to separate Christ's spirit from the origin of this transmission. Some will be found who may perhaps reply on behalf of others, and say what impresses even me to some extent. Although no one's spirit is 'in the loins of his ancestor,' a tithe was imposed on Levi, who was in the loins of Abraham 'according to the flesh,' and not on Christ, who was there 'according to the flesh.' Levi was there with respect to the seminal principle† by which he was to enter his mother through sexual intercourse. With respect to this principle Christ's flesh was not there, although Mary's flesh was there in this respect.

†*seminale ratio.* Augustine thinks of this as a kind of germinal existence of the fully achieved creature.

Therefore, neither Levi nor Christ was in Abraham's loins according to the spirit; 'according to the flesh,' however, both Levi and Christ [were there], but Levi according to carnal craving, Christ solely according to his physical substance. Since both a visible corporeality and an invisible principle exist in a seed, both of these traveled down from Abraham, and even from Adam himself, all the way to Mary's body, because it too was conceived and born in this way. Christ took the visible substance of his flesh from the flesh of the Virgin, but the principle of his conception came not from a man's seed but far otherwise and from above. Consequently, according to what he received from his mother he too was in Abraham's loins.

Tithes were imposed on [Levi] in Abraham; although only 'according to the flesh,' yet he was in his loins in the same way that Abraham himself was in his father's [loins]. In other words, he was born of his father Abraham just as Abraham was born of his own father—undoubtedly through a law in his members at war with the law of his mind,† and through an invisible craving—although the chaste and proper rights of marriage do not permit this to be the prevalent factor, except insofar as they are able to provide for the continuing of the race as a result of it.

†Rm 7:23

Tithes were not imposed there on one whose flesh did not derive the inflamed wound, but the material remedy, from this source. Since the tithe was connected to the prefiguring remedy, what paid the tithe in Abraham's flesh was what was cured; it was not the source of the cure. The flesh—not of Abraham alone, but also of that first and earthly human—had both the wound of the transgression and the remedy for the wound. The wound of the transgression was in the law of the members at war with the law of the mind, a law transmitted, so to speak, from that [flesh] by the seminal principle throughout their whole physical posterity. The remedy for the wound, in what came from that [flesh] without the operation of concupiscence, was in the bodily material alone. It was taken from the Virgin through a divine principle of conception and formation, for the sake of an association with death without wickedness, and a model of resurrection without falsehood.

—from the *Literal Commentary on Genesis* 10.30*

453. 'The Lord has sworn and will not repent. You are a priest forever according to the order of Melchizedek.' Those who read [Scripture] know what Melchizedek brought out when he blessed Abraham,† and if they already partake of it they see a sacrifice of this kind now offered to God throughout the whole world. God's oath is a rebuke to the skeptical, and the fact that God 'will not repent' is an indication that he will not change this priesthood. The priesthood according to the order of Aaron he did change.

†Ps 110:4 (**Heb 7:17, 21**); Gn 14:18–19

God does not repent as humans do, just as he does not get angry like humans, or get jealous like humans; he does everything like God. God's repentance does not follow a mistake. God's anger is without the heat of an agitated mind. God's mercy is without the wretched heart of the compassionate, from which it gets its Latin name.† God's jealousy is without spite. God's repentance means a change, unexpected by humans, of things that lie in his power. God's anger is retribution for sin. God's mercy is his goodness in giving help. God's jealousy is his providence, by which he does not permit those he holds subject to love with impunity what he forbids.

†*Misericordia*, from *miserum cor* (wretched heart).

—from *Against the Opponent of the Law and the Prophets* 1*

454. *Finding fault with them [God] says, 'Behold, the days are coming, says the Lord, and I will bring about for the house of Israel and for the*

*452. *De Gen. ad Litt.* 10.19–20; CSEL 28,1: 321,14–324,15
*453. *Contra Adv. Leg. et Prophet.* 1.20.39–40; CC 49: 70,1071–71,1079. The first paragraph repeats section 386.

whole house of Judah a new covenant . . . by giving my laws in their mind and writing them on their heart, and I will be their God, and they will be my people.'† †**Heb 8:8–10** (Jer 31:31–33)

Why does [the psalmist] pray that the Lord lay down a law for him, if it 'is not laid down for the righteous'? It 'is not laid down for the righteous' in the way it was laid down for a stubborn people 'on tablets of stone' and not 'on fleshly tablets of the heart'—in accord with the old covenant from Mount Sinai which bears children into slavery,† not in accord with the new covenant, of which it is written by the prophet Jeremiah, 'Behold, the days will come, says the Lord, when I will bring about for the house of Israel and for the house of Judah a new covenant, not according to the covenant I drew up for their ancestors . . .' †Ps 119:33, 32; 2 Co 3:3; Ga 4:24

You see how [the psalmist] wants the Lord to lay down a law for him—not as it was laid down 'for the unrighteous and disobedient,' who belonged to the old covenant, 'on tablets of stone,' but as it is given in minds and written on hearts for the holy children of the free woman—that is, of Jerusalem on high—the children of the promise, the children of an eternal inheritance—by the Holy Spirit, as by the finger of God; not [a law] they can retain in memory and neglect in life, but one they may know by understanding and carry out by loving, in the breadth of love, not in the narrowness of fear.

—from the treatise on Psalm 118, where it says,
'Lay down a law for me, O Lord'*

455. When we read, 'Behold, the days are coming, says the Lord, and I will bring about for the house of Israel and for the house of Judah a new covenant . . . and I will be their God, and they will be my people,'† undoubtedly he is prophesying of the Jerusalem to come, whose reward is God himself. To possess God and to belong to God, is the supreme and total good there. †Jer 31:31–33 (**Heb 8:8–10**)

—from *On the City of God* 17.3*

---

*454. *En. in Ps* 118.11.1; CC 40: 1696,11/33 passim. Repeats most of section 401.
*455. *De Civ. Dei* 17.3; CC 48: 553,24–554,37 passim

†**Heb 11:17–19**

456. *By faith Abraham, when put to the test, offered up Isaac . . . for this too he brought him forward as a type.*†

As a type of whom, if not of the one of whom the Apostle says, 'Who did not spare his own Son, but handed him over for us all'? Therefore as the Lord carried his own cross, so Isaac too carried to the place of sacrifice the wood on which he was to be laid.†

†Rm 8:32; Jn 19:17; Gn 22:6

—from *On the City of God* 16.32*

†**Heb 12:16** (Gn 25:32–33)

457. *Let there be no fornicator or profane person, like Esau, who sold his birthright for a single meal.*†

Here we learn that in eating food a person is to be faulted not for a kind of food but for immoderate greed.

—from *On the City of God* 16.37*

*456. *Ibid.* 16.32; CC 48: 536,29–537,37 passim
*457. *Ibid.* 16.37; CC 48: 541,5/7

BIBLIOGRAPHY

Latin/English titles, with references to English translations (in the following series: Ancient Christian Writers; Fathers of the Church; Library of Christian Classics; Loeb Classical Library; The Nicene and Post-Nicene Fathers, series 1; Classics of Western Spirituality: Augustine of Hippo; *Works of Saint Augustine: A Translation for the 21st Century*).

Ad Orosium Contra Priscillianistas et Origenistas/To Orosius, Against the Priscillianists and the Origenists (Works I/18), 439

Confessiones/Confessions (LCL, NPNF 1, et al.), 113, 127, 146, 164, 198, 327, 363, 396, 437

Contra Adversarium Legis et Prophetarum/Against the Opponent of the Law and the Prophets (Works I/18), 8, 104, 181, 183, 228, 233, 386, 397, 440, 453

Contra Duas Epistolas Pelagianorum/Against Two Letters of the Pelagians (NPNF 5), 48

Contra Epistolam Petiliani/Against the Letter of Petilianus (NPNF 4), 342

Contra Epistolam Secundini Manichaei/Against the Letter of the Manichaean Secundinus, 72, 365

Contra Faustum Manichaeum/Against Faustus the Manichaean (NPNF 4), 65, 180, 232, 249, 272, 294, 312, 334, 374, 376, 378, 441

Contra Gaudentium/Against Gaudentius, 288

Contra Iulianum/Against Julian (FC 35), 58, 297

Contra Mendacium/Against Lying (FC 16, NPNF 3), 265, 330

Contra Secundam Iuliani Responsionem/Unfinished Work Against the Second Reply of Julian, 23, 24, 35, 36, 37, 38, 40, 49, 59, 86, 87, 92, 96, 98, 102, 242, 352, 399

De Adulterinis Coniugiis/On Adulterous Marriage (FC 27), 161, 162, 163

De Baptismo Contra Donatistas/On Baptism, Against the Donatists (NPNF 4), 278, 331, 382, 427, 428, 429

De Bono Coniugali/On the Good of Marriage (FC 27, NPNF 3), 412
De Civitate Dei/On the City of God (FC 8, 14, 24, LCL 411–417, NPNF 2, et al.), 78, 84, 90, 109, 129, 148, 151, 174, 175, 200, 208, 211, 216, 220, 239, 244, 248, 271, 283, 289, 300, 322, 323, 362, 390, 394, 410, 414, 438, 443, 446, 455, 456, 457
De Consensu Evangelistarum/On the Harmony of the Gospels (NPNF 6), 204, 305
De Correptione et Gratia/On Rebuke and Grace (NPNF 5), 413
De Diversis Quaestionibus ad Simplicianum/On Various Questions, to Simplician (LCC: *Earlier Writings*), 52, 54, 56, 88, 93, 95, 97, 224, 226
De Diversis Quaestionibus LXXXIII/On Eighty-Three Questions (FC 70), 51, 63, 71, 178, 218, 255, 264, 303, 343, 345, 448
De Doctrina Christiana/On Christian Doctrine (NPNF 2, et al.), 117, 202, 227, 275, 389, 398
De Dono Perseverantiae/On the Gift of Perseverance (NPNF 5), 80
De Genesi ad Litteram/Literal Commentary on Genesis (ACW 41–42), 137, 197, 203, 284, 298, 315, 329, 384, 409, 416, 452
De Genesi Contra Manichaeos/On Genesis, Against the Manichaeans (FC 84), 141
De Gestibus Pelagii/On the Actions of Pelagius (NPNF 5), 85, 290
De Gratia et Libero Arbitrio/On Grace and Free Will (NPNF 5), 7, 10, 14, 75
De Moribus Ecclesiae Catholicae/On the Practices of the Catholic Church (FC 56, NPNF 4), 83
De Natura et Origine Animae/On the Soul and Its Origin (NPNF 5), 188
De Nuptiis et Concupiscentia/On Marriage and Concupiscence (NPNF 5), 33, 236
De Perfectione Iustitiae Hominis/On the Perfection of Human Righteousness (NPNF 5), 333, 358, 393
De Praedestinatione Sanctorum/On the Predestination of the Saints (NPNF 5), 25, 77, 108, 223, 268, 314
De Sermone Domini in Monte/On the Lord's Sermon on the Mount (ACW 5, FC 11, NPNF 6), 3, 121, 172, 173, 176, 182, 185, 191, 212, 221, 257, 286, 296, 436
De Trinitate/On the Trinity (FC 45; LCL: *Late Works*, incomplete; NPNF 3; Works I/5), 2, 28, 29, 32, 45, 67, 79, 111, 112, 135, 138, 150, 154, 165, 166, 167, 186, 187, 199, 209, 210, 229, 230, 237, 276, 280, 319, 321, 324, 344, 349, 360, 364, 369, 372, 383, 385, 420
Enarrationes in Psalmos/Explanations of the Psalms (ACW 29–30; abridged in NPNF 8), 11, 12, 13, 15, 16, 17, 18, 19, 21, 22, 26, 60, 68, 105,

107, 114, 116, 118, 123, 125, 130, 134, 140, 153, 155, 159, 160, 189, 194, 238, 240, 247, 254, 256, 310, 326, 335, 336, 337, 338, 354, 355, 356, 387, 395, 401, 408, 418, 421, 425, 434, 442, 444, 445, 447, 449, 450, 454

Enchiridion/Enchiridion (ACW 3; FC 2; NPNF 3), 31, 42, 44, 50, 103, 152, 156, 158, 170, 243, 252, 285, 309, 313, 366, 406, 431

Epistolae/Letters—note that some letters are referred to as books—(FC 12, 18, 20, 30, 32, 81; selected letters in LCL 239 and NPNF 1; letters 147 and 187 in Paulist), *40*, 351; *55*, 353; *82*, 177, 263, 266, 292, 293, 299; *98*, 392 ; *120*, 136; *130*, 73, 139, 361; *140*, 316; *147* (Paulist), 142, 201, 231, 317, 403, 404; *149*, 320, 373, 375, 377, 405; *157*, 34, 39, 41, 101, 206, 234, 350; *186*, 81, 205, 267; *187* (Paulist), 371 ; *190*, 207; *194*, 9, 74, 76, 89, 91, 94, 110, 282; *205*, 213, 215; *214* (NPNF 5), 157; *215*, 43; *217*, 245; *228*, 258; appendix *20*, 261

In Ioh. Ep./Commentary on the First Letter of John (abridged in LCC: *Later Works*; NPNF 7), 6, 99, 100, 126, 128, 222, 253, 270, 304, 357, 417, 451

Quaestiones Evangeliorum/ Questions on the Gospels, 4, 122, 131

Sermo/Sermon (Works 3/1–10; selections in ACW 15; FC 11, 38; NPNF 6), *2*, 20, 328; *3*, 291; *37*, 277; *71*, 145, 193, 426; *131*, 347; *151*, 219; *153*, 53, 55; *154*, 57, 61, 259, 302; *155*, 62, 64, 66, 69; *156*, 70, 274, 400; *160*, 307; *162*, 168; *176*, 402; *177*, 415, 419, 422; *197*, 5, 133, 149, 262, 287, 370; *205*, 301; *229*, 184; *236*, 27; *268*, 318; *278*, 169; *283*, 144; *293*, 407; *298*, 433; *299*, 241, 432, 435; *302*, 119, 120; *330*, 269; *334*, 82; *341*, 132, 332, 367, 388; *350*, 196; *362*, 214, 217, 379, 381, 424; *Guelferb. 3*, 115; unnumbered, 30, 46, 124, 171, 195, 235, 260, 279, 308, 325, 339, 388, 391, 411, 430

Tract. In Ioh./Commentary on the Gospel of John (FC 78, 79, 88, 90, 92; NPNF 7), 47, 106, 143, 147, 179, 190, 192, 224, 246, 250, 251, 273, 281, 295, 306, 311, 340, 341, 346, 348, 359, 368, 380, 423

Quodvultdeus: *Contra Quinque Hereses*/Against Five Heresies, 1

CISTERCIAN TEXTS

Bernard of Clairvaux

- Apologia to Abbot William
- Five Books on Consideration: Advice to a Pope
- Homilies in Praise of the Blessed Virgin Mary
- Letters of Bernard of Clairvaux / by B.S. James
- Life and Death of Saint Malachy the Irishman
- Love without Measure: Extracts from the Writings of St Bernard / by Paul Dimier
- On Grace and Free Choice
- On Loving God / Analysis by Emero Stiegman
- Parables and Sentences
- Sermons for the Summer Season
- Sermons on Conversion
- Sermons on the Song of Songs I–IV
- The Steps of Humility and Pride

William of Saint Thierry

- The Enigma of Faith
- Exposition on the Epistle to the Romans
- Exposition on the Song of Songs
- The Golden Epistle
- The Mirror of Faith
- The Nature and Dignity of Love
- On Contemplating God: Prayer & Meditations

Aelred of Rievaulx

- Dialogue on the Soul
- Liturgical Sermons, I
- The Mirror of Charity
- Spiritual Friendship
- Treatises I: On Jesus at the Age of Twelve, Rule for a Recluse, The Pastoral Prayer
- Walter Daniel: The Life of Aelred of Rievaulx

John of Ford

- Sermons on the Final Verses of the Songs of Songs I–VII

Gilbert of Hoyland

- Sermons on the Songs of Songs I–III
- Treatises, Sermons and Epistles

Other Early Cistercian Writers

- Adam of Perseigne, Letters of
- Alan of Lille: The Art of Preaching
- Amadeus of Lausanne: Homilies in Praise of Blessed Mary
- Baldwin of Ford: Spiritual Tractates I–II
- Gertrud the Great: Spiritual Exercises
- Gertrud the Great: The Herald of God's Loving-Kindness (Books 1, 2)
- Gertrud the Great: The Herald of God's Loving-Kindness (Books 3)
- Guerric of Igny: Liturgical Sermons I
- Helinand of Froidmont: Verses on Death
- Idung of Prüfening: Cistercians and Cluniacs: The Case for Cîteaux
- Isaac of Stella: Sermons on the Christian Year, I–[II]
- The Life of Beatrice of Nazareth
- Serlo of Wilton & Serlo of Savigny: Seven Unpublished Works
- Stephen of Lexington: Letters from Ireland
- Stephen of Sawley: Treatises

MONASTIC TEXTS

Eastern Monastic Tradition

- Besa: The Life of Shenoute
- Cyril of Scythopolis: Lives of the Monks of Palestine
- Dorotheos of Gaza: Discourses and Sayings
- Evagrius Ponticus: Praktikos and Chapters on Prayer
- Handmaids of the Lord: Lives of Holy Women in Late Antiquity & the Early Middle Ages / by Joan Petersen
- Harlots of the Desert / by Benedicta Ward
- John Moschos: The Spiritual Meadow
- Lives of the Desert Fathers
- Lives of Simeon Stylites / by Robert Doran
- The Luminous Eye / by Sebastian Brock
- Mena of Nikiou: Isaac of Alexandra & St Macrobius
- Pachomian Koinonia I–III (Armand Veilleux)
- Paphnutius: Histories/Monks of Upper Egypt
- The Sayings of the Desert Fathers / by Benedicta Ward
- Spiritual Direction in the Early Christian East / by Irénée Hausherr
- The Spiritually Beneficial Tales of Paul, Bishop of Monembasia / by John Wortley
- Symeon the New Theologian: TheTheological and Practical Treatises & The Three Theological Discourses / by Paul McGuckin
- Theodoret of Cyrrhus: A History of the Monks of Syria
- The Syriac Fathers on Prayer and the Spiritual Life / by Sebastian Brock

CISTERCIAN PUBLICATIONS

TITLES LISTING

Western Monastic Tradition

- Anselm of Canterbury: Letters I–III / by Walter Fröhlich
- Bede: Commentary...Acts of the Apostles
- Bede: Commentary...Seven Catholic Epistles
- Bede: Homilies on the Gospels I–II
- Bede: Excerpts from the Works of St Augustine on the Lettrs of the Blessed Apostle Paul
- The Celtic Monk / by U. Ó Maidín
- Life of the Jura Fathers
- Maxims of Stephen of Muret
- Peter of Celle: Selected Works
- Letters of Rancé I–II
- Rule of the Master
- Rule of Saint Augustine

Christian Spirituality

- The Cloud of Witnesses: The Development of Christian Doctrine / by David N. Bell
- The Call of Wild Geese / by Matthew Kelty
- The Cistercian Way / by André Louf
- The Contemplative Path
- Drinking From the Hidden Fountain / by Thomas Špidlík
- Eros and Allegory: Medieval Exegesis of the Song of Songs / by Denys Turner
- Fathers Talking / by Aelred Squire
- Friendship and Community / by Brian McGuire
- Gregory the Great: Forty Gospel Homilies
- High King of Heaven / by Benedicta Word
- The Hermitage Within / by a Monk
- Life of St Mary Magdalene and of Her Sister St Martha / by David Mycoff
- Many Mansions / by David N. Bell
- Mercy in Weakness / by André Louf
- The Name of Jesus / by Irénée Hausherr
- No Moment Too Small / by Norvene Vest
- Penthos: The Doctrine of Compunction in the Christian East / by Irénée Hausherr
- Praying the Word / by Enzo Bianchi
- Rancé and the Trappist Legacy / by A. J. Krailsheimer
- Russian Mystics / by Sergius Bolshakoff
- Sermons in a Monastery / by Matthew Kelty
- Silent Herald of Unity: The Life of Maria Gabrielle Sagheddu / by Martha Driscoll
- The Spirituality of the Christian East / by Thomas Špidlík
- The Spirituality of the Medieval West / by André Vauchez
- Tuning In To Grace / by André Louf
- Wholly Animals: A Book of Beastly Tales / by David N. Bell

MONASTIC STUDIES

- Community and Abbot in the Rule of St Benedict I–II / by Adalbert de Vogüé
- The Finances of the Cistercian Order in the Fourteenth Century / by Peter King
- Fountains Abbey and Its Benefactors / by Joan Wardrop
- The Hermit Monks of Grandmont / by Carole A. Hutchison
- In the Unity of the Holy Spirit / by Sighard Kleiner
- The Joy of Learning & the Love of God: Essays in Honor of Jean Leclercq
- Monastic Odyssey / by Marie Kervingant
- Monastic Practices / by Charles Cummings
- The Occupation of Celtic Sites in Ireland / by Geraldine Carville
- Reading St Benedict / by Adalbert de Vogüé
- Rule of St Benedict: A Doctrinal and Spiritual Commentary / by Adalbert de Vogüé
- The Rule of St Benedict / by Br. Pinocchio
- St Hugh of Lincoln / by David H. Farmer
- The Venerable Bede / by Benedicta Ward
- What Nuns Read / by David N. Bell
- With Greater Liberty: A Short History of Christian Monasticism & Religious Orders / by Karl Frank

CISTERCIAN STUDIES

- Aelred of Rievaulx: A Study / by Aelred Squire
- Athirst for God: Spiritual Desire in Bernard of Clairvaux's Sermons on the Song of Songs / by Michael Casey
- Beatrice of Nazareth in Her Context / by Roger De Ganck
- Bernard of Clairvaux: Man, Monk, Mystic / by Michael Casey [tapes and readings]
- Bernardus Magister...Nonacentenary
- Catalogue of Manuscripts in the Obrecht Collection of the Institute of Cistercian Studies / by Anna Kirkwood
- Christ the Way: The Christology of Guerric of Igny / by John Morson
- The Cistercians in Denmark / by Brian McGuire
- The Cistercians in Scandinavia / by James France
- A Difficult Saint / by Brian McGuire
- A Gathering of Friends: Learning & Spirituality in John of Ford / by Costello and Holdsworth
- Image and Likeness: Augustinian Spirituality of William of St Thierry / by David Bell

- Index of Authors & Works in Cistercian Libraries in Great Britain I / by David Bell
- Index of Cistercian Authors and Works in Medieval Library Catalogues in Great Britian / by David Bell
- The Mystical Theology of St Bernard / by Étienne Gilson
- The New Monastery: Texts & Studies on the Earliest Cistercians
- Nicolas Cotheret's Annals of Cîteaux / by Louis J. Lekai
- Pater Bernhardus: Mentor of Martin Luther... / by Franz Posset
- A Second Look at Saint Bernard / by Jean Leclercq
- The Spiritual Teachings of St Bernard of Clairvaux / by John R. Sommerfeldt
- Studies in Medieval Cistercian History
- Studiosorum Speculum / by Louis J. Lekai
- Three Founders of Cîteaux / by Jean-Baptiste Van Damme
- Towards Unification with God (Beatrice of Nazareth in Her Context, 2)
- William, Abbot of St Thierry
- Women and St Bernard of Clairvaux / by Jean Leclercq

MEDIEVAL RELIGIOUS WOMEN

edited by Lillian Thomas Shank and John A. Nichols:

- Distant Echoes
- Hidden Springs: Cistercian Monastic Women (2 volumes)
- Peace Weavers

CARTHUSIAN TRADITION

- The Call of Silent Love / by A Carthusian
- The Freedom of Obedience / by A Carthusian
- Guigo II: The Ladder of Monks & Twelve Meditations / by Colledge & Walsh
- Halfway to Heaven / by R.B. Lockhart
- Interior Prayer / by A Carthusian
- Meditations of Guigo II / by A. Gordon Mursall
- Prayer of Love and Silence / by A Carthusian
- Poor, Therefore Rich / by A Carthusian
- They Speak by Silences / by A Carthusian
- The Way of Silent Love (A Carthusian Miscellany)
- Where Silence is Praise / by A Carthusian
- The Wound of Love (A Carthusian Miscellany)

CISTERCIAN ART, ARCHITECTURE & MUSIC

- Cistercian Abbeys of Britain
- Cistercians in Medieval Art / by James France
- Studies in Medieval Art and Architecture / edited by Meredith Parsons Lillich *(Volumes II–V are now available)*
- Stones Laid Before the Lord / by Anselme Dimier
- Treasures Old and New: Nine Centuries of Cistercian Music (compact disc)

THOMAS MERTON

- The Climate of Monastic Prayer / by T. Merton
- Legacy of Thomas Merton / by P. Hart
- Message of Thomas Merton / by P. Hart
- Monastic Journey of Thomas Merton / by P. Hart
- Thomas Merton/Monk / by P. Hart
- Thomas Merton on St Bernard
- Toward an Integrated Humanity / edited by M. Basil Pennington

CISTERCIAN LITURGICAL DOCUMENTS SERIES

- Cistercian Liturgical Documents Series / edited by Chrysogonus Waddell, ocso
- Hymn Collection of the...Paraclete
- *Institutiones nostrae:* The Paraclete Statutes
- Molesme Summer-Season Breviary (4 volumes)
- Old French Ordinary & Breviary of the Abbey of the Paraclete (2 volumes)
- Twelfth-century Cistercian Hymnal (2 volumes)
- The Twelfth-century Cistercian Psalter
- Two Early Cistercian *Libelli Missarum*

STUDIA PATRISTICA

- Studia Patristica XVIII, Volumes 1, 2 and 3

CISTERCIAN PUBLICATIONS

HOW TO CONTACT US

Editorial Queries

Editorial queries & advance book information should be directed to the Editorial Offices:

- Cistercian Publications
  WMU Station
  1201 Oliver Street
  Kalamazoo, Michigan 49008

- Telephone 616 387 8920
- Fax 616 387 8921

How to Order in the United States

Customers may order these books through booksellers or directly by contacting the warehouse at the address below:

- Cistercian Publications
  Saint Joseph's Abbey
  167 North Spencer Road
  Spencer, Massachusetts 01562-1233

- Telephone 508 885 8730
- Fax 508 885 4687
- e-mail cistpub@spencerabbey.org
- Web Site www.spencerabbey.org/cistpub

How to Order from Canada

- Novalis
  49 Front Street East, Second Floor
  Toronto, Ontario M5E 1B3

- Telephone 416 363 3303
  1 800 387 7164
- Fax 416 363 9409

How to Order from Europe

- Cistercian Publications
  Mount Saint Bernard Abbey
  Coalville, Leicester LE67 5UL

- Fax 44 1530 81 46 08

Cistercian Publications is a non-profit corporation. Its publishing program is restricted to monastic texts in translation and books on the monastic tradition.

A complete catalogue of texts in translation and studies on early, medieval, and modern monasticism is available, free of charge, from any of the addresses above.